Growth and Change: America, 1898–1952

Edited by

John M. Carroll
Walter A. Sutton
Frank W. Abbott
David C. Smith

Kendall/Hunt
Publishing Company
Dubuque, Iowa

B   404061   01

Contents

Preface

Growth and Conflict presents fourteen original essays concerning the response of the United States to the early years of the twentieth century. The scope of the essays is broad, stretching from the emergence of the United States as a world power in the last days of the 19th century through the American attainment of the pinacle of power at the end of the second great war of this century. In those years, the United States underwent many changes—from rural nation to urban nation; from a homogenous to a pluralistic culture; from a production economy to a consumer economy; from a limited actor in world affairs to the star in the center of the stage. Each change created tensions in the society, and those tensions created the conflicts which were the growing pains of the modern era.

This volume is organized into two major sections, one on politics and diplomacy and the other on social and economic developments. The sections are organized chronologically to supplement most major textbooks of American history. In each essay, the authors, all practicing historians, have attempted to relate the events of the past to the present time.

Professor Robert Righter surveys the opening years of this century and focuses on Theodore Roosevelt as the symbol of the new age. Professor William Gibbs examines the Progressive movement as a part of the reform tradition of America, while Professor Thomas Leonard looks at the development of an American presence in the world. Professor Leonard's overview is supplemented by the essays of Professor Peter Buckingham on American diplomacy from the end of World War I to the beginning of World War II. More focused views of American foreign policy appear in Professor Mark Gilderhus's examination of Pan-Americanism and Professor Nelson Dawson's treatment of American views of the Soviet Union. Section One is completed by Professor J. K. Sweeney's essay on the growth of presidential power in the United States.

Section Two concerns the economic and social development of the nation. Professor Larry Lankton examines the impact of the automobile and the consumer economy on American prosperity, while Professor Donald Zellman looks at the social implications of the same period. Professor Jeffrey Samson describes the developing American love affair with sports and recreation. Professor Judy Litoff surveys the rise of the American woman as an active participant in the political and social life of the nation, while Professor Gary Kremer covers the emergence of the black as a visible part of the society. Professor David Smith focuses on popular culture as revealed by phonograph recording and radio broadcasting. Professor Jane Stephens concludes Section Two with her essay on the shift in American thinking from deterministic to relativist philosophies.

In each section, and throughout the book, the recurring theme is the growth of the American nations and the way the nation responded to the conflict which those changes brought.

Part I
American Politics and Diplomacy, 1898–1952

In his first inaugural address in 1913, President Woodrow Wilson summed up the new age which America had entered. "We have," the President said, "been refreshed by a new insight into our own lives. . . . We have come now to the sober second thought. The scales of heedlessness have fallen from our eyes. We have made up our minds to square every process of our national life with the standards we so proudly set up at the beginning and have always carried at our hearts. Our work is a work of restoration." In the first four decades of the twentieth century, the United States worked at bringing a new sense of community to the nation. It transformed itself into a responsible industrial power and into a respected world power. It extended itself to other nations in this hemisphere and involved itself in European and Asian affairs, ending three-quarters of a century of non-involvement. The nation saw the traditional relationships of power shifting as strong presidents made Washington the center of government and the executive branch the primary force. Wilson's words of reform heralded the Progressive effort to force the nation to come to grips with the centralizing impact of industrialization and the release of pent up energies in a struggle to create a better, fairer society. As society developed along industrial lines, so government grew.

The essays in this section focus on those changes which accompany the growth and development of the United States in the twentieth century. Rightly or wrongly, the active America moved steadily toward a future different from that imagined by the founding fathers. Rightly or wrongly, the growth of Presidential power caused a new importance to attend the quadriennial hooplas which marked the American people's selection process for its chief executive. Rightly or wrongly, the implications of industrialization forced the United States to alter its view of the American role in the world and its relations with other nations.

Each change, each development forced upon the nation basic policy decisions. The choices posed by those questions created the great debates by which America charted its future. How should the society respond to industrialization? Should it allow business to take its course unhindered by the actions of the government, or should government intervene in the private sector to

1

establish rules of competition? How should the Constitution be viewed as an organic instrument of government? Should it change through interpretation or only through amendment? Should the election of the President be turned directly over to the people, or should the electoral college remain to remind the nation of limits to majority rule? Should the United States pursue globalism, or should it limit its incursions into the world? In these four decades, the United States began to answer those questions.

America and Americans on the Eve of the 20th Century

Robert W. Righter
University of Wyoming

"It is exhilarating to feel the nation's muscles expand and harden," wrote *Saturday Evening Post* editor, Maurice Thompson. On the eve of a new century Americans had good reason to celebrate their accomplishments. The brash, exuberant, young nation had, indeed, come a long way since its birth just a little over one hundred years earlier.

The country had attained a sectional truce—if not unity—and the differences between the North and the South began to pale as the leaders who fought the Civil War retired from positions of power. What seemed more relevant was the industrial revolution. It touched the lives of almost every American. The revolution created mighty corporations, immense cities, factories, mills, mines, and a new landscape criss-crossed with railroads, telephone wires, and roads. An immense wilderness had been—in a century—bent to the will of this energetic young nation in which anything seemed possible. Those accepted concepts and ideas, such as democracy, individualism, capitalism, Anglo-Saxon blood, power, progress, and abundance, were credited with creating a new world power which would take its rightful place on the world stage.

For many Americans there seemed to be a divine guidance and purpose in their success. Albert Beveridge, senator from Indiana, expressed the sentiments of many. Rising in the Senate on January 9, 1900, the brilliant young orator declared: "Of all our race, God has marked the American people as His chosen Nation to finally lead in the regeneration of the world. This is the divine mission of America," continued the senator, "and it holds for us all the profit, all the glory, all the happiness possible to man. We are trustees of the world's progress, guardians of its righteous peace." Profit, glory, happiness, progress, and peace—these were important ideas at the turn of the century, as they are today. However, while today we are often uncertain if we have the keys to unlock the benefits of such ideas, to Beveridge it was clear that divine purpose was at work to reward the emerging nation.

The concept of higher purpose was useful to those wishing to explain the nation's sweep across the continent, with its concomitant/cruelty and displacement of Native Americans. One newspaper editor, Theodore Marburg, wrote in 1898 that any atrocities of that movement were both understandable and justified. "When the white man came to America there were about 500,000

More and more people were moving from the country to the city. The attractions of Long Beach, California, about 1900 illustrate some of the reasons. (Courtesy of National Archives.)

Indians in what now constitutes the United States. Today," continued Marburg, "there still remain 225,000. We have then brushed aside 275,000 Indians, and in place of them have this population of 70,000,000 of what we regard as the highest type of modern man." There was a purpose and a duty to civilization in all this, and it was Marburg's contention that "any nation which blocks the way of human progress must expect to be brushed aside by more powerful and vigorous blood."

So there the nation was on the eve of a new century. Supremely confident in its ideas and actions, such an exceptionally bold nation might almost be considered a 3,500 mile wide Camelot, stretching from sea to shining sea.

Leaders of this new Camelot were equal to the promise. It seemed almost apocalyptical when President William McKinley—a Civil War officer and an

4

"old-guard" conservative politician—died of a gun shot wound in September, 1901, the third president to be assassinated in less than forty years. Yet in his place rose Theodore Roosevelt, a man who seemed right for the new age and the new century.

Roosevelt was unhampered by personal memories of the Civil War. His own military experience had been in the Spanish American War, and there was a vast difference between the two wars. The former had been an American tragedy, tearing apart families, communities, geographic sections, and the union of states. The latter represented an American triumph, perhaps the most popular war in the nation's history. The adversary, Spain, was in the final throes of decline when young America dealt a final knock out blow. It was as if an eighteen year old took on an eighty-eight year old. The war was brief and successful: only some 250 American lives lost, Spain was thrashed and left prostrate, and American imperialistic objectives in Cuba and the Philippines obtained. It was, as diplomat John Hay described it, "a splendid little war."

Roosevelt's antics during the war—bordering between adolescent enthusiasm and comical naivete—give us some idea of the personality of the man who would soon lead the nation. Lieutenant Colonel Roosevelt determinedly brought together the First Volunteer Cavalry, a most unlikely combination of cowboys, bad men from the West, polo players, steeplechase riders from the private clubs of New York, and a few well-heeled adventurers from such ivy league colleges as Harvard, Yale, and Princeton. The "Rough Riders," as the press called them, trained in San Antonio under the ebullient leadership of Roosevelt. He enjoyed the task of readying his men for action, but he was always in a hurry, fearful that he might miss his chance to fight. "It will be awful if we miss the fun," he confided in a letter to his older sister. He didn't, and at Cuba's San Juan hill, or more accurately Kettlehill, the victory of the "Rough Riders" catapulted their leader into the national limelight.

This sort of physical exertion and enthusiasm was characteristic of Roosevelt. Whether boxing at Harvard, riding the range in North Dakota, leading a charge up San Juan Hill, camping in Yosemite Valley with naturalist John Muir, or hunting in Africa, Roosevelt lived his life with gusto and exuberance. His friend Cecil Spring Rice wrote in 1904 that, "You must always remember that the President is about six."

Of course Spring-Rice referred to his enthusiasm, not his mentality. Roosevelt was no intellectual lightweight. His choice of friends included such learned men as Henry Adams, Henry Cabot Lodge, and Rudyard Kipling. He wrote for *Century* and *Scribner's Magazine,* two of the most highly respected magazines of his day. He was well-versed in natural history as well as American history. His efforts at writing, including *The Naval War of 1812* and the four-volume *The Winning of the West,* were well-received, although some of his other historical efforts were too superficial and too opinionated to have lasting value.

Thus when Roosevelt became president at forty-two, the youngest president in the nation's history to that time, his vigor matched that of the nation.

Nowhere was this more evident than in foreign policy, which at times seemed nothing more than an extension of his charge up San Juan Hill. It is generally acknowledged that the Spanish American War marked America's emergence as a world power. Roosevelt made sure that the rest of the world understood that fact.

The Panama Canal offers an example of Roosevelt in action. When he came to power, "His Accidency," as he was sometimes called by his enemies, moved quickly to clear away diplomatic roadblocks with England, signing the second Hay-Pauncefote Treaty of 1901, which allowed the United States to construct, own, and fortify the canal.

Having dealt with England, Roosevelt and his Secretary of State, John Hay, turned their attention to Colombia, which owned the Isthmus of Panama. Colombia was hesitant, and Roosevelt was impatient. When it became evident that Colombia would not immediately accept American terms, Roosevelt became enraged, and rather than continue negotiations he let it be known that the United States would not allow a Panamanian revolt to fail. Rebels orchestrated a revolt, and when the Colombian government sent troops to suppress it, the U.S.S. *Nashville* prevented the soldiers from landing, using the thinly-veiled excuse that they must keep the isthmus opened to commerce. On November 4, 1903, one day after the revolt, Roosevelt authorized recognition of the new nation of Panama. Fifteen days after the bogus revolt, the Hay-Bunau-Varilla Treaty was signed, conveying to the United States in perpetuity a zone ten miles wide in return for a payment of $10,000,000 and $250,000 a year.

Some Americans decried such piratical tactics, but when the *Literary Digest* analyzed the news of some seventy American newspapers, it found that fifty-three favored the *coup* while only seventeen criticized it. America was flexing its muscles, and Roosevelt correctly gauged that such blatant imperialistic action would be well-received by the voting public. Later he proclaimed: "I took the Canal Zone and let Congress debate. . . ."

Whether dealing with Colombia, Venezuela, Cuba, England, or Germany, Roosevelt liked to follow an old West African proverb: "Speak softly and carry a big stick, you will go far." Latin America felt the sting of the "big stick" when Roosevelt modified the Monroe Doctrine, a change which became known as the Roosevelt corollary (1904). The corollary stated that when Latin American countries acted irresponsibly ("chronic wrongdoing" was the phrase), the United States might have to act as an international police power. In other words, the "northern colossus," as the United States was often called, might have to land U.S. Marines and take over the government. In the next 20 years we invoked the corollary often, much to the dismay of our southern neighbors.

In policing the western hemisphere the new American navy was always prominent. Roosevelt studied naval history and the strategic importance of naval power fascinated him. Before becoming president he served as Assistant Secretary of the Navy, advocating the building of "a dozen new battleships, half of them on the Pacific Coast." He never quite attained his wish, but nevertheless by the close of Roosevelt's presidency the United States Navy was second only to that of Great Britain. To impress Japan as well as the rest of the world, in 1907 Roosevelt proposed sending the entire fleet of sixteen battleships on an around the world cruise. Some congressmen protested such an audacious display of military power, but Roosevelt had his way. The voyage proved a spectacular success, spreading goodwill in Australia, Japan, and then to the Mediterranean nations. On another level the presence of the great fleet surely signified to any doubters that America had come of age.

Roosevelt brought the same vigor to the nation's internal problems as he did to foreign policy. His most challenging task was to make the American capitalistic system work. Certainly many Americans questioned an economic structure in which the rich seemed to get richer and the poor, poorer. In the 1880s and 1890s the "captains of industry" consolidated both money and power, and even incorporated a respectable social theory called Social Darwinism, which emphasized the survival of the fittest. While industrial leaders wallowed in wealth and new found prestige, laborers made little headway, and American farmers, the backbone of the 19th Century economy, struggled for survival.

By 1892 these frustrated farmers had organized the Populist party, challenging the established order. They advocated radical changes, including nationalization of railroads and formation of people's cooperatives to guarantee farm crop prices. They championed an 8-hour day for labor, a graduated income tax, and the adoption of the initiative and referendum procedures to make the government more responsive to the people. These were extremist positions in the 1890s, and some of them still are in our own age. Established leaders worried about the appeal of the Populists and such leaders as Mary E. Lease of Kansas, who urged farmers to "raise less corn and more hell." It was clear to some moderates such as Roosevelt, that to avoid revolution, reform must be initiated.

Actually Roosevelt did very little to aid directly the farmers of America. He did sign the Elkins Railroad Act (1903), which strengthened the hand of the Interstate Commerce Commission in controlling railroad rates. Also, to aid western farmers and ranchers he supported passage of the Reclamation Act of 1902, which funneled large amounts of federal dollars into irrigation projects.

Perhaps more important than legislation was the tone which he set. For instance, one section of the Reclamation Act stipulated that no landowner could irrigate more than 160 acres of land with federal reclamation project water. Large landowners protested, but before the Commonwealth Club of San Francisco Roosevelt defended the 160 acre limitation in broad, theoretical, but unmistakable terms:

> I wish to save the very wealthy men of this country and their advocates and upholders from the ruin that they would bring upon themselves if they were permitted to have their way. It is because I am against revolution; it is because

I am against the doctrines of the Extremists, of the Socialists; it is because I wish to see this country of ours continued as a genuine democracy; it is because I distrust violence and disbelieve in it; it is because I wish to secure this country against ever seeing a time when the "have-nots" shall rise against the "haves". . . .

Such rhetoric indicates the approach of Roosevelt and the Progressives to the problems posed by industrialism, monopoly, and the concentration of power. Whether he was advocating the 160 acre limitation on water or cracking down on the Rockefeller interests, Roosevelt believed that he was saving the system, and saving the wealthy from themselves. Affluent Americans had to make concessions and release their stranglehold on farmers, laborers, and the political process. To those who vehemently opposed organized labor, he preached a middle course, advocating "the right of laboring men to join a union . . . without illegal interference." This might not satisfy such labor leaders as Samuel Gompers or radicals as Eugene V. Debs, but it was more than most businessmen would concede.

While farmers faced hardships, black people, approximately ten percent of the nation's population, encountered a hostile world strewn with barriers to economic success and a life free from fear. While granted freedom and the rights of citizenship after the Civil War, blacks found by the 1890s that the promise of freedom and equality was a cruel hoax, and that they were mere pawns in a political game between Republicans and Democrats. When the game ended, southern whites reasserted their supremacy with legal segregation. Voting rights were stripped away, and the illusion of economic freedom was replaced by the debt-peonage system in which the harder black farmers worked the more in debt they seemed to fall. Some black farmers became virtually reinslaved.

Racial violence accompanied reinslavement as lynchings and burnings of blacks increased dramatically in the South during the 1890s. Continuing this grisly trend, between 1900 and 1914 more than 1100 blacks were murdered, most—but not all—in the southern states. Death by such brutal means as burning-at-the-stake and hanging bespoke the determination of whites to demonstrate to blacks their place in American society. Young whites, who often witnessed such violence, also learned the nature of the racial relationship which was the cornerstone of the southern way of life. It would take the better part of the new century to begin to undo this polarized racial heritage.

To be a black leader at the turn of the century was surely a thankless task. Amidst an atmosphere of hopelessness and hostility, ex-slave Booker T. Washington took up the task, preaching forgiveness and reconciliation. Emerging from a background of slavery and rural poverty, Washington's program was practical rather than idealistic. He acknowledged white racism, urged his people to accept the situation, work diligently, and hope attitudes would change. He founded Alabama's Tuskegee College, with its focus on agricultural training, manual arts, and hard work.

Between 1880 and 1910 women working outside the home increased from 2.5 million to 7 million. Here women are trimming currency at the Dept. of the Treasury. (Courtesy of National Archives.)

Washington rose as the spokesman for blacks following his famous "Atlanta Address," given in 1896 before a predominantly white audience. It was the first time that a black person had been invited to give a major address to prominent whites. Washington urged businessmen to employ southern blacks, proclaiming that "in all things that are purely social we can be as separate as the fingers, yet one as the hand in all things essential to mutual progress." To blacks he counselled, "the opportunity to earn a dollar in a factory just now is worth infinitely more than the opportunity to spend a dollar in an opera-house." Thus, Washington argued equal economic opportunity while he condoned segregation. His speech drew a roar of approval from the crowd.

Such a conciliatory attitude drew criticism from black leaders who believed that Booker T. Washington had either sold out, or simply did not understand the depth of white racism. W. E. B. Dubois, a Harvard-educated black leader, denounced Washington for his capitulation to racism and his tacit acknowledgement that blacks would act as docile laborers for the foreseeable future. DuBois urged a different course. He believed that ambitious and talented members of his race must educate themselves to be leaders. Furthermore, blacks must press for social, political and economic equality. The Niagara Movement (1907) and the National Association for the Advancement of Colored People (1910) were both dedicated to equality and vigorous protest of lynching and mob violence. They reflected DuBois' more militant stance. But success would be many decades away, for the "melting pot" of America, so accessible to some immigrants, steadfastly resisted the one people that came involuntarily to this new world.

Indians fared no better than blacks. Continually displaced throughout the 19th Century, whites coveted more and more of their land. They lost not only land, but lives. The 1900 Census registered the low point of Native American populations, before or since. As editor Theodore Marburg noted, many Indians were "brushed aside" in the march of civilization and progess.

Those that survived may well have envied the dead. Many factors contributed to the abysmal condition of American Indians, but one was especially important. The General Allotment Act of 1887, or the Dawes Act as it was popularly known, authorized the carving up of reservation lands into individual land allotments: 160 acres for a head of family, and 80 acres to each adult single person. Surplus tribal land, after allotment, was opened to white settlement. The motives of land speculators who supported the act are clear, but the enthusiasm of Indian reformers needs an explanation. They fervently believed that assimilation into white society was the answer for the Indians, and that tribal governments and reservations were impediments to that process. To accelerate assimilation, the Dawes Act undercut tribal government and encouraged farming through private land ownership. It didn't work, and actually more Indians tilled the soil before the act than after it.

Although the reformers' objectives went unfulfilled, those who coveted Indian land were well-rewarded. Between passage of the Dawes Act and its repeal in 1934, Indian land shrunk from 150 million acres to about 48 million acres, and much of this desert land.

Yet not all Indian lands were allotted, and some reservations actually expanded. Between 1900 and 1908 four additions to the Navajo Reservation added several million acres. Nor did the Dawes Act destroy the culture of Native Americans. While whites were trying one thing, Indians were doing another. In large numbers they embraced the Native American Church, whose doctrines combined Christianity with native religious traditions, including the use of peyote. Furthermore, tribes began to work together to better their collective condition. This Pan-Indian movement resulted in the formation of the Society of American Indians in 1911. Indian peoples were showing the resiliency and determination to survive.

Women did not face the difficult world of blacks and Indians, but they too knew discrimination. Consistently women received lower pay for equal work. They were often denied access to education. Nor did they have direct political power. Women could not vote, and by custom they were not expected to run for public office. Politics was viewed as a dirty business unbefitting any well-bred woman.

Men and women embraced the cult of domesticity, which had as its basic tenet that women found fulfillment through matrimony and maternity. Marriage offered protection and economic security. It offered some power and influence, for it provided access to the ruling males. But above all it offered women a chance to achieve their mission: to raise children and make their homes a sanctuary of love and moral purity.

Nevertheless, at the turn of the century, women's world was changing. Many left the home for the larger community. The poor found jobs as secretaries, as textile workers, as hotel workers, and in other service industries. In 1880 only 2.5 million women worked outside of the home, but by 1910 that number had swelled to 7 million. The affluent expanded their horizons by joining social and service clubs like the American Association of University Women (organized in 1881) and the Daughters of the American Revolution founded in the 1890s. The General Federation of Women's Clubs received a national charter in 1901, and soon boasted over a million members. By 1904 the organization took on a new, more strident position when Sarah Decker announced: "Ladies . . . Dante is dead . . . and I think it is time that we dropped the study of his inferno and turned our attention on our own." As the 20th Century took hold, women throughout the nation heeded Sarah Decker's call, resulting in the right to vote (19th Amendment) in 1920, and the fight for equal rights which continues to this day.

Theodore Roosevelt devoted little effort to ending these discriminatory practices in the nation. He did have liberal tendencies, but they were often tempered by political pressure. For instance, one evening he invited Booker T. Washington to the White House for dinner, but southerners protested, and he never repeated the offer. As indicated above, the president directed his considerable energy toward making the free enterprise system work. He earned a reputation as a "trust-buster" when he took action which successfully broke up the Northern Securities Company, a mammoth railroad holding company dominated by such business moguls as J. P. Morgan, John D. Rockefeller, James J. Hill, and E. H. Harriman.

During Roosevelt's administration the Attorney General's office did move against forty-four alleged trusts and monopolies. Businessmen were put on their guard. However, the president was no socialist, but he did realize the free enterprise system must be somewhat competitive to guarantee fair consumer prices. Some public services, of course, would be provided through big and complex monopolies. Roosevelt recognized that telegraph and telephone service, urban transportation systems, and electrical and heating systems, were best organized by one company. The type of integration and cooperation required did not lend itself to competition. With such services, Roosevelt argued, the solution was government regulation by an impartial, independent commission.

The use of the nation's natural resources did require regulation. During the 19th Century conservation and careful disposal of public lands and resources seemed unnecessary. The nation's resources appeared bountiful and well-nigh inexhaustible. Americans were a people of plenty and living in a land of superabundance. However, by the eve of the new century some Americans realized that the idea of superabundance was a dangerous myth which Americans could no longer perpetuate. The result was a heightened concern for conservation. These early conservationists wanted to end the flagrant waste of timber and water resources. They also wished to prevent the monopoly of valuable resources. Iron ore, crude oil, and timber lands were falling into the hands of a few people.

In 1891 in response to these ideas Congress passed the Timber Reserve Act, allowing the president to establish forest reserves by executive decree. In the 1890s Presidents Benjamin Harrison and Grover Cleveland set aside a few reserves, but it was under President Roosevelt that the national forest system took shape. Roosevelt, with the assistance of dynamic conservation leaders such as Gifford Pinchot, established well over 100 million acres of forest reserves. To manage this grand wooded estate the United States Forest Service was launched in 1905, with Pinchot as Chief Forester.

The establishment of the national forests represented a new federal land policy. In the 19th Century the policy was one of disposal. "Uncle Sam's" land policy centered on transferring public land into private hands. However, slowly land policy turned from disposal to retention and management. New terms, such as "wise use," "mutliple use," and "sustained yield," crept into the American lexicon. Trained experts began long range planning for the most efficient use of the remaining resources. Theodore Roosevelt warned the nation in 1908 that it was running out of minerals, iron ore, and coal. In a sense the *fin de siecle* marked, if not the end of abundance, at least a premonition of an age of scarcity.

One resource that became scarce was uninhabited land. During the 19th Century the nation took great pride in transforming wilderness land into productive farm land. By the 20th Century, however, the land was largely settled and Americans became a frontierless society. This caused some anxiety, for many believed with historian Frederick Jackson Turner that the frontier was instrumental in forming such American characteristics as love of democracy, individualism, and optimism.

In light of such anxiety some Americans thought it wise to retain some wilderness as a hedge against an overcivilized, over urbanized society. Thus was born another branch of the conservation movement: the preservation movement. Contrary to Gifford Pinchot, who believed that "the first principle of conservation is development . . ." such men as Robert Underwood Johnson, editor of *Century Magazine,* and naturalist John Muir advocated no use of some of the land. What they meant was no *economic* use, such as lumbering, mining, grazing, farming, or water development. Called preservationists, these Americans prodded Congress to establish national parks and a National Park Service (1916) dedicated to preserving some scenic areas in their natural state for future generations. From these beginnings has grown a strong movement to protect a small percentage of the land from commercial use.

Certainly the urge to preserve some of the American landscape was associated with another phenomena of the age: the rise of the city. A nation which found its roots in the farmhouse was now moving to city tenements. A people who had gauged their lives by nature's seasons and the rising and setting sun now found life's metronome in the repetitive regularity of the factory whistle and the time clock. Furthermore, the old customs were confused by a flood of immigrant groups with different language and customs. Many Americans wondered if all this change was entirely for the better.

Yet, the city had an undeniable appeal. The city at the turn-of-the-century represented the future. It offered opportunity, and in a certain sense, a new frontier. In the 19th Century ambitious young Americans turned to the land for wealth and success, but in the 20th Century the city—whether New York, Chicago, or San Francisco—offered the best chance for rapid advancement. Americans flocked to the city for opportunity, culture, and excitement. Symphonies, theaters, art exhibits, and all sorts of entertainment added a new dimension to life. Some urban dwellers enjoyed the chance to choose from a wide range of services, including doctors, churches, stores, and schools. Finally, many city persons enjoyed the relative anonymity of the city, which was, of course, the antithesis of farm and small town living.

However people felt about the city, it had become a fact of American life. As one authority commented: "Cities like sex are here to stay." Ironically, rapid advances in agricultural technology and techniques helped make the city possible. In 1787 it required the labor of nine farming families to feed one urban family. But by the mid-20th Century eight urban families could subsist quite nicely on the labor of one mechanized farm family. The industrial revolution meant people were no longer bound to the soil. Statistics confirmed the fact. While only 13 percent of Americans lived in cities in 1850, that figure surged upward to 60 percent by 1950.

So the nation faced problems with the dawn of a new century, but the majority of Americans were optimistic. Writing of 19th Century America, historian Henry Steele Commager explained that "nothing in all history had ever succeeded like America, and every American knew it." And, Americans fervently believed the past was mere prologue to a glittering future. They looked forward to a new one hundred years which would bring national greatness and individual wealth—provided you had the good fortune to be a white male.

And why shouldn't Americans be optimistic? They had conquered a continent in practically the wink of an eye. They had farms to feed the western world with wheat and corn. Cities, such as Chicago and San Francisco, hummed with commercial activity, while providing cultural and intellectual activities as well. The American West, that great expanse of land between the two cities, offered a landscape comparable in scope to the peoples' hopes, dreams, and expectations. The West was spacious and spectacular, from the wonders of Yellowstone to the vast sweep of the Grand Canyon, and so was the American vision.

As if to match such spectacular natural history, Americans loved to boast of their collective achievements. They trumpeted their successes to the world, and backed up their boasts with statistics. Whether it was tons of wheat, acres of land, numbers of skyscrapers, children in school, or miles of railroad lines, Americans spoke in superlatives that no nation in the world could equal. The statistics were simply a microcosm of a new reality: the United States had come of age.

Sources and Suggested Readings

Bailey, Thomas, *A Diplomatic History of the American People* (1955).
Braeman, John, *Albert J. Beveridge: American Nationalist* (1971).
Brown, A. Theodore, Charles N. Glaab, *A History of Urban America* (1967).
DeConde, Alexander, *A History of American Foreign Policy* (1963).
DuBois, W. E. B., *The Souls of Black Folks* (1903).
Franklin, John Hope, *From Slavery to Freedom* (1974).
Goodwyn, Lawrence, *The Populist Moment* (1978).
Kerber, Linda, Jane DeHart Mathews, *Women's America: Refocusing the Past* (1982).
Morgan, H. W., *America's Road to Empire* (1965).
Pringle, Henry F., *Theodore Roosevelt* (1931).
Washington, Booker T., *Up From Slavery* (1900).
Weinberg, Albert K., *Manifest Destiny* (1935).
Wiebe, Robert H., *The Search For Order: 1877–1920* (1967).

Progressivism:
The Political Transition

William E. Gibbs
New Mexico Military Institute

The role that government should play in society is one of the most hotly debated political issues of the last two decades. Some, usually called conservatives, argue that government plays too great a role, thus obstructing natural growth and imposing a burden on the American taxpayer. One representative of this point of view has stated: "Government is not the solution; it is the problem." Others, usually known as liberals, insist that government should continue to play its essential role in managing social change, as it has throughout much of the twentieth century. Their conflict revolving around the role of government has its roots in the first two decades of this century, the Progressive Era, when the role of government underwent a critical transition from that of an inactive caretaker and watchdog of public affairs to an active participant establishing and guiding the course of the nation. In other words, the progressives produced, both in form and function, the modern political state of today.

During the event-filled years of Teddy Roosevelt and Woodrow Wilson, many sought to gain sufficient political power to enable them to manage the dynamic forces of change triggered by the nation's revolutionary industrial transformation of the previous thirty years, 1870–1900. Those engaged in these endeavors, the progressives, differed in their socio-economic background, motivation, place of origin and objectives. Many were from the middle class, and a few even possessed upper class credentials. Some represented the impoverished urban immigrants of the East, while others reflected the interests of the rural farmers of the West and South. A moralistic strain, rooted in fundamentalist Protestantism, elicited a sense of duty which compelled some to cry out like an evangelist for a return to the values of an agrarian yesterday; while others called impassionately for the application of scientific management to prepare more efficiently for an industrial tomorrow. With this great diversity, it is not difficult to understand why some historians have argued that this ill-defined and unsystematic clamor did not constitute a movement.

Nevertheless, while they differed in composition and disagreed as to impulses and objectives, there was general agreement as to method. Clearly, the various progressive groups recognized that the increasing use of collective action, primarily through the political state, to gain control and to direct change was an idea whose time had arrived. Throughout the early years of the century, these reformers organized into fragile, often shifting, coalitions both to acquire political power and to use that authority to give some order and direction to a society adrift. This process also involved the progressive effort to streamline and to refine political institutions as instruments to direct social change. As a result of these efforts, new operating procedures were developed which led to the bureaucratic political state of today with its powerful executive, numerous regulatory commissions and extensive public interest-group involvement.

This modern managerial state was built to establish a new order after the breakdown of the old, nineteenth century social order. In the period after the Civil War, the nation had industrialized very rapidly. Railroads blanketed the country, and the steel industry easily outdistanced its European competitors. Petroleum, more and more concentrated in the hands of the able and ambitious John D. Rockefeller, mushroomed into a major industry. The timely arrival of vast numbers of European immigrants facilitated this transformation by providing the necessary labor force. Immigrants or the children of these immigrants, frequently living in deplorable tenement houses, made up seventy-five percent of the population of New York, Chicago, Cleveland, and Boston by the turn of the century. Such conditions made it clear to many that a value system, which worked well in the first half of the nineteenth century to regulate a rural, agrarian society, did not meet the needs of the rapidly emerging industrial giant. By World War I, the rapid economic transformation of society seemed to the young journalist, Walter Lippmann, to have set the country adrift, and many sought to acquire some mastery over this precarious condition.

The industrial transformation of society was accompanied by a simultaneous intellectual assault upon the nineteenth century value system. Even those in the ivy towers of college campuses recognized that society was "out of sync" and began to attack the old remedies and to prescribe new. Many college professors attacked those ideas which endorsed unrestricted individualism operating in a free, competitive marketplace controlled by the laws of nature. As a result, social Darwinism and ideas associated with the concept of laissez-faire became the objects of special criticism. Young scholars from various disciplines cranked out critical commentary on nature's supposed immutable laws of human behavior. Social scientists such as Richard T. Ely of the University of Wisconsin and Lester Ward of Brown University argued that man could undertake to control rather than simply be controlled by his environment. Philosophers William James and John Dewey insisted that the truth of an idea was based upon the success of its operation in the laboratory of life. Consequently, this philosophy, known as pragmatism, came to be based upon human actions rather than philosophical abstraction. Jurists Oliver W. Holmes, Jr., and Louis Brandeis challenged the idea that the law was fixed, stating that it, too, changed in response to the needs of society. Historians, likewise, began to challenge the time-honored interpretations of the past. Charles A. Beard shook the foundations of the traditionalist interpretation of creation of the Constitution when he argued in his *An Economic Interpretation of the Constitution*

(1913) that the founding fathers may have been inspired by their own economic concerns rather than selfless national interest.

Late nineteenth century scholars such as Ely, Ward, James and Holmes generally agreed that social institutions were constantly changing and that man could, through collective action, intervene to control and manage that change. To most academics of that era, government was the most logical institution to undertake the administration of social change. Few had faith, however, that the corrupt, party dominated, status quo-oriented political systems operating in the 1880's and 1890's would even address let alone remedy the grave problems confronting the nation. Many, especially those reflecting middle class values, insisted that government would have to be cleansed both of conservative and corrupt impurities as well as converted, along business lines, into an efficient managerial machine. Once in place, this instrument, they reasoned, could effectively manage social change, especially if it systematically applied scientific expertise.

It would be accurate to observe that an intellectual strategy for change did not of itself necessarily establish the right conditions to generate a reform movement. The temperament or mood of the country at the end of the century, however, was very receptive. Specifically, the decade of the 1890's, often erroneously pictured as "gay," provided the necessary ingredients of fear, anxiety, and despair which created that climate of opinion responsive to efforts to establish a new system of order.

Few periods have been so filled with turmoil and anxiety as the 1890's. With the Populist presidential campaign of 1892, the farmers' outcry for attention could be heard from Boston to San Diego. Calling for such "extreme" measures as a graduated income tax, direct election of senators, government ownership of the means of communication, the Populists frightened many. Mainstream industrial America breathed a collective sigh of relief when the Republican candidate, William McKinley, defeated the "wildman of the West", William Jennings Bryan, in 1896. At the same time, moreover, the United States experienced its most serious depression to date. With unemployment running as high as twenty percent and because of labor violence at the Homestead Steel plant in 1892 and during the Pullman Strike in Chicago in 1894, many even feared revolution. The middle class particularly felt threatened not only by labor violence from below but also from the concentration of capital (monopolies) from above. Between 1898 and 1902 this country experienced the most rapid period of corporate consolidation ever recorded. Two-thousand-five-hundred firms merged, and the first billion dollar concern, U.S. Steel, made its appearance. Big business appeared to be unrestrained in its quest to get even bigger.

The fluid climate of confusion brought together numerous elements of discontent. Specifically, various groups of the aggrieved came together because of their agreement upon one point—the unregulated economy was not working and some form of direct regulation appeared to be the logical alternative.

Coincidentally, a new form of what we would call investigative journalism greatly increased public awareness of the consequences of change without direction. Anticipated by Jacob Riis' exposure of the misery of the urban poor in *How the Other Half Lives* (1890) and Henry Demarest Lloyd's attack upon Standard Oil in *Wealth Against Commonwealth* (1894), these writers, whom Teddy Roosevelt referred to as muckrakers, burst upon the scene in 1902. Aided by reduced printing costs, cheap paper and a more literate and receptive mass-audience, magazines like *McClure's* and *Everybody's* provided a forum for young writers. Bernstein and Woodward's exposure of the Watergate scandal in the 1970's may have been based upon the example provided by journalists such as Lincoln Steffens, Ida Tarbell, Ray Stannard Baker, and Upton Sinclair. Their book length exposés, including Steffens' *Shame of the Cities,* Tarbell's *The History of the Standard Oil Company,* Baker's *Following the Color Line* and Sinclair's *The Jungle,* circulated detailed accounts of corruption of political officials, monopolies, discrimination against black Americans, and fraudulent claims of patent medicines, and unsanitary conditions in the meat packing industry. Their journalistic style, while a bit heavy on lamentation and light on remedy, pointed out the great disparity between American ideals and American social realities. It also touched the nation's nerves—nerves already frayed by the disconcerting decade of the nineties.

Coordinated efforts to establish some control over the flow of change through government intervention basically originated in that area of most immediate economic and social damage—the city. The approach employed by urban progressives in tackling their problems is significant for it established a process of intervention and control which helped shape the strategies employed by both state and national governments. Here the need for change was met by a technique which worked, at least on the local level.

The new middle class, squeezed from both above and below, provided the driving force behind urban reform. Occasionally aligned with labor, immigrant groups, intellectual types, the middle class primarily moved to make government more responsive to the people—specifically to the middle class. In this effort to establish what has come to be called direct democracy, its leaders sought to strip political parties and the bosses of power. They directed their attacks at city councils and legislative bodies, which they believed to be controlled by corrupt party officials who were the pawns of big business. This led in some instances to the restructuring of city governments by placing authority in commissions and city managers rather than city councilmen. By 1913, over 300 cities had adopted the commission plan and in the 1920's the city manager plan became equally popular. Urban progressives also placed additional trust in elected executive officers and reform mayors like Hazen Pingree of Detroit, Tom Johnson of Cleveland, and Sam "Golden Rule" Jones of Toledo. Although these men exercised considerable power, they too were subject to close scrutiny by "Leagues" of citizens and various "good government" groups.

Urban reform activists generally reflected the progressive interest in efficiency. In effect, they envisioned running city government on the corporate model. Mayors were to be managers who worked through committees of experts to run the cities scientifically. As a result, independent commissions staffed by professionals took over such responsibilities as constructing tax schedules, establishing transit and utility rates, and generally maintaining efficient service. This process did produce some meaningful results, and a number of cities established regulatory control over utilities, sometimes referred to as "gas and water" socialism. Pressured by representatives of various public interest groups such as representatives of settlement houses, civic federations, and bureaus of municipal research, numerous city governments moved to improve the safety of the work place, especially for women and children. The Triangle Shirtwaist Fire of 1911, which killed 146, mainly women, in New York, raised such a public outcry that both state and city governments enacted stricter building codes.

Contrary to the urban experiences, progressivism on the state level was essentially a twentieth century phenomena. It also differed in that it can be more specifically associated with one individual, Governor Robert La Follette of Wisconsin. Signs of discontent were much in evidence in Wisconsin, but they did not coalesce as a reform movement until "Fighting Bob" became governor in 1900. La Follette, influenced by Richard Ely and other social scientists located just down the street at the State University, turned his state into a laboratory of progressive reform. Other states such as Oregon, Minnesota, and New York soon followed La Follette's and Wisconsin's lead.

Many spokesmen for state interests, like their urban colleagues, argued that government must be made more responsive to public opinion in order to function as an effective instrument of social change. To accomplish this, Wisconsin introduced the initiative and referendum which permitted citizens to circumvent an unresponsive state legislature. By 1920 virtually every state had some form of citizen participation in the law-making process. Various measures directed at political corruption were also passed. These included the direct primary, which reduced the influence of party bosses by providing the rank and file party member with an opportunity to elect candidate of their choice. By 1916 all but three states had direct primaries. Another less used method was the direct recall of elected officials. Wisconsin also passed a Corrupt Practices Act, in addition to limiting campaign expenditures and lobbying activities.

Even more than their urban counterparts, state progressive leaders sought to administer change through the regulatory commission. Sharing the belief in scientific management, La Follette organized a number of independent, nonpartisan commissions staffed with college-trained experts. These regulatory agencies supervised rates and services for public utilities and transportation corporations as well as enforced policy decisions in matters of business, health, education, taxation, correction and conservation. According to progressive thinking, this system would enable the best minds to bring their intelligence to bear on the problems before them.

Strong executive leadership surfaced in other states as well. Using a similar political strategy, they, too, were able to gain control and direct the flow of change. Governors Albert Cummins of Iowa and Hiram Johnson of California succeeded in their efforts to regulate railroads. Governor William U'Ren of Oregon even secured passage of legislation regulating the working hours of women. In 1908 this legislation was successfully defended before the Supreme Court in the case of *Muller v. Oregon* by a progressive activist and future justice, Louis Brandeis. The Court's action in recognizing the right of a state to protect its workers led to the enactment of worker protection legislation in a number of additional states. Two-thirds established some type of employer liability insurance by 1916. By that date, this type of state action was generally assisted by data provided by such federal agencies as the Census Bureau and the newly created Department of Labor.

The progressives also registered significant gains in the South, especially in the area of business regulation. Although little was done to address the problem of child labor, southern progressives passed numerous measures to make democracy more direct through legislation providing for initiative, referendum, and the direct primary. Still, the South, remembering the Populist efforts to enlist Negro voting support, took great pains to keep the Afro-American disfranchised, making the direct primary an all white affair. This is not surprising since many of the progressive leaders of the South, such as James K. Vardaman of Mississippi and Hoke Smith of Georgia, were confirmed racists committed to keeping the Negro in "his place."

It would be inaccurate to infer that this was a condition unique to the South, for progressivism was a "white-only" phenomena throughout most of the country. During these years, 1900–1920, pseudoscientific claims purporting to prove black inferiority or its counterpart, white superiority, were widely made. Many, therefore, began to argue that maybe the Southerners had the right answer to the so-called "Negro Problem". Progressive leaders on the federal as well as state level regularly mirrored this sentiment and consequently were either openly hostile or at best indifferent toward the plight of the Negro. As a result, they frequently acquiesced to the application of the "southern solution" to remedy the race situation and virtually ignored persistent acts of discrimination (disfranchisement) and violence (lynching) directed at black Americans.

Progressivism on the state and local levels was able at best to employ only a piecemeal approach or it might be argued that they had limited goals. By 1912 conservative interest groups such as the National Association of Manufacturers were mounting effective resistance to continued government intervention. The reforms had gone far enough for this group. The tide of reform on the state level had to some degree ebbed, and most of the foremost progressive leaders, Robert La Follette, Albert Cummins, Hiram Johnson, had moved on to Washington, often as a result of the direct election of senators, to carry on and broaden the struggle.

The increasing awareness that some of the nation's problems were too big to handle or either the local or state level aroused many to call for action on the part of the national government. Even Thomas A. Edison, generally assumed to be preoccupied with a new experiment, observed "We've stumbled along for a while, trying to run a new civilization in old ways, but we've got to start to make this world over." In the first years of the twentieth century, the young man in the White House, Theodore Roosevelt, was not beyond believing that he was just the man "to make this world over." In need of a cause as well as a constituency, Teddy tuned in to the temper of the times and became the progressive movement's loudest cheerleader. Years spent in the West, about which he wrote several books, acquainted him with the exploitative practices of the railroads and the need for conservation. His role as Police Commissioner of New York exposed him to the deplorable conditions of the city, and he feared these could lead to revolution if not altered. Most important, Roosevelt, both by personality and by philosophical disposition, believed that government could and should intervene to manage change in America.

Roosevelt's appointed successor, William H. Taft, weighing nearly 300 pounds, did not have the energy or sympathy with the progressives's new managerial state to provide dynamic leadership. Quite frankly, Taft much preferred the company of conservative Republican senators like Nelson Aldrich of Rhode Island to the boisterous and self-righteous La Follette. While Taft did not provide leadership to the movement, he did not generally attempt to obstruct the efforts of the progressives to redefine the function and role of government. In fact, some of the most significant achievements were accomplished within the Taft years.

During Taft's first year in office, 1909, the publicist, Herbert Croly, published a book which not only provided a mid-stream evaluation of progressivism but also offered valuable insights into the directions its supporters should follow. In this important book, *The Promise of American Life,* Croly identified and confirmed the strategy of greater government involvement. Reflecting earlier scholarship, Croly pointed out that Americans had been forced to abandon the Jefferson ideal of individualism operating in a society regulated by natural laws functioning free from government interference. Croly, in its place, resurrected the thinking of Alexander Hamilton when he called for a new optimism based upon national purpose attainable through the guidance of an active political state.

The election of 1912, which elected Taft's Democrat opponent, Woodrow Wilson, provided an extensive hearing for Croly's thinking. Although Wilson was somewhat conservative by nature, especially on questions of race and women's rights, he, nonetheless, had solid progressive credentials as a governor of New Jersey. The campaign was complicated when Taft, even without progressive support, won the Republican nomination, causing Roosevelt to bolt the party to form the Progressive (Bull Moose) Party. Matters were further complicated when the Socialists put forth their own rather formidable candidate, Eugene V. Debs. The campaign, which did provide a rare opportunity for the American people to choose, soon settled into a race between Roosevelt and Wilson. In this confrontation, the question of the proper role of government became a significant issue between them. Roosevelt's campaign, which often sounded more like a crusade, developed a program, "New Nationalism," which leaned heavily upon Croly's suggestions, calling for an assertive federal government working through specialists to regulate large corporations rather than break them up. Although he was known as the "Trust Buster," Roosevelt demonstrated while in office, especially in agreements such as that made with U.S. Steel to buy the Tennessee Coal and Iron Company, that he preferred to work out regulatory arrangements. Wilson's program, "New Freedom," supported an active government, but he professed in 1912 to prefer to use the administrative machinery to break up rather than regulate the trusts. It is noteworthy that both accepted the new role of government, and in time it became obvious that their differences were primarily rhetorical, for Wilson by the time he was reelected in 1916 had moved his administration into a regulatory relationship with business not unlike that proposed by Croly.

During the years from Roosevelt through Wilson's first term (1901–1917), progressivism operated on the national level much as it functioned on both local and state levels. Consequently, it lends itself to a similar analysis. Initially, this involves the identification of efforts to establish more direct democracy and then the recognition and explanation of various measures designed to restructure the process of governing. Finally, it considers efforts of this newly emerging managerial state to address society's ills.

Actions taken to make democracy more direct and thus the national government more responsive to the people produced significant results during the Progressive Era. The most important measures were the seventeenth and the nineteenth amendments. The former provided for the direct election of senators, taking election from the hands of state legislators, whom most progessives considered notoriously venal. The amendment was introduced during the Taft presidency and became law in 1913. The latter, the nineteenth amendment, culminated a long campaign for the vote for women. Although Wilson only begrudgingly gave it his support, it was introduced, nonetheless, and became law in 1920. Other state measures, constructed to give the people more political leverage, were also considered at the national level. These included the direct primary as well as the initiative and referendum which Roosevelt and the Bull Moose Party incorporated into their platform in the campaign of 1912.

The process of governing, as it did on both state and local levels, underwent significant change during this important transitional period. The progressive preference for government by the executive provided the occasion for strong presidents to actually usurp prerogatives previously exercised by legislative bodies. Certainly, Roosevelt and Wilson and to a lesser degree Taft rejected the passive role played by their Gilded Age predecessors and acted decisively in new areas, formulating public policy, setting an agenda for Congress, and even in directly shaping public opinion. These presidents also played a far greater role in both the formulation and administration of foreign policy. While some people continued to oppose this type of assertive leadership, many willingly responded to the managerial presidency.

Both Roosevelt and Wilson certainly shared the progressive commitment to bureaucratic efficiency, and, like their urban and state counterparts, both extensively used regulatory commissions and agencies staffed with nonpartisan experts. This sharp change in administrative approach has had considerable impact on the conduct of affairs of government. Since these administrative bodies often had both investigative and enforcement powers, they actually assumed some of the traditional functions of the legislative branch. As a result, political parties, which had historically operated to secure control of legislative bodies, began to wane in importance, and special interest groups, which began to lobby before the regulatory commissions, began to wax in influence. Offices filled with professional lobbyists representing the Farmers Union, the American Federation of Teachers, the U.S. Chamber of Commerce, and other similar interest groups began to appear in Washington. As a result of these changes, the function and form of twentieth century national politics which operates today took definite shape during these progressive years.

This newly emerging managerial state not only resembled its state and local counterparts in composition and structure but also in function. As with progressive mayors and governors, the progressive presidents used the political state as an instrument to effect social change and to establish social control. Consequently, the concentration of capital in the form of monopolies, which many considered a threat to both democracy and capitalism, came in for considerable attention. In order to establish his political turf as well as his reputation, Roosevelt prosecuted and forced dissolution in 1904 of the Northern Securities Holding Company. Teddy thus acquired his "Trust Buster" title which stayed with him in spite of the fact that both Taft and Wilson prosecuted more trusts. Several measures followed in these productive, prewar years to extend the government's authority over business. In 1903, Roosevelt established the Bureau of Corporations which had the authority to subpoena information from corporations necessary for prosecution under the Sherman Antitrust Act of 1890. Wilson's Federal Trade Commission (1914) and the Clayton Antitrust Act (1914) further equipped the government to undertake such prosecution. On numerous occasions, moreover, these regulatory agencies simply used the threat of investigation to successfully deter excessive and illegal consolidation.

As might be expected, the much-hated railroads came in for their share of federal regulatory attention. The Hepburn Act (1906) passed during the second Roosevelt administration moderately strengthened the Interstate Commerce Act by authorizing the Interstate Commerce Commission to set rates as well as outlaw rebates. The Mann-Elkins Act (1910), passed under Taft, further strengthened the Commission. These regulatory controls grew into outright nationalization of the railroads during World War I.

Various measures specifically added to the federal government's authority to exercise control over certain social conditions. The Pure Food and Drug Act and the Meat Inspection Act (1906), the latter to some degree the product of Roosevelt's reading of Upton Sinclair's muckraking account, *The Jungle,* equipped the government to intervene to protect public health. Other such measures included the Mann Act (1910), passed under Taft, which attacked prostitution and several pieces of labor legislation such as the Child Labor Act (later declared unconstitutional) and the Adamson Act (1916). The latter two laws were passed during Wilson's first term and extended the authority of the federal government to regulate working conditions, thus they had social impact. Frequently state legislation in these same areas was stronger and buttressed the federal effort. This was particularly the case in Maine, Pennsylvania, and Wisconsin.

Probably the most important measures to extend the managerial authority of the federal government were those establishing the conservation program, the Federal Reserve system and the national income tax. Beginning with the Newlands Act (1902), which used federal money acquired from the sale of land to establish irrigation projects in the West, conservation measures, initially administered by Roosevelt's chief forester, Gifford Pinchot, reclaimed and returned millions of acres to the national reserve. Although the controversy between Pinchot and Taft's Secretary of the Interior, Richard A. Ballinger, contributed to the split between Taft and Roosevelt, new conservation measures continued to be passed which substantially increased the responsibility of the federal government to manage the land. The Federal Reserve Act (1913) sought to establish a system to control the supply of money and credit by setting up a system of twelve regional banks supervised by a central bank in Washington. With this Wilsonian measure, the national government's regulatory role would extend, especially after the Depression in the thirties, to the money supply itself. The Sixteenth Amendment (1913) permitted the federal government to tax incomes in order to fund its increased activities as well as to try to effect a redistribution of the wealth. It is significant to note that these measures increased the government's primary role to operate in a preventive rather than in a remedial capacity. In other words, the progressive managerial state began to acquire the authority to remove the causes of problems rather than simply address the effects.

After 1914 international affairs diverted much of the progressives' as well as President Wilson's attention. With the exception of a politically motivated spurt of legislation in 1916, Wilson's domestic reform program was complete. Entrance into World War I, however, provided a splendid opportunity for the progressive approach to government to prove its worth. Managerial government with its emphasis on a strong executive administering through professionally staffed committees adapted most suitably to the wartime situation. Progressive offspring such as the War Industries Board, headed by Bernard M. Baruch, assumed responsibility for increasing manufacturing efficiency. Herbert Hoover's Food Administration mobilized agricultural production, and the Committee on Public Information, directed by George Creel, managed as well as manufactured public opinion toward the war.

While some progressives, most notably Robert LaFollette and Jane Addams, opposed intervention in Europe, others, such as Theodore Roosevelt, resorted to their oft-used rationales to justify participation. In the minds of the latter, intervention was simply another example of government intervention to impose order; this time it happened to be upon a post-industrial world gone amuck. Woodrow Wilson certainly saw it that way through his professorial, pince-nez spectacles. In justifying United States involvement, he used typically idealistic progressive rhetoric referring to the encounter as a "war to end all wars" and a "war to make the world safe for democracy." This, however, had rather unfortunate results for a military victory could hardly achieve those lofty goals. Expectations were not met, frustration ensued and many began to question the value both of the war effort and of the progressive approach in general. The rejection of the League of Nations, which many progressive reformers saw as a vehicle to intervene internationally to again impose their idea of order, prompted the well-known editor of the *Emporia Gazette,* William Allen White, to write "the strains of war and the frustration of peace shattered the progressive movement." Just as Georgia politician, Tom Watson, noted earlier with reference to populism and the Spanish-American War, the sweet voice of the bird of reform was drowned out in the blare of the bugle.

The decade of the twenties, to some degree, confirmed White's judgment. The progressive impulse to establish social justice certainly never revived very strongly. The burgeoning consumer society siphoned off many activist groups, especially the professionals and small businessmen, who had earlier supported such causes. "Main Street" ideals, so aptly identified in Sinclair Lewis' novels, *Main Street* (1920) and *Babbitt* (1922), replaced them. The predisposition to intervene politically in society in addition to the product of the application of the progressive method, the managerial state, nevertheless, remained intact. Unfortunately, both served equally well during these postwar years those forces of social coercion in their quest through prohibition (Eighteenth Amendment) and immigration restrictions (Johnson Act, 1921; National Origins Act, 1924) to create a culturally homogeneous society.

The twenties demonstrated that the progressive reform impulse might have waned but the apparatus created to translate this inspiration into social reality remained in place readily available to whomever had the political power to use it. This was certainly the case when Franklin D. Roosevelt used the managerial state operating through inumerable expert committees, frequently called alphabet agencies, to organize American efforts at mastering the Depression in the thirties and the Axis powers in the forties.

Over the years, historians have differed greatly in their evaluation of the Progressive Era. Some see it as simply an effort on the part of conservative groups to turn back the clock to the individualist setting of the nineteenth century. Others insist that it was designed to curb the intense competition

American doughboys in action in France during World War I. (Courtesy of National Archives.)

emerging in the twentieth century. Many have challenged claims that it was a social reform movement, insisting that it did little to alleviate the hardships of the poor and in fact contributed substantially to making life more difficult for Afro-Americans and other minority groups. While assessing the entire progressive record continues to be both difficult and controversial, the fact remains that much of what the progressives did still influences our lives. Reform mayors, frequently doing battle with political machines, continue to hold forth in city halls across the country. In addition, city codes remain filled with regulatory measures controlling the work place and building practices. Governors, like "Fighting Bob" La Follette, still get elected by attacking the "interests". To do so, however, they must first win their party's direct primary. Presidents, even the conservative ones, continue to curry public favor by fondly recalling the deeds of Teddy Roosevelt and Woodrow Wilson. Once more, our daily lives are filled with vestiges of progressives' labors. For instance, it would not be at all surprising to pick up a local newspaper which might include on the front page some reference to new meat inspection procedures along with a discussion of the fact that more and more women are running for the United States Senate. The page treating recreational activities might make some reference to additional camping facilities in one of the national parks. In the business section, there might be considerable commentary concerning the recent prosecution of a giant corporation for violation of antitrust laws. Of course there might be some unappealing reminders of the progressive years especially if the paper commented on the magnitude of the federal income tax.

The legacy of the Progressive Era does not consist, however, of just reforms and reformers but primarily of an attitude toward the role of government and its sponsored institution, the managerial state. In the transitional period between 1900 and 1920, Americans invested in government the responsibility for resolving the problems associated with rapid economic and social change. Simultaneously, the bureaucratic state based upon a strong executive managing society through nonpartisan and largely independent regulatory commissions evolved to meet the newly acquired responsibilities. This attitude and this institution have remained most formidable throughout the twentieth century. In spite of the efforts of some politicians to "get government off our backs", it is not likely soon to go away, and in fact, most people are conditioned to accept government controls, as needs arise.

Sources and Suggested Readings

Blum, John Morton, *The Progressive Presidents* (1980).
Buenker, John D., John C. Burnhan, Robert Crunden, *Progressivism* (1977).
Buenker, John D., *Urban Liberalism and Progressive Reform* (1973).
Croly, Herbert, *The Promise of American Life* (1909).
Chambers, James Whiteclay, *The Tyranny of Change: America In the Progressive Era, 1900–1917* (1980).
Gould, Lewis, ed., *The Progressive Era* (1974).
Kennedy, David, *Progressivism: The Critical Issues* (1971).
Link, Arthur, and Richard L. McCormick, *Progressivism* (1983).
Lippmann, Walter, *Drift and Mastery: An Attempt to Diagnose the Current Unrest* (1914).
Nugent, Walter R. K., *From Centennial to World War: American Society, 1876–1917* (197).
O'Neill, William L., *The Progressive Years: America Comes of Age* (1975).
Schiesl, Martin J., *The Politics of Efficiency: Municipal Administration and Reform in America, 1880–1920* (1977).
Unger, Irwin, *The Vulnerable Years: The United States, 1896–1917* (1977).
Wiebe, Robert H., *The Search For Order* (1967).

American Foreign Policy: From Regionalism to Globalism

Thomas M. Leonard
University of North Florida

The emergence of the United States as a global power began in 1898, 122 years after independence. Prior to the Civil War, United States expansion was largely a westward movement, essentially continental and anti-colonial. Following the war, while most Americans concentrated upon the development of the West and industrialization east of the Mississippi River, new factors influenced the nation's foreign policy. There was a resurgence of Manifest Destiny—the idea that the U.S. had a God given mission to extend the area of freedom overseas. Americans rationalized that their democratic institutions should be extended to less fortunate peoples and that the United States had a responsibility to insure that backward countries and peoples be protected from European imperialism. Interest in new markets paralleled the nation's industrial development. This was particularly true in the 1890s, when the western frontier closed. There was acute agrarian distress, and the depression of 1893 caused commercial leaders to lose confidence in the belief that domestic markets would continue to provide for national prosperity. Accompanying this "outward look," there was a need for securing the areas of expansion. Large merchant and naval fleets were needed, along with coaling stations in order to sustain communication lines. Imperialism led to war with Spain and to America's gaining an empire.

After the Spanish American war, American policy continued to be imperialist. One of its major goals was a canal across central America. The ninety day voyage of the cruiser *Oregon* around the tip of South America to the Caribbean Sea during the war dramatized the military advantage of a canal. In 1898, President William McKinley, referring to the canal, told Congress that "our national policy now more imperatively than ever calls for its control by this government." The U.S. desire for a canal came at a time when Britain was fighting the Boer War in Africa and facing an aggressive German policy on the continent, and thus was anxious for new friendships. As a result, the British acquiesed to the U.S. request for abrogation of the Clayton-Bulwer Treaty of 1850, which called for joint control. A new treaty, the 1901 Hay-Paunceforte agreement resulted.

Subsequently, American officials determined to construct a canal through Panama, then a province of Colombia, but the Colombian senate rejected the Hay-Herran treaty on the grounds that compensation was inadequate. The treaty's rejection caused the Panamanians, long discriminated against by the Colombians, to intensify their demand for independence. President Theodore Roosevelt did nothing to discourage the independence movement. When the Panamanians revolted on November 3, 1903, U.S. marines were readily available to protect the trans-isthmian railway, but in the process they prevented Colombian troops from suppressing the revolt. Three days later, recognition was extended to Panama, and on November 18, 1903, Secretary of State John Hay completed negotiations with Philippe Bunau-Varilla, providing for U.S. construction of a trans-isthmian canal.

The interoceanic canal pleased the expansionists, and it also brought new considerations to American foreign policy. Given their histories of political instability and financial mismanagement, the Caribbean peoples were considered inferior by the Americans. These same factors threatened the canal's security. Such fears contributed to the U.S. rationalization that it must establish a protectorate over the region. President Roosevelt affirmed this policy in his annual message to Congress in December, 1904. He explained that flagrant cases of wrongdoing or impotence would force the United States reluctantly to intervene as an international police power. Termed the "Roosevelt Corollary" to the Monroe Doctrine, it justified United States actions in the Caribbean through 1920, by which time a protectorate over the region was established.

Roosevelt's "corollary" expressed what already was being practiced. Although the 1898 Teller Amendment disclaimed any intention to annex Cuba, subsequent decisions gave the United States wide latitude over Cuba's internal affairs. The 1901 Platt Amendment was incorporated into the Cuban constitution and later embodied in a treaty. Accordingly, Cuba could make no treaty impairing its independence or incur foreign debt beyond its means. Also, the Americans gained the right to intervene in Cuba to maintain public order, sponsor sanitation programs, and build a naval base. Secretary of State Elihu Root explained that these measures were necessary for the security of the anticipated Panama Canal. Until World War I, the U.S. Army administered Cuba with a "moral suzerainty," suppressing guerilla revolts, supervising the writing of a new constitution and electoral code, and building roads, schools and sanitation facilities. The island's stability encouraged further private U.S. investment, while Cuban sugar enjoyed a reduced tariff on the mainland, Cubans came to resent the substitution of United States for Spanish authority.

Similar authority was found in the 1903 Hay-Bunau-Varilla treaty with Panama, which permitted the United States to act "as if it were sovereign" in the canal zone, guarantee Panamanian independence, and maintain public order in the republic. In application, the U.S. served as arbiter of the Panamanian-Costa Rican boundary dispute, settled in favor of the latter; prevented Panama from granting railroad and harbor concessions to foreign interests; assumed control of radio and civil aviation in Panama; and sent troops into the republic on three different occasions to quell public disorder and supervise the 1908, 1912 and 1918 elections. As with Cuba, the U.S. used moral righteousness to protect its interests.

The threat of European intervention in 1904 in the Dominican Republic resulted in the application of Roosevelt's "corollary." Beset by civil war, the Dominicans feared German, Spanish, and Italian intervention to protect their citizens and investments. When the war ended in 1905, the Europeans sought United States assistance with debt collection from the Dominicans. The Americans willingly obliged, establishing a customs receivership in 1905. Roosevelt asserted that such actions prevented financial calamity and European intervention.

The same was not true of President Woodrow Wilson's Dominican venture in 1916. The republic was beset by turmoil and corruption following the 1911 assassination of President Ramón Cáceras, which strongly influenced Wilson's determination to restore constitutional order. Marines were landed to protect American citizens and property, and supervise presidential elections. However, Captain Henry Knapp declared martial law, and within a year began supervision of a moral crusade which included construction of educational and sanitation facilities, roads and communication systems, fiscal reform and constitutional government. Like Cuba and Panama, the Dominican Republic became a United States protectorate.

The events leading to intervention in Haiti differed from those in the Dominican Republic, but the results were the same. When violence erupted in July, 1915, following the assassination of President Vilbrun Guillame Sam, President Wilson easily justified the dispatch of Admiral William Caperton with five companies of troops to restore order. Caperton declared martial law, established a client government, and forced a treaty upon Haiti granting the U.S. wide discretion over that nation's internal affairs. Caperton was replaced by Army Colonel Littleton Waller and Major Smedley Butler, who by 1919 directed the elimination of guerrilla opposition and established a national guard to maintain public order. A new constitution, written in the State Department and opening agricultural lands to foreign investments, was forced upon Haiti. The U.S. actions in Haiti secured the Caribbean's island perimeter.

Wilson's moral crusade, however, failed in Mexico. By 1913 some 50,000 Americans lived in Mexico, with investments totaling about one billion dollars. At the time of his inauguration, Wilson was confronted with an intensely nationalistic "government of butchers" headed by Victoriano Huerta, who had deposed and assassinated President-elect Francisco Madero. With U.S. private interests threatened, Wilson determined to install a democratic and pro-American government in Mexico City. When nonrecognition failed to dislodge Huerta, Wilson, in February, 1914, lifted the existing arms embargo, thus permitting supplies to reach Huerta's opponents. Subsequently, jingoism increased on both sides, and fighting finally erupted on April 21, 1914, when Wilson ordered the American occupation of Vera Cruz to prevent delivery of German arms to Huerta's government.

With war threatening, Wilson was pleased with the Argentine, Brazilian and Chilean mediation offer. Mexico nationalism, opposed to any type of intervention in its domestic affairs, was at cross currents with Wilson's objectives, causing the mediation effort to fail. In July, 1914, Huerta fled to Spain, replaced by conservative General Venustiano Carranza. With order restored and U.S. interests apparently secure, recognition was extended to the Carranza government in October, 1915.

Peace did not come to Mexico. Carranza, not a reformer, soon found himself under attack by *caudillas* throughout the countryside. Among the most notable was Francisco Villa, whose strong anti-American sentiment caused him to ransack the town of Columbus, New Mexico, March 9, 1916, killing 17 Americans. In response, Wilson ordered General John Pershing to capture Villa. With nearly 12,000 men, Pershing marched some 300 miles into Mexico in unsuccessful pursuit. With the coming of World War I, Wilson was forced to abandon his Mexican initiative.

While the Americans clearly defined the Caribbean in terms of regional self interest, and pursued their goals relatively free of European competition, the same was not true in the Pacific. Economic contact can be traced to 1784, after which the attraction of trade with China increased. The opening of Japan in 1854 accelerated economic interest in the entire Far East. The completion of the transcontinental railroad in 1869 served as a stimulus to trade with Australia and New Zealand. After the Civil War the missionary desire to "civilize" the Asians fell in line with the expansionists push for a Pacific empire.

The first step towards establishing a prominent position in the Pacific was the uncomfortable arrangement in 1889 with Great Britain, which withdrew in 1899, and Germany to estabilsh a protectorate over Somoa, an important coaling station for U.S. ships trading in the southwest Pacific. The second step was Hawaii, annexed in the midst of the Spanish-American War, July 7, 1898. Interest in Hawaii began in the 1820s and with the development of sugar which enjoyed reduced U.S. tariffs after 1875. The attempt at annexation in 1854 was rejected by the Senate, and in 1893 by anti-expansionist President Grover Cleveland. Although President McKinley initiated a new annexation treaty in July, 1897, it took Admiral George Dewey's victory at Manila Bay on May 1, 1898, to demosntrate the greater importance of Hawaii as a coaling station and as the first line of Pacific defense.

The final significant acquisition in the Pacific was the Philippine Islands, which few Americans considered important during the 1890s. Following Dewey's victory over the Spanish at Manila Bay, the American forces were hesitant and did not take the city of Manila until August. When peace negotiations began in Paris in October, 1898, McKinley's instructions were vague, alluding only to the strategic and commercial advantages of Luzon, with its port at Manila. In reality, McKinley, an expansionist, was waiting for public opinion to catch up with him. It did. As expected, long time expansionists—Beveridge, Hearst, Lodge, and Mahan—clamoured for annexation. They gained support from the business community. Although originally against the war, it now recognized the advantages of the Philippines. Various Chambers of Commerce and the *Wall Street Journal* spoke of expanded markets and profits in the Far East, with the Philippines as an operational base to the entire Asian mainland. As the evidence began to pile up on behalf of strategic and economic interests,

After the Spanish American War U.S. forces occupy the Philippine Islands. (Courtesy of National Archives.)

the Americans also came to judge the Filipinos not capable of self government. To sanctify annexation, McKinley announced that there was nothing left to do but "uplift and civilize and Christianize" the Filipinos. The St. Louis *Post Dispatch* was more accurate when it stated that "we want this colony."

From 1899 to 1917, particularly to 1910, U.S. activities in Asia intensified. China became the center of attention. Businessmen, financiers and railroad builders saw profits in China's underdeveloped interior; missionaries envisioned converting millions of Chinese to Christianity; idealists hoped to plant democracy on the mainland; and naval officers wanted coastline bases. Economic interest, however, was the most dominant element of American policy towards China.

United States interests in China were threatened by the imperial designs of other nations that already had carved out spheres of influence. The British followed by the Germans, Russians and Japanese, established monopolies in China's most lucrative areas. When U.S. interests in China developed during the Spanish-American War in 1898, it found itself nearly shut off from the mainland. As a result, the U.S. found an open door, whereby there would be equal treatment of trade in China.

The British with their interests also threatened, were interested in a co-operative policy. When Alfred E. Hippisley, a British employee in China, broached the subject to his long time American friend William W. Rockhill in 1899, he found a receptive ear. Rockhill served as an informal advisor to Secretary Hay, also an expansionist and strong anglophile. During the summer of 1899, the three threshed out a memorandum sent to Britain, Germany, Russia, France, Japan, and Italy. The note was not designed to protect China; nor did it object to spheres of influence. Rather, the note served U.S. interests by asking each nation not to discriminate against other countries in their spheres in regard to tariffs, harbor dues, and railroad rates. In effect, an Open Door. With the exception of Italy, which had no sphere of influence in China, each nation returned a qualified response. Undaunted, Hay announced that all had accepted the Open Door, and his bluff was not called. Hay's action may have strengthened McKinley's position against the anti-imperialists, but it brought no practical benefits to China.

Economic self-interest, not concern for China or its people, motivated the second Open Door note in July, 1900. Expanding upon the first note, Hay now called for recognition of Chinese territorial integrity and administrative unity. Couched in terms that U.S. policy was "to seek a solution" to the two problems, the second note did not call for or receive an answer. Because of Japanese and Russian encroachments in China and of America's military weakness, the question became one of how to keep the door open.

In the decade and a half that followed the Open Door notes, the United States government and private citizens suffered frustrations, disappointments, and failures in China. Reverses occurred in investment schemes and trade patterns, which were further aggravated by the 1911 Chinese revolution and Japan's growth as an Asiatic power.

Among the businessmen who looked to China for profits were E. H. Harriman, J. P. Morgan, John D. Rockefeller, and Jacob Schiff. President William Howard Taft's Secretary of State, Philander C. Knox, saw the government and business sharing common interest in Asia, but by the time he took office in 1909, U.S. enthusiasm for projects in China began to wane. Their combined efforts however, were not productive. Trade with China remained less than three percent of the total value of U.S. trade by 1917.

President Wilson extended recognition to the Chinese Republic in May 1913 following Sun Yat-sen's revolution. Despite being the first great power to do so, the United States remained isolated in China by 1917. Unable to gain influence through moral suasion or economic investment, the United States

"Dawn of Day in the Antilles" (1898); The Flag as symbol of American Imperialism. (Reproduced from the collections of the Library of Congress.)

lost out to the growing power of Japan. Because of limited natural resources and a large population, Japan began looking outward by the turn of the century, joining the great powers in the race for colonies, particularly in China.

Viewing the Russians as their chief competitors, the Japanese set out to check Russian advances. Diplomacy failed and war came in 1904 with the Japanese attack upon the Russian stronghold at Port Arthur. The Russo-Japanese War provided President Roosevelt with an opportunity to secure U.S. interests in the Pacific, especially from Japanese advances. Roosevelt wanted Russia strong enough to remain a counter force to the Japanese in Asia and Japan too weak to challenge the Open Door. Thus, he approved the agreement reached between his Secretary of War, William Howard Taft and Japanese Foreign Minister, Taro Katsura in July, 1905, whereby Japan pledged not to attack the Philippines and the U.S. recognized Japan's suzerainty over Korea.

Roosevelt next served as an "honest broker," resulting in the 1905 Portsmouth Treaty, which ended the Russo-Japanese War. The treaty was generous to Japan, confirming her Korean role, granting her the Russian mining and railroad interests in Southern Manchuria, and the possession of the southern half of Sakhalin Island, but the treaty did not provide an anticipated indemnity. Japanese hostility immediately followed, which thereafter characterized relations with the United States.

The U.S. belief in Japanese racial inferiority further strained relations. The 1906–1907 "yellow peril" fear throughout California best illustrated the U.S. attitude. Only direct pressure from President Roosevelt prevented the segregation of Japanese school children—all 93—in San Francisco. His subsequent "Gentleman's Agreement" prevented the migration of Japanese coolie labor to the United States. The Japanese were not pleased.

Continued Japanese bellicosity significantly contributed to Roosevelt's decision to send the navy on a global cruise in 1908. The Japanese reluctantly invited the fleet to stop at Yokahama. Quiet diplomacy also prevailed. On November 30, 1908, Secretary of State Elihu Root and Japanese Minister Kogoro Takahira reached a diplomatic agreement. It provided for the maintenance of the status quo in the Pacific, respect for each other's territorial possessions in the region, a pledge to uphold the Open Door in China, and support by peaceful means the independence and integrity of China. In desiring to establish more cordial relations with Japan, however, Roosevelt actually weakened the Open Door principles, by not clearly limiting Japanese rights on the mainland.

World War I further strained United States-Japanese relations. First, Secretary of State William Jennings Bryan failed to persuade the belligerents to maintain the status quo in the Far East. Next, Japan, invoking the 1902 treaty with Britain, declared war on Germany, seizing control of the Shantung Peninsula. Also, by agreement with Britain, and subsequently with other European powers, the Japanese occupied German controlled islands. Finally, in January, 1915, the Japanese issued a secret ultimatum to China known as the Twenty-One Demands. The ultimatum sought to establish Japan's political and economic supremacy in China. The Chinese turned to their American friends, whose diplomatic pressure forced the Japanese to back down on its political but not its economic demands. Japan further solidified its Far Eastern position with the Lansing-Ishii Agreement in November, 1917. While pledging to uphold the Open Door, the agreement specified that "territorial propinquity creates special relations between countries . . . and consequently . . . the United States recognizes that Japan has special interests in China, particularly in the part to which her possessions are contiguous." While the U.S. emphasized the Open Door, the Tokyo government interpreted the agreement to mean U.S. recognition of paramount Japanese interests in China. Furthermore, Japan believed that exploitation of China could continue, provided no territory was annexed.

The United States was unable to achieve its objectives in Asia. Lacking sufficient power to implement its policy, no gains were made in China or in the effort to restrict Japanese expansion. The continued belief that China would become Asia's major power and, therefore, that its integrity he maintained, caused perilous conditions for the United States in Asia.

As the United States' global power grew, its most important contacts with Europe resulted from a conflict of interests in the Far East and Latin America. Although scant attention was given to European affairs, the U.S. was not truly isolated from the continent. It remained America's largest trading partner; immigration strengthened cultural and personal links; and occasional crisis generated official and public attention.

Except for President Roosevelt's role in convening the 1906 Algeciras Conference to settle territorial conflicts in Morocco, the United States remained an observer of the shifting European balance of power in the early twentieth century. Few Americans shared Roosevelt's belief that the United States could no longer remain aloof from European conflicts, which might lead to war, and affect America's global interests. Nor did most Americans understand Roosevelt in 1911 when he observed that "we ourselves are becoming, owing to our strength and geographic situation, more and more the balance of power of the whole globe." By 1914 most Americans still were not interested in European affairs.

The popular aloofness was evident when the Austrian Archduke, Franz Ferdinand was assassinated in June 1914 and war erupted in August. President Woodrow Wilson reflected this sentiment in his August 4, 1914, neturality proclamation. "The United States must be neutral in fact as well as in name. . . . We must be impartial in thought as well as action," he asserted. Events over the next three years, however, brought the U.S. into war. These events reenforced American sentiments developed since the 1880's, which were decidedly pro-British.

Wilson's great passion was to exert moral leadership in world affairs, and in that capacity he hoped to serve as an honest broker in bringing that conflict to an end. Wilson sent his most intimate advisor, Edward M. House, on two peace missions to Europe. In January, 1915, the Germans appeared anxious at the possibility of a negotiated settlement, but the British were not. When the British delayed House in London until March, the German desire disappeared. A year later House again returned to Europe and reached an agreement with British Foreign Minister Sir Edward Grey in February. The decidedly pro-Allied memorandum provided that the British and French, at the opportune moment, would propose that Wilson initiate a conference, and if Germany refused or the conference failed, the U.S. would *probably* enter the war on the Allied side. Wilson underscored the word probably before approving the agreement, thus not making a binding pledge. The opportune moment never came because British and French forces were unable to seize a battlefront advantage.

Frustrated, Wilson appealed for a negotiated settlement in a note directed to the belligerents on December 18, 1916, six days after the Germans issued an unexpected statement declaring their willingness to discuss a peace settlement. Confident of a victory, the Germans determined that rejection of the offer was cause to renew the offensive. Because the notes came so close together, the British and French incorrectly suspected collusion, rejected negotiations, and pursued instead indemnities and destruction of Germany.

Wilson made one last effort on January 22, 1917. He called for "peace without victory," based upon the equality of nations, freedom of the seas and world disarmament, all to be accomplished through a league of nations. Wilson's idealism fell on deaf ears.

United States economic policies, on the other hand, significantly contributed to its entry into the war. Not fully recovered from the 1907 economic setback, U.S. conditions were further worsened by the loss of German markets once war broke out. At first, Wilson proclaimed that neutrality, permitted the Americans to sell material to both sides on a cash basis only, and initially rejected any plans for financial assistance to the belligerents. Soon out of funds, the Allies, along with U.S. bankers pressured for a policy change. Following the resignation of Secretary of State William Jennings Bryan, an ardent neutral, Wilson informed bankers they could make loans. By the time the U.S. entered the war in 1917, nearly $2.3 billion was advanced to the Allies, but only $27 million to the Germans. Trade figures until 1917 revealed a 290% increase in U.S.-Allied trade and a 93% increase with the Central powers. Prosperity was distinctly tied to the Allied side.

The American response to neutral rights violations also clearly indicated its pro-Allied attitude. Neither the British nor the Germans accepted Wilson's position, that as a neutral, the U.S. had the right to trade unmolested with the belligerents. The British moved quickly. The North Sea was declared a military area and it was mined. Ships were stopped on the high seas and seized if carrying contraband, an ever widening list of goods that eventually included foodstuffs and textiles. The British also created a Black List, censored neutral mail, and cut the trans-Atlantic cable to the continent. London did not take U.S. protests seriously and generally persuaded the Americans that such actions were essential for winning the war.

More alarming was the German use of submarines, considered immoral and illegal. Secretary Bryan's suggestion that all U.S. ships and citizens stay out of the war zones, was dismissed by Wilson on the grounds that freedom of the seas must be upheld. Germany was to be held in "strict accountability" for the loss of any American lives to submarines. Wilson's position hardened following the sinking of the *Lusitania* May 7, 1915, by a German submarine. Despite a harsh public stance, German submarine commanders secretly were instructed not to attack passenger liners. The Germans again softened in August, 1915, when the *Arabic* was sunk and agreed to pay an indemnity. Calm prevailed for seven months until March, 1916, when the *Sussex* was torpedoed. Wilson was adamant. The sinking of another passenger ship would because for severing diplomatic relations with Germany, he declared. With one condition, the Germans yielded—that Britain relax its food blockade of Germany. Wilson accepted the submarine pledge as binding, but ignored the attached condition.

That event gave the impression of a Wilsonian diplomatic victory, but in reality Wilson backed himself into a corner. While the British release of the Zimmermann note, a German lure to bring Mexico into the war against the United States, and the 1917 revolution in Russia, which potentially would end fighting on the eastern front, were important factors, it was the submarine that served as the immediate catalyst to U.S. entry. On January 31, 1917, Germany announced the resumption of unrestricted submarine warfare. From March 12 to 19, 1917, three U.S. ships were torpedoed. Wilson's hand was forced. He asked for and received from Congress a declaration of war.

The submarine brought war to the United States in 1917, but its attitudes and policies during the preceding thirty years made it more sympathetic to the British cause, as demonstrated by financial and trade patterns from 1914 to 1917. Germany had long been perceived as a rival, and therefore found it difficult to gain American sympathy.

The United States contributions to World War I completed its development into a global power. The policies of Presidents Roosevelt, Taft, and Wilson continuously moved the U.S. in that direction. Confident of its superior system, and economically energetic, the United States sought dominant political influence as it reached around the globe. Policies met with varied success. The Caribbean became a regional sphere of influence, Pacific interests were on tenuous ground, and the European connection, because of the war, became more tightly knit.

Sources and Suggested Readings

Beale, Howard K., *Theodore Roosevelt and The Rise of America to a World Power* (1956).

Cooper, John Milton, *The Warrior and the Priest: Woodrow Wilson and Theodore Roosevelt* (1983).

Dobson, John M., *America's Ascent: The United States Becomes a Great Power, 1880–1914* (1978).

Gregory, Ross, *The Origins of American Intervention in The First World War* (1971).

Iriye, Akire, *Pacific Estrangement: Japanese and American Expansion, 1897–1911* (1972).

Link, Arthur S., *Woodrow Wilson: Revolution, War and Peace* (1979).

Marks, Frederick W., *Velvet and Iron: The Diplomacy of Theodore Roosevelt* (1979).

May, Ernest R., *Imperial Democracy: The Emergence of America as a Great Power* (1961).

May, Ernest R., *World War and American Isolation, 1914–1917* (1957).

Munro, Dana G., *Intervention and Dollar Diplomacy in The Caribbean, 1900–1921* (1964).

Scholes, Walter V., and Marie V. Scholes, *The Foreign Policy of the Taft Administration* (1970).

From Versailles Through the Great Depression

Peter H. Buckingham
Southwest Texas State University

In December 1918, as the U.S.S. *George Washington* steamed toward Europe carrying the American peace delegation, President Woodrow Wilson became apprehensive about what the coming months and years would bring. "What I seem to see—I hope I am wrong—" he told a friend, "is a tragedy of disappointment." As it turned out, the subsequent peace disappointed almost everyone, Wilson included. When the terms of the Treaty of Versailles became known, Marshall Ferdinand Foch made a prophecy of his own, tragically accurate, commenting: "This is not Peace. It is an Armistice for twenty years."

Many of Wilson's admirers and detractors viewed him as an idealist hoodwinked by crafty, stripe-trousered diplomats of the Old World. In reality, the President was a hard-headed realist with a clear understanding of what had to be done at the Paris Peace Conference in order to assure future world tranquility and continued American prosperity. Like so many of his fellow citizens, Wilson had an unshakable faith in the uniqueness of the United States, feeling that American society had been born late enough to escape the difficult transition from feudal to modern liberal institutions and values. The purer and more rational American version of liberal-capitalism, characterized by government stability, civil liberties, the promise of upward mobility, and free enterprise could be offered to the world, Wilson believed, as an alternative both to European imperialism, which had caused so much misery in the past, and to the new and even more frightening specter of revolutionary socialism sweeping through Russia and into Eastern Europe.

Wilson and his advisers well knew that the fight for "a just democracy throughout the world" based on the American model would not be easy. The triumphant Allies thirsted for revenge against the beaten Central Powers, while V. I. Lenin, leader of the Russian Bolsheviks, was urging the workers of Europe to follow the revolutionary socialist example. Once the peace conference convened in January 1919, the President gave top priority to the creation of a League of Nations as the best means of bringing about a more liberal world order and a stable peace. The most controversial part of the League's constitution was Article X, in which member nations promised to respect and defend the territorial integrity of all other members. Because of this collective security provision, potential aggressors could be crushed before war spread. But

Wilson and his principal advisers at the Paris Peace Conference; Edward M. House, Robert Lansing, The President, Henry White, and Gen. Tasker H. Bliss. The President's refusal to include a prominent Republican in the Delegation contributed to the partisan outcry against the Treaty of Versailles. (Courtesy of Herbert Hoover Presidential Library.)

American adherence to Article X meant an end to the traditional policy, followed since the days of George Washington, of avoiding foreign alliances, and, as Wilson soon discovered, many Americans were determined not to become entangled in the quarrels of Europe.

Although the statesmen at Paris supported the President's League of Nations, they refused to go along with other aspects of the Wilsonian peace regarding territorial adjustments and fair treatment of Germany. Consequently, the Treaty of Versailles was a compromise between the traditional peace of the victors and an impartial settlement. Wilson was unable to stop France, Britain, and Japan from partitioning German and Turkish colonial possessions along the lines of secret wartime treaties. The Americans did prevent the French from dismembering Germany in return for a promise of automatic military aid in the event of another German invasion and acceptance of the use of high reparations to keep the Germans in a state of artificial inferiority. In spite of his avowed anti-colonialism, Wilson never intended for the peace to be the instrument of liberation for all peoples; rather, he hoped to make the imperialist empires of Europe more humane, liberal, and peaceful, gradually, through the League of Nations. With the world more stable and trading restrictions eliminated, industrial nations could compete with one another without spilling blood or exploiting underdeveloped areas. The rules of this Open Door competition, as Wilson understood, benefitted the strongest economic competitor, that is, the country with the most surplus capital, the United States.

By the time Wilson returned home in July 1919, he found a hostile coalition of political and ideological enemies arrayed against the treaty. Republican majority leader Henry Cabot Lodge, an old-line imperialist, negotiated a temporary alliance with the "irreconcilables," a group of senators opposed to America's abrupt departure from traditional political isolation from Europe. Confident that the people were with him, Wilson set out on a "swing around the circle" speaking tour by train, only to suffer a paralyzing stroke a few days after his return to Washington.

Biding his time in the hope that the American people, already disillusioned with the great crusade overseas and increasingly fearful of revolutionary socialism at home, would turn on Wilson, Lodge finally reported the Treaty of Versailles to the Senate, along with fourteen reservations designed to water down the commitment to collective security and, hence, to insure future American freedom of action. All efforts to effect a compromise between Wilson and Lodge failed. Twice the Senate voted and twice enough Democrats remained loyal to the ailing President to vote against the treaty with the Lodge reservations, which meant no treaty at all since the majority leader's coalition was strong enough to block any other ratification schemes.

Wilson had refused to meet Lodge halfway in the hope that the 1920 presidential campaign might be transformed into a "great and solemn referendum" on the treaty. It turned out to be neither; Republican billboards dotted the countryside proclaiming "Let us be done with this wiggle and wobble," a slogan which set the tone for a contest between two former newspaper publishers from Ohio, Warren G. Harding and James M. Cox. Ironically, Harding won by wiggling and wobbling his way through the campaign, telling both pro and anti-League forces what they wanted to hear.

In time, the new Republican administration broke the stalemate between Congress and the President over foreign policy, but the international "normalcy" of Harding, Secretary of State Charles Evans Hughes, and their successors had much more in common with Wilsonian internationalism than either side would have cared to admit. The Republicans claimed credit for a return to the traditional American policy of freedom from entangling alliances; yet, during his last eighteen months in office, it was Wilson who began the trend toward political isolation from Europe by refusing to participate in treaty-related diplomatic conferences because of disillusionment with the greed of the victorious Allies.

Furthermore, moderate Republicans such as Lodge, Hughes, and Secretary of Commerce Herbert Hoover shared Wilson's belief in America as the rightful moral and economic leader of the world. While the new policymakers hoped to focus on a conservative domestic program of tax cuts, a balanced budget, reduced government spending, and protection of American industries, they saw also that there would be no real economic normalcy at home without a revival of trade. In the 1920s, Republicans advocated the idea that peace and prosperity could be achieved, not through the imperfect League of Nations (tied to a status quo dictated by the Allies of Paris), but by a series of limited, piecemeal American-led initiatives, including conferences on the reduction of arms, the codification of international law, a world court system, and, following in Wilson's footsteps, revival of the Open Door policy as an alternative to the commercial imperialism of Europe.

The World War destroyed the balance of power which existed until 1914 in the Far East, bringing on a Japanese-American confrontation in its place. In order to leash Japanese expansionist ambitions and put an end to a financially wasteful three-cornered naval race among the United States, Japan, and Britain, Hughes invited concerned Pacific powers to the Washington Naval Conference of 1921–1922. In the Five Power Pact, the Secretary forced the Japanese to accept a position of inferiority in capital ships (vessels of 10,000 tons and smaller bottoms toting guns larger than 8 inches in bore diameter) at a fixed ratio of 5–5–3 compared to Britain and the United States (525,000 tons each for the Anglo-Saxon powers and 315,000 tons for Japan). The Four Power Pact scrapped the old Anglo-Japanese alliance in favor of a vague arrangement whereby the United States, Japan, Britain, and France agreed to respect the status quo in the Pacific and consult in case of outside aggression. All nations attending the conference pledged in the Nine Power Pact to respect the commercial and territorial integrity of China.

The treaties made a good beginning at arms reduction, but China had been left unprotected. A decade later, when Japan began to behave aggressively in East Asia, Hughes would be much criticized for failing to deal with the realities of international politics. In 1921, it seemed to make more sense to bring Japan into the world economic system which Hughes was building, rather than to confront the Japanese over China, a move neither the Senate nor the public would countenance in an age of growing political isolationism.

Secretary Hughes also spent much time and effort seeking to stabilize relations among the industrial nations of Europe. After signing separate peace agreements with Germany, Austria, and Hungary, the United States tried to orchestrate a rational settlement of the German reparations problem. Mindful of those in his own party, who, like Senator William E. Borah, feared that America would be sucked into the vortex of European imperialism and militarism, Hughes resorted to the use of unofficial diplomatic observers, bankers, and corporate leaders to do his bidding. Through a combination of patience, skill, and American financial power, the United States finally convinced the French in 1924 (and again in 1929) to modify their strategy of keeping the Germans in a state of artificial inferiority through the payment of crushing indemnities, no small task since the Anglo-Saxon powers had abandoned their promise of automatic military support for France in case of invasion. As a final incentive for the Europeans to agree to the Dawes Plan (1924), Hughes, taking a cue from Wilson, held the Allies accountable for their war debts. Thus the Secretary of State triumphed where the former President had failed in imposing on Europe a limited reparations settlement based on Germany's capacity to pay, but only at the cost of setting up a system of circular payments. American bankers lent Germany money to rebuild itself as a means of paying the Europeans reparations, and the Allies, in turn, used part of the money to repay their war debts to the United States.

Wilson had hoped to use the League of Nations to help remove national economic barriers to the flow of trade and to provide equal access to all world markets. Hughes could not use that avenue; instead, he approached the challenge of creating an Open-Door world through a series of bilateral treaties. The Harding administration faced another handicap because Congress insisted upon raising the tariff at a time when the State Department was trying to persuade other countries to open their doors to American products. Hughes set out with hopes high to align the antiquated American commercial treaty system (and its emphasis on protectionism) with the Open Door policy. Beginning with Germany, the Secretary of State negotiated a series of pacts designed to give and receive all third party privileges granted to another country (most-favored-nation treaties). The high tariff, congressional reservations demanding the right to protect the American merchant marine, and continuing European evasions of Open Door provisions frustrated Hughes (and his successors, Frank B. Kellogg and Henry L. Stimson) in their Republican approach to a Wilsonian ideal.

The 1920s was a decade in which Americans depended on paper, and millions of private citizens found themselves caught up in an orgy of speculation in stocks and bonds while the State Department relied heavily on treaty-making to create a law-bound world. The culmination of this "paper-mania" was reached with the Kellogg-Briand Pact. As part of France's never ending search for security against Germany, Foreign Minister Aristide Briand proposed to Secretary of State Kellogg that the two countries sign a treaty promising never to go to war against one another. Justifiably concerned over France's attempt to lure America into European politics through a seemingly innocent device, Kellogg balked at the request. A majority of the American people, though, favored the idea of outlawing war as an easy way of contributing to world peace. To negate Briand's proposal and still satisfy the public, the Kellogg suggested that all nations be invited to sign the treaty. On August 27, 1928, representatives from around the world gathered to sign this "international kiss," promising to renounce war as an instrument of policy and to settle their disputes peacefully. The Kellogg-Briand Pact was hailed as a great step forward, but the lack of enforcement provisions left peace at the mercy of nations dissatisfied with the status quo.

The paper prosperity of the late 1920s, based on inflated stock values, collapsed in late 1929 and eventually brought the paper peace down with it. As the Great Depression spread through most of the world, nations became too preoccupied with domestic problems to follow through effectively on the promising first steps toward permanent peace taken under Wilson and Hughes. The reparation settlement began to unravel in the spring of 1931 with economic crises in Austria and Germany, forcing a break in the circle of payments. Reluctantly, President Herbert Hoover proposed a one-year moratorium on both reparations and war debt payments. After that, Germany paid no more indemnities, and only Finland continued to meet its modest debt obligations. No single event did more to embitter the American public against Europe than the default on debts. As industrial nations scrambled to put up trade barriers to protect domestic markets and as world trade shrank, Americans came to look upon foreign trade as unreliable and even undesirable. The limited internationalism of the 1920s yielded quickly to profound isolationism in the 1930s.

Japan was no exception to the trend toward national autarky (or self-sufficiency) as a means of coping with the world economic crisis. A small nation (with less land area than the state of Texas and a population of 65 million), Japan had taken advantage of Chinese weakness early in the century and become dominant in Manchuria, a mineral-rich province of Northeast China. Friction between China and Japan developed in the late 1920s as General Jiang Jieshi emerged as the apparent winner in a long and bloody power struggle. On September 18, 1931, a group of Japanese officers stationed with the Kwantung army in Manchuria engineered an incident at Mukden as a pretext for dismembering the region from China.

Americans had long thought of themselves as special friends of China; yet, Secretary of State Stimson could only wait for events to unfold in spite of the Japanese challenge to the Nine Power Treaty and the Kellogg-Briand Pact. After issuing an ineffectual note of protest, the Secretary convinced Hoover to allow an American diplomat to represent the United States temporarily at the League of Nations. When Japan ignored a League Council resolution calling for its withdrawal from Manchuria, the Council appointed a commission of inquiry. On January 7, 1932, Stimson, impatient with the League's lack of assertiveness and frustrated by Hoover's veto of economic sanctions, wrote a note putting Japan on notice that the United States would not recognize Manchuria as Japanese property. The "Stimson Doctrine" was hardly original; Secretary of State William Jennings Bryan had said much the same thing in 1915 in a written protest over Japan's Twenty-One Demands against China, and it was but the latest in a series of attempts by American officials (Hay, Roosevelt, Knox, and Wilson) calling for the Open Door and protection of Chinese territorial integrity. Like the others, Stimson's doctrine was doomed to failure. Japan paused long enough to issue an insolent reply before attacking Shanghai three weeks later.

After the bombardment of Shanghai, the European powers and President Hoover did next to nothing, save to endorse the Stimson Doctrine. By that time, the Secretary of State had already made another statement, this one in a letter addressed to Senator Borah, but aimed, for different reasons, at China (encouragement), the American public (enlightenment), the League (advice), Britain (arousal), and Japan (admonishment). Once again invoking the Open Door, Stimson scolded the Japanese for violating the Nine Power Pact and the Kellogg-Briand treaty, implying that the United States might respond with a naval buildup in the Pacific and fortification of Guam and the Philippines. Undaunted by the American bluff, Japan consolidated its Chinese holdings, creating the puppet state of Manchukuo and pulling out of the League on grounds of persecution.

Stimson's moral condemnation of Japan did not prove satisfactory as an instrument of policy. He made the effort because in a period of isolationism there was no other alternative to complete silence. Something had to be said in defense of the Open Door, for it might be violated again elsewhere. He believed that moral nations, like moral men, should live life by certain rules or be castigated for their actions. The Manchurian crisis laid bare the weakness of the "paper peace" built up in the 1920s. In a world wracked by depression and lingering bitterness over the status quo peace of the victors, the notion that foreign policy need no longer be based on power proved a dangerous illusion.

Just as continuity rather than transformation was the rule when Wilsonianism yielded to normalcy, a smooth transition in foreign policy occurred between Hoover and Franklin D. Roosevelt in 1933. Like Hoover, Roosevelt had once been a pro-League Wilsonian, but by the time of his presidency, FDR had long since repudiated his former boss' ideals. Bowing to political expediency, Roosevelt chose during his first term to concentrate his energies on the New Deal, a domestic crusade against the Great Depression.

The new President made American priorities clear when he torpedoed the World Economic Conference of 1933 with the announcement that the United States would not support a scheme for international currency stabilization,

Hoover and Roosevelt ride to FDR's Inauguration, 1933. In spite of personal animosities, Roosevelt continued many of Hoover's foreign policies. (Courtesy of Franklin D. Roosevelt Presidential Library.)

even on a temporary basis, thus perpetuating the trend toward national autarky. FDR and Secretary of State Cordell Hull did reverse Hoover's high tariff policies, inaugurating a reciprocal trade program which swapped American tariff reductions on select items in return for foreign reductions on American surplus goods on an unconditional most-favored-nation basis, a policy first tried by Republicans in the 1890s and then by Wilson and Hughes after World War I.

The Roosevelt administration fared no better in the area of world disarmament than had Hoover and Stimson. In an attempt to move the World Disarmament Conference off dead center, delegate Norman Davis presented a modified proposal (originated by the previous administration) whereby the United States would consult with other nations in case of a threat to peace and promise not to interfere with any economic sanctions against an aggressor. When isolationist leaders in Congress indicated their opposition to this small gesture in the direction of collective security, FDR withdrew the proposal. Subsequent disarmament projects met with abject failure, dispelling the optimism of the early 1920s.

Most Americans reacted with horror as a new armaments race spiraled among the great powers. Peace groups, angered by the lack of progress toward disarmament, along with isolationist politicians, began to rewrite history in their search for a way to keep the nation out of the next war. Senator Gerald P. Nye of North Dakota headed a special committee investigating the arms trade, and while the final voluminous report equivocated, the public was left with the impression that greedy and amoral munitions makers and bankers had suckered Wilson into the World War to protect their selfish interests. To make certain that this tragedy could not be repeated, Congress passed a neutrality law in mid-1935 which FDR felt would help him to conduct foreign policy more on the basis of the national interest. The heart of this measure featured an arms embargo which forced the government to suspend the sale of war implements (but not food or raw materials) to any and all belligerents. A provision limiting the life of the law to six months was added to the behest of the President in the hope that Congress would give him more discretionary powers when permanent legislation came up for discussion.

In October 1935, many Americans were grateful for the new law when a serious crisis rocked Europe. Well aware that Britain and France had failed to stop Germany's Nazi leader Adolf Hitler from rearming openly in violation of the Treaty of Versailles and, hungry for an easy foreign triumph, the Italian fascist dictator, Benito Mussolini, invaded the African kingdom of Ethiopia. Immediately, the United States slapped an embargo on the export of arms to the warring parties, at the same time warning Americans not to travel on belligerent ships. Roosevelt and Hull acted quickly to encourage the tepid League, which voted only mild sanctions against Italy. In a move designed to further prod the world body into action, the administration risked the emnity of Italian-Americans (a key voting bloc in the New Deal political coalition) by asking big business not to increase trade with either belligerent. But France and Britain ignored Roosevelt's gesture, choosing instead to follow a policy of appeasement for fear of driving Mussolini further into Hitler's camp. After this brief flirtation with collective action, the United States retreated behind further neutrality legislation.

President Roosevelt signed into law on February 29, 1936, a one-year extension of the previous Neutrality Act with an additional provision banning bank loans to nations at war after failing to convince Congress to give him some discretion over what could be embargoed. A week later, gambling that the great powers would not stop him, Hitler marched German troops into the Rhineland in defiance of the Versailles pact. When Britain and France stood by idly, partly out of the conviction that the peace treaty had been too harsh and partly out of fear of the German anti-semitic fanatic, Americans congratulated themselves for erecting the shield of neutrality.

The world received a preview of the general conflict to come during the Spanish Civil War of 1936–1939. Eager for potential allies, Hitler and Mussolini supported fascist military rebels, while the Soviet Union sent aid to the Spanish Loyalists. The State Department cooperated with an Anglo-French arms embargo, a policy which led indirectly to a fascist victory in early 1939, since the Soviets could not hope to match the help given to General Francisco Franco's forces.

In early 1937, with Europe sliding toward war, Congress worked to tighten up the Neutrality Act without undercutting the limited economic recovery brought on by the New Deal. A compromise was struck between forces advocating strict neutrality and greater flexibility in presidential discretion: now, belligerents could purchase anything but armaments, so long as they paid cash and transported their goods in their own ships. The Neutrality Act of 1937 continued the ban on loans to warring nations and forbade Americans from traveling on belligerent vessels. American neutrality had been achieved, albeit at a high cost, for potential aggressors knew in advance exactly what the world's most powerful industrial democracy would do in the event of war.

Meanwhile, another incident led to a full-scale war between China and Japan. Roosevelt, understanding that neutrality would favor Japan (owing to China's inability to utilize the "cash and carry" provision), refused to invoke the Neutrality Act in the Pacific. He also joined in the European appeasement of Japan at the Brussels conference, signalling that nothing would be done to aid the Chinese. Still, the President had come to realize that a world dominated by fascists in Europe and Japan in Asia would be neither pleasant nor safe for future overseas economic expansion. Cautiously testing the political waters, FDR delivered a speech in Chicago on October 5, 1937, suggesting rather vaguely that aggressor nations, like persons with a communicable disease, ought to be quarantined for the good of all. Public reaction was mixed, less isolationist than FDR had anticipated, but the lack of a clear consensus provided the President with the rationale for taking a middle ground, which meant the continuation of a passive policy.

Growing bolder as Germany rearmed, Hitler moved to dominate Central Europe in 1938. After forcing Austria to merge with the Reich, the German Führer demanded the cession of western Czechoslovakia as his price for peace. Roosevelt supported British Prime Minister Neville Chamberlain's determined appeasement policy with a telegram reading simply "Good Man" when the British agreed to meet with Hitler at Munich. The settlement, designed to turn Hitler eastward toward the Soviet Union, was a German triumph; it also awakened many Americans, Roosevelt included, to the fact that strict neutrality had not well served long range American interests.

Once Hitler violated the Munich Agreement by swallowing up the remainder of Czechoslovakia, the only real hope for peace lay with an Anglo-French-Soviet alliance guaranteeing the territorial integrity of Hitler's next target, Poland. Mutual suspicions doomed this alternative to failure and led

Soviet dictator Joseph Stalin to pursue a Russian version of appeasement. A worried German career diplomat (of one-quarter Jewish ancestry) provided the United States with information on the secret German-Soviet talks. Unfortunately, the State Department issued only veiled warnings to Britain and France. On August 23, 1939, FDR sent off telegrams to Hitler, the President of Poland, and the King of Italy offering his services as a conciliator. It was too little, too late; the Nazi-Soviet Non-Aggression Pact had already been signed and with it went the twenty year armistice.

For the next 27 months—between Hitler's invasion of Poland and the Japanese attack on Pearl Harbor—Americans debated what the nation should do about the new world war. Ever the astute politician, Roosevelt inched the United States away from neutrality and toward an alignment with the besieged western democracies. Slowly, a new consensus began to emerge in the administration, the business community, and among significant portions of public opinion. America's angry and heartbroken retreat from world politics after the Versailles peace was perceived by more and more people as irresponsible and counterproductive. Neutrality came to be seen as the moral equivalent of appeasement. The only way to make things right again was to launch a new crusade to regenerate a world too unstable for a foreign policy based merely on paper treaties and the Open Door.

Sources and Suggested Readings

Buckley, Thomas H., *The United States and the Washington Conference* (1970).
Burns, Richard Dean, and Bennett, Edward M., eds., *Diplomats in Crisis: United States-Chinese-Japanese Relations, 1919–1941* (1974).
Divine, Robert A., *The Reluctant Belligerent: American Entry Into World War II* (1979).
Duroselle, Jean-Baptiste, *From Wilson to Roosevelt: Foreign Policy of the United States, 1913–1945* (1963).
Ferrell, Robert H., *American Diplomacy in the Great Depression: Hoover-Stimson Foreign Policy, 1929–1933* (1957).
Hawley, Ellis W., *The Great War and the Search for a Modern Order, A History of the American People and Their Institutions, 1917–1933* (1979).
Leffler, Melvyn P., *The Elusive Quest: America's Pursuit of European Stability and French Security, 1919–1933* (1979).
Levin, N. Gordon, Jr., *Woodrow Wilson and World Politics: America's Response to War and Revolution* (1968).
Link, Arthur S., *Wilson the Diplomatist: A Look At His Major Foreign Policies* (1957).
Parrini, Carl P., *Heir To Empire: United States Economic Diplomacy, 1916–1923* (1969).
Payne, Howard C., Raymond Callahan, and Edward M. Bennett, *As the Storm Clouds Gathered: European Perceptions of American Foreign Policy in the 1930s* (1979).

Pan-American Visions: From Wilson to Truman

Mark T. Gilderhus
Colorado State University

The proponents of Pan Americanism in the United States have always extolled the merits of political and economic integration within the western hemisphere. For them, the cultivation of closer, more intimate ties with the countries of Latin America had self-evident virtue and necessarily would serve a mutual interest in peace, prosperity, and security. They reasoned that the creation of a functioning, regional system would benefit all participants by providing for the arbitration of disputes, the expansion of trade and investment, and the diminution of European influences. But, as it turned out, the promise always exceeded the actuality. Success proved difficult, and efforts to implement such goals sometimes had unanticipated outcomes.

Pan Americanism always had more appeal in the United States than in Latin America. The advocates argued their case by affirming the existence of a common bond among all Americans. The historian Arthur P. Whitaker described it as "the western hemisphere idea," according to which a unique community had developed out of a shared history, geography, and ideology—that is, the experience of republicans in the New World rebelling against the monarchists of the Old. In contrast, the disparities of wealth and power more impressed the Latin Americans. They worried that too close an affiliation with "the colossus of the North" might result in their submergence. Early in the 1820s, Simón Bolívar, the liberator of South America, advised close cooperation among the newly independent Spanish-American states in order to ward off domination by the United States. Such mistrust also caused Latin Americans to shy away in 1889 when Secretary of State James G. Blaine proposed the creation of a customs union and a system of compulsory arbitration. The so-called "dependency theorists" in the present day have given credence to such fears by insisting that the inequality of relationships in the western hemisphere has exploitative consequences for Latin America, draining away resources, and holding the region in thrall to an alien authority.

The issue has great importance. Whether a strong, stable state in close proximity with weaker, more disorganized ones can function in any sense as an equal is a controversial question. Just what the United States intended to accomplish with its support of Pan Americanism, and what it actually brought about, are subjects of ongoing debate. Gradually a regional, inter-American system took shape. The impact of the First World War achieved some of the desired results by realigning Latin American economies away from Europe and toward the United States. Later, the experiences of the Great Depression and the Second World War contributed to the establishment of a formal means of political consultation. But throughout, the discussion over aims and consequences persisted. The Latin Americans could never be sure whether Pan Americanism was an instrument of partnership or imperial control.

The War with Spain in 1898 introduced many changes in inter-American relations. The victory consolidated United States' hegemony in the Caribbean and encouraged more aggressive forms of behavior, resulting in the establishment of five protectorates in Cuba, Panama, Haiti, Nicaragua, and the Dominican Republic, and also in the practice of military intervention. As President Theodore Roosevelt put it in his "Corollary" to the Monroe Doctrine in 1905, "Chronic wrongdoing . . . may in America, as elsewhere, ultimately require intervention by some civilized nation." The exercise of "an international police power" served several purposes. It maintained order, safeguarded the interest in trade and investment, and rendered unnecessary any forceful measures by the Europeans. Through the use of "preventative intervention," the United States would act as Europe's bill collector and make the western hemisphere secure.

Such methods treated the Caribbean region as a sphere of influence and angered Latin American patriots, who protested against the violation of their national sovereignty. To dissipate the ill will, Woodrow Wilson, upon becoming the president, shifted tactics and tried to win over his critics. He enthusiastically endorsed the Pan American formula. He intended, first, to reduce the European economic presence in Latin America by expanding United States trade and investment. To such ends, his administration encouraged national banks to put branches in Latin American cities and steamship lines to extend their routes. The completion of the Panama Canal in 1914 encouraged such efforts. Wilson also invited the Latin Americans to join with him in a new kind of regional association. He calculated specifically that cooperation with the larger, more stable countries could assist in impressing upon the smaller, less stable ones the need for discreet behavior. At a minimum, they must respect the rights of foreigners, pay their debts, and maintain an orderly, peaceful environment. His attention centered on the largest powers—Argentina, Brazil, and Chile.

In response to the outbreak of the First World War in Europe, the Wilson administration mounted an ambitious program. Late in 1914, Colonel Edward M. House, the president's friend and confidant, urged "a constructive international policy . . . to weld North and South America together." Hoping to show that "friendship, justice, and kindliness were more potent than the mailed fist," he wanted to develop "a model" to aid the Europeans in keeping the peace after the war. The negotiation of a Pan-American treaty in conjunction with the ABC countries (Argentina, Brazil, and Chile) might accomplish this task. According to House's plan, it would require the peaceful arbitration of disputes and guarantee collectively the political independence and territorial integrity of each state under republican forms of government.

EUROPE: "If I had only done that!"

A political cartoon depicting inter-American cooperation at the time of the Great War in Europe. Westerman, *Ohio State Journal* (Columbus), 1916.

Another effort ran parallel. Wilson also wanted to work out a new definition of the Monroe Doctrine. First articulated in 1823, this traditional and hallowed creed declared the western hemisphere off limits to European intrusions, and further, according to the Roosevelt Corollary, allowed the United States to employ unilateral interventions in order to keep the Europeans out. Wilson hoped to enlist the aid of other Latin American states in a multilateral version. If conditions in some country became unsettled and threatened to provoke the Europeans to action, the United States and its associates in the western hemisphere should cooperate in putting things right. Such a plan would undercut objections to intervention by implicating the Latin Americans in the practice.

As it turned out, the effort came to nothing. After two years of sporadic negotiation, Chile blocked the Pan-American treaty out of concern that it might involve outside powers in the Tacna-Arica dispute with Peru, a legacy of the War of the Pacific in the 1880s. Wilson's own acts—the interventions in Mexico, Haiti, and the Dominican Republic—destroyed the credibility of a revised Monroe Doctrine. Relations remained difficult throughout the First World War. When the United States entered the conflict in April 1917, thirteen Latin American countries either declared war on Germany or broke diplomatic relations. But seven stayed neutral, including the troublesome pair, Mexico and Argentina*; indeed, they revived the alternative favored by Bolívar and urged the need for a Pan-Hispanic confederation of Spanish-speaking countries to curb the United States. Wilson's experiment in redesigning the political structure of the western hemisphere had failed.

In contrast, economic integration advanced markedly during the war. For Latin Americans, the onset of hostilities resulted in serious dislocations by disrupting the customary trading and investment patterns. Great Britain and Germany traditionally had supplied much of Latin America with markets, capital, and finished goods. Because of the war, neither country could carry out the usual role. Indeed, they had to liquidate investments in order to finance the fighting. Latin Americans had to search elsewhere for places to sell the raw produce of agricultural enterprise and extractive industries. The United States responded to the opportunity by replacing Great Britain as the dominant, economic power. By the end of the war, it accounted for more than forty percent of Latin America's imports and exports. The magnitude of trade and investment multiplied several times over, and the trend continued into the next decade. By 1929, United States' investments totaled $5,429,000,000, about a billion more than the British, the nearest competitor.

The war confirmed the ascendency of the United States in the western hemisphere, and Republican administrations during the 1920s intended to maintain it. Under Presidents Harding, Coolidge, and Hoover, the United States promoted trade and investment and relied on the unilateral use of power

*Declared war: Brazil, Cuba, Costa Rica, Guatemala, Haiti, Honduras, Nicaragua, Panama.
 Broke diplomatic relations: Bolivia, Dominican Republic, Ecuador, Peru, Uruguay.
 Remained neutral: Argentina, Chile, Colombia, Mexico, Paraguay, El Salvador, Venezuela.

to insure the requisite conditions of order and stability. They had little regard for Wilson's notions of collective responsibility and found multilateral formulas unacceptable. For example, they saw no point in giving a Pan American definition to the Monroe Doctrine. As Secretary of State Charles Evans Hughes put it in 1923, "the Monroe Doctrine is distinctively the policy of the United States," and the government "reserves to itself its definition, interpretation, and application."

The issue of paternalistic practices carried out unilaterally, nevertheless, provoked acrimonious discussions. At two International Conferences of American States, the first in Santiago, Chile, in 1923, the second in Havana, Cuba, in 1928, Latin American delegates insisted upon bringing up political subjects, in spite of United States' efforts to keep them off the agendas. Latin Americans especially complained about the legacies of past interventions in Cuba and Panama, the presence of United States Marines in Haiti and Nicaragua, and the ongoing difficulties with Mexico. They wondered whether the United States would send in troops again.

Delegates from the United States denied that any inconsistency existed in simultaneously adhering to the Monroe Doctrine and also respecting the sovereign independence of neighboring countries. At Havana, the head of the delegation, the former Secretary of State Charles Evans Hughes, argued bluntly that "the difficulty" in inter-American relations resulted not from any threat of "external aggression" but from the internal collapse of sovereignty within the various Latin American countries. As he lamented, "What are we to do when government breaks down and American citizens are in danger of their lives? Are we to stand by and see them killed because a government . . . can no longer afford reasonable protection?" In such instances, he insisted, any government must defend its nationals. Significantly, he provided justification under the right of "interposition" and not "intervention."

In spite of such claims, subtle changes took place by the end of the 1920s. Although Republican administrations publicly upheld reliance on unilateral methods, they used them sparingly in practice and, indeed, gradually backed away from them. American forces left the Dominican Republic in 1924. Later, President Hoover withdrew the soldiers from Nicaragua and devised a plan to get them out of Haiti. Moreover, in 1930, the so-called *Clark Memorandum,* the work of Under Secretary of State J. Reuben Clark, disassociated the right of intervention from the Monroe Doctrine. Clark held that lawless conditions could justify intervention, but he would not sanction it under the terms of the Monroe Doctrine.

Though never an official policy, the *Clark Memorandum* gave evidence of a different kind of thinking. External circumstances had changed, and with them, the calculations of statecraft. The United States had premised the need for intervention on the presence of a European threat. In the 1920s, one no longer existed. In addition, policymakers wondered about the cost effectiveness of military intervention. Critics questioned whether the returns made it worthwhile to occupy other countries and sometimes to fight against insurgents. Finally, the anti-Yankee sentiments spawned by intervention sometimes became virulently nationalistic. In Mexico, for example, the Constitution of 1917 vested ownership of mineral resources with the nation and threatened American, British, and Dutch oil producers with expropriation. The issue precipitated a chronic wrangle until 1938, when President Lázaro Cárdenas put the provision into force and relieved the companies of their properties. Since leaders in the United States had no wish to see such manifestations elsewhere, some reasoned that less blatant forms of political supervision might mute the level of assertiveness and reduce the extent of the danger.

The "Good Neighbor" policy of the 1930s grew out of such considerations and also represented a response to the Great Depression. The collapse of foreign trade, compounded by high tariffs in the United States, had deadly effects in Latin America. Exports to the United States fell off from $1,014,127,000 in 1928 to $316,040,000 in 1933, a decline of about two-thirds. Economic misery accumulated with heaps of unsold commodities on the docks and resulted in waves of political instability. Established governments fell from power all over Latin America in 1930, arousing concern in the United States that radical nationalists might take control and emulate the Mexican example.

Some historians have located the beginning of the Good Neighbor policy in the Hoover presidency. Admittedly, during a visit to ten Latin American countries after his election in 1928, Herbert Hoover criticized past practices. Once in office, he also refrained from intervention. But he responded less emphatically to the effects of the Great Depression and, indeed, made them worse by accepting the highly restrictive Hawley-Smoot tariff in 1930. For such reasons, the responsibility for initiating the Good Neighbor policy more properly resides with Franklin D. Roosevelt's administration. As president, Roosevelt popularized the term, really a cliché, and gave substance to it. His moves indicated an important and subtle shift in the tactics of foreign policy.

Roosevelt drew on Pan-American traditions in formulating the Good Neighbor policy. During the First World War, he had served as assistant secretary of the navy and had absorbed some of Wilson's views. For example, in 1928, he published an article in the prestigious quarterly journal, *Foreign Affairs,* in which he attacked traditional practices in the Caribbean and urged the United States to renounce forever "arbitrary intervention in the home affairs of our neighbors." Instead, he advanced one of Wilson's pet schemes, the idea of "collective intervention." If "evil days" and "disorder and bad government" should fall upon "one of our sister nations" and require "a helping hand," a group of American states, presumably under United States leadership, should undertake the necessary response.

When Roosevelt became the president early in 1933, the Depression had ravaged Latin America. Moreover, contingents of Marines still occupied Haiti; the United States maintained outright protectorates in Cuba and Panama and controlled the finances of Nicaragua and the Dominican Republic. During the next eight years, the Roosevelt administration liquidated these remnants of

Room for All under the New Umbrella

Pan-American harmony amidst a world torn apart by war in 1916. (Charles L. (Bart) Bartholomew, *Minneapolis News,* ca. 1916. Reprinted with permission of The Minneapolis Star and Tribune Company. All rights reserved.)

past interventions and promised to abstain from similar practices in the future. The pledge of nonintervention became a central feature. Overall, the Good Neighbor policy is best explained as a response to the Great Depression. Roosevelt intended to use foreign policy to combat economic collapse at home. To obtain markets and cheap resources in Latin America, he proposed to give up direct forms of political control in return for economic favors. In the expectation that Latin Americans would respond reciprocally, he advised, "Give them a share. They think they are just as good as we are, and many of them

59

are." Nevertheless, they would have to comport themselves according to traditional rules with proper regard for the rights of property and trade. Since indirection could accomplish a great deal, he sacrificed some of the appearances of power while retaining much of the substance.

The commitment to nonintervention came about in two steps. At the Seventh International Conference of American States at Montevideo, Uruguay, in 1933, the Latin Americans supported a declaration to the effect that "no state has the right to intervene in the internal or external affairs of another." Secretary of State Cordell Hull endorsed it but attached a reservation, noting that international law did permit intervention in certain instances. The qualification could have rendered his action meaningless, but it did not. At the next Inter-American Conference in Buenos Aires in 1936, the United States accepted without condition or qualification a prohibition introduced by Mexico, declaring as "inadmissible the intervention of any one of them, directly or indirectly, and for whatever reason, in the internal or external affairs of any other of the Parties." The United States thus embraced nonintervention but, intriguingly, the phraseology, specifically the injunction against "the intervention of any one of them," left open the possibility of a joint action. The influence of Woodrow Wilson lived on.

The economic component of the Good Neighbor policy centered on the negotiation of reciprocal trade agreements and the activities of the Export-Import Bank. The Reciprocal Trade Agreements Act of June 1934 reversed Republican policy by authorizing the president to negotiate bilateral agreements providing for the mutual reduction of tariff barriers by as much as fifty percent. In the same year, the Export-Import Bank came into existence, a creation of the National Industrial Recovery Act. As a dispenser of international credit, it bolstered American exports by requiring the recipients to expend the loans upon the purchase of goods in the United States. Such measures enabled the United States to regain some of the commerce lost since 1929. Full recovery had to await the onset of the Second World War.

The commitment to nonintervention underwent two tests late in the decade. In 1937, the Bolivian government confiscated the property of the Standard Oil Company as part of a plan to court Argentina with oil concessions. In 1938, the Mexican government expropriated foreign-owned petroleum holdings after the companies defied an official ruling in a labor dispute. In each instance, the United States employed diplomatic pressure, insisting upon just compensation for the losses of its citizens, but refrained from using force. The Mexican case was especially significant. It struck North Americans as a terrible precedent. In response, petroleum corporations mounted a campaign in support of intervention and also refused to ship or sell Mexican oil. Mexico countered by flirting with Germany, Italy, and Japan, hoping to acquire tankers and markets. The problem had a double-barreled implication. The Roosevelt administration wanted to halt the advance of radicalism and economic nationalism in Latin America but not at the cost of forcing Mexico into an association with the Axis powers. In the end, the president's unwillingness to support the most extravagant claims of the oil producers and the discreet performance of the American ambassador, Josephus Daniels, resulted in an acceptable settlement. After first claiming $450 million as the rightful compensation, the oilmen backed off and agreed to take $24 million.

The outbreak of war in Europe in September, 1939, again had important consequences in the western hemisphere. Defense issues demanded attention, and the economic dependence of Latin America upon the United States became even greater. Indeed, "the northern colossus" acquired ever more leverage and control, parlaying economic aid and the promise of loans into additional tariff reductions and other favors. Powerful incentives for correct behavior, such devices aided in persuading the Bolivians and the Mexicans to resolve the petroleum disputes.

The degree of political intimacy also increased. Throughout the war years, the United States attempted to guarantee "continental solidarity" under its leadership. At a meeting of foreign ministers at Panama City in the fall of 1939, the American republics proclaimed their neutrality in the European conflict and also tried to insulate the western hemisphere against "hostile acts" by declaring it off limits. Another meeting at Havana in July, 1940, reaffirmed the "no-transfer" rule so that Germany could not acquire colonies in the western hemisphere. The foreign ministers also agreed to the principle of collective security, according to which they would regard an attack against one as an attack against all and would, in such an event, consult together to determine the proper reaction.

In arranging for the defense of the western hemisphere, the United States wanted little military contribution from Latin America but expected to acquire military and naval bases in important areas. Requests to put United States troops in Panama, outside the Canal Zone, and also in the northeastern "bulge" of Brazil, presumably an area vulnerable to German threats, provoked some opposition in Latin America, but in each instance, the Roosevelt administration got its way. The United States also wanted Latin American governments to crack down on pro-German elements so that clandestine activities would not present any dangers. The easing out of German and Italian commercial enterprises opened new business opportunities for the United States. The move into civil aviation in the Andean region, previously dominated by the Germans, provides an example.

When the United States formally entered the war after the Japanese attack on Pearl Harbor, most of Latin America followed suit. Except for Argentina and Chile, both of which remained neutral during much of the conflict, all of the other states either severed diplomatic ties with the Axis powers or declared war on them. The latter included the nine Central American and Caribbean countries and also Mexico, Brazil, Colombia, Venezuela, and Bolivia. Only Mexico and Brazil sent armed forces overseas. The United States discouraged the others but coordinated joint-defense efforts through various boards and agencies and dispensed military aid and assistance through Lend-Lease. Such arrangements fostered good will in the military establishments of Latin America and also made possible the seizure of political power by military officers in many countries during the 1950s.

The implications of wartime relations worried Latin Americans. The mounting influence of the United States and their own heavy reliance on raw exports especially caused concern. What could they expect after the war when demand fell off and conditions changed? Would the United States step in with aid in support of economic development and diversification? What also of political relationships? How would Latin America fit into the Allies' plans for the reconstruction of the world? What also of the presumed dominant role of the Great Powers? Latin Americans particularly wondered how the proposed United Nations would affect them and their regional interests. They hoped to find ways to constrain United States' power and also to shape the behavior of the northern neighbor according to their needs. But they feared that the developing rift between the United States and the Soviet Union would result in their subordination.

Such questions attracted much attention as the war drew to a close. At the Inter-American Conference on Problems of War and Peace in Mexico City in February, 1945, the diplomats wrote the so-called "Act of Chapultepec," in which they endorsed again the idea of collective security but this time applied it within the hemisphere to acts of aggression by any American state. Presumably this provision would deter any resort to unilateral intervention. Economic issues also stirred discussion. Latin Americans wanted specific assurances that the United States would assist them in making the transition from war to peace. Instead, they got exhortation and advice. They should keep tariffs low, encourage investment, and rely on private enterprise. Such responses foreshadowed the low priority assigned to Latin America by the United States during the early stages of the Cold War.

As the split with the Soviet Union deepened after the Second World War, policymakers in Washington wanted to consolidate relations with Latin America, maintain their favored position, and keep things quiet so that they could concentrate on other issues in Europe and Asia. In the late 1940s, neither the power of the Soviet Union nor the influence of international communism posed much threat in Latin America. Nevertheless, the United States hoped to align the countries in the region against the Soviet Union. A solid voting bloc in the United Nations, for example, could prove useful; but any such effort entailed a tactical puzzle. How could the United States call the shots in the western hemisphere without encouraging the Soviet Union to do similarly in eastern Europe? Another problem also existed. What of the threat of indigenous radicalism? Leaders in the United States worried that internal instability and revolutionary ferment might dash their plans to organize the hemisphere.

The leaders in the Truman administration responded ambitiously, seeking to maintain the *status quo* within the region while retaining the prerogative to employ United States power elsewhere around the globe. They wanted it both ways. As historian David Green explained, they desired "a closed hemisphere in an open world." While excluding alien presences, they also intended to shore up defenses against economic nationalism and accomplish what Green called "the containment of Latin America." To secure United States interests, they would strike a *de facto* alliance with the ruling elites and traditional oligarchies against the advocates of radical change.

The United States subsequently moved to accomplish these goals at a sequence of international conferences and found its purposes and ambitions pitted against those of Latin America in odd and complicated ways. Many Latin Americans wanted a more formal political organization in the region, hoping to use it as a restraint against the United States, but feared, nevertheless, that Washington would find ways to manipulate and dominate it. A formula worked out at the San Francisco Conference late in the spring of 1945, Article 51 of the United Nations Charter, permitted the American republics to make arrangements for regional defense without violating the integrity of the international organization. Subsequently, the "Rio Pact"—the product of a conference in the Brazilian capital in August 1947—authorized collective self-defense against armed attacks and also against "an aggression which is not an armed attack," the latter, presumably, a reference to subversion by communists or other radicals. Some months later in the spring of 1948, the Ninth International Conference of American States at Bogotá, Colombia, brought into existence the Organization of American States. It achieved formal organization in the inter-American system after half a century and instituted a regular means of political consultation. The charter reaffirmed long-established principles, including the ideals of hemispheric solidarity, representative government, peaceful settlement of disputes, and nonintervention. According to Article 15, "No State or group of States has the right to intervene, directly or indirectly, for any reason whatever, in the internal or external affairs of any other States." It coexisted in uneasy equilibrium with the requirements of the Rio Pact, leaving quite murky the relationship between nonintervention and the repulsion of aggression.

No similar initiatives addressed economic issues after the war. Just as Latin Americans had feared, the transition to peace put them in a terrible squeeze. The drop in demand for their raw products reduced their earnings, while the cost of finished, imported goods increased steadily. Latin Americans appealed to the United States for long-term programs of aid and assistance to bring about economic development but received no satisfaction. A Marshall Plan for Latin America never came about. Officials in the Truman administration had higher priorities elsewhere.

The Pan American movement achieved something of a culmination during the Truman years. It had accomplished many of the stated goals, including a large measure of political and economic integration, but had not always fulfilled the expectation of mutual benefits. As a result, profound differences divide scholars who try to understand the consequences. Apologists generally applaud the development of formal political arrangements to safeguard the region against aggressive threats and the willingness of the United States to embrace nonintervention. They also see the structure of economic relations—trading raw materials for finished goods—as a defensible division of labor.

The critics, in contrast, interpret Pan Americanism as a deception enabling the United States to perpetuate neo-colonial relationships. According to them, the resulting condition of economic dependence is inherently exploitative, the result of trading low-cost exports for high-cost imports. Moreover, they refuse to take seriously the United States' commitment to nonintervention. No matter what the provisions of the OAS charter, the United States found ways to overthrow governments of Guatemala in 1954 and the Dominican Republic in 1965. Such acts hardly signified a readiness to accept equality among sovereign states. The controversy still persists, whether Pan Americanism is best understood as a system of friendly association or subtle dominion.

Sources and Suggested Readings

Bemis, Samuel Flagg, *The Latin American Policy of the United States, An Historical Interpretation.* New York: W. W. Norton & Co., Inc., 1967, first published, 1943.

Chilcote, Ronald H., and Joel Edelstein, eds., *Latin America: The Struggle with Dependency and Beyond.* Cambridge, Mass.: Schenkman Publishing Co., 1974.

Connell-Smith, Gordon, *The United States and Latin America, An Historical Analysis of Inter-American Relations.* New York: John Wiley & Sons, 1974.

Davis, Harold Eugene, John J. Finian, and F. Taylor Peck, *Latin American Diplomatic History, An Introduction.* Baton Rouge: Louisiana State University Press, 1977.

Gilderhus, Mark T., "Pan-American Initiatives: The Wilson Presidency and 'Regional Integration,' 1914–1917." *Diplomatic History,* 4 (Fall 1980), pp. 409–424.

Gilderhus, Mark T., "Wilson, Carranza, and the Monroe Doctrine: A Question in Regional Organization." *Diplomatic History,* 7 (Spring 1983), pp. 103–115.

Green, David, *The Containment of Latin America: A History of the Myths and Realities of the Good Neighbor Policy.* Chicago: Quadrangle Books, 1971.

Mecham, J. Lloyd, *The United States and Inter-American Security, 1889–1960.* Austin: University of Texas Press, 1967.

Parkinson, F., *Latin America, The Cold War, & The World Powers, 1945–1973.* Beverly Hills: Sage Publications, 1974.

Stuart, Graham H., and James L. Tigner, *Latin America and the United States.* 6th ed. Englewood Cliffs, N.J.: Prentice-Hall, Inc., 1975.

Whitaker, Arthur P., *The Western Hemisphere Idea: Its Rise and Decline.* Ithaca, N.Y.: Cornell University Press, 1954.

The Role of Presidential Leadership

J. K. Sweeney, Professor of History
South Dakota State University

Presidential leadership is often defined as the courage to provide what is needed as opposed to what is wanted, or to exercise options which would not normally be the choice of ordinary persons. It also includes the ability to anticipate situations, to educate the electorate concerning new obligations, and the willingness to transform ideas and procedures previously thought radical into respectable alternatives. Of course, the process of problem solving is untidy, occasionally long, and frequently disorderly. Change is normally evolutionary rather than revolutionary, and may be compared to the manner in which babies walk—falling forward and catching themselves before hitting the ground. Moreover, leadership must be distinguished from decision-making, which identifies those elements and individuals responsible for particular results.

Decision-makers are normally more numerous than a cursory look at institutional structures would suggest, and their motivations are often more obscure or trivial than might be generally presumed. "Watergate" was, in the final analysis, a "third-rate burglary," yet it served as the catalyst to eject from office a president in possession of an overwhelming electoral mandate. Furthermore, the results of most decisions are often vastly different from those originally projected, and many are the actual culmination of decisions made at lower levels which prevent real choices in policy. Most would agree with Harry S. Truman that a chief executive can push buttons and give orders, but all too often nothing happens! It is only necessary to examine the Cuban Missile Crisis and the matter of the missile bases in Italy and Turkey in order to be convinced of this essential fact. President Kennedy was under the impression, later dispelled, that his previous order to dismantle those bases was sufficient to produce the action.

Then again, the president was not intended to function as the institutional leader of the United States government. That function was reserved for the Congress as a collective body. The delegates to the Philadelphia convention in 1787 were well aware of the reality of executive tyranny, as demonstrated by the indictment of George III in the Declaration of Independence as the ultimate villain. Therefore, the delegates assumed the president would be the chief administrator and, if necessary command the army and navy, while Congress led the nation after the manner of the Confederation legislature. But

Theodore Roosevelt Speaking in New Castle, Wyoming, in 1903. (Reproduced from the Collections of the Library of Congress.)

committees are a poor mechanism for making difficult decisions, or any decisions. More importantly, the early presidents, especially Washington and Jefferson, were not content to perform in the limited fashion envisaged by the authors of the Constitution, nor were they willing to see the nation drift through the storms of controversy created by European wars and the needs of commerce and security. The tradition of an independent chief executive was dramatically reinforced by Andrew Jackson. Jackson functioned on a grand scale, and proved equal to two-thirds of both Houses of Congress in their efforts to overturn presidential vetoes. The War between the States, industrialization, and the emergence of the United States as a global power also enhanced the powers and responsibilities of the office. Presidents became heroic, larger-than-life figures thought capable of miracles. Indeed, they are often expected to supply unprecedented remedies for all the various ills facing the nation. This is obviously an unrealistic expectation, but it provides a framework in which presidents are expected to act.

Yet, the nature of the American political system is such that it does not normally operate to produce "leaders." Any action taken before a national consensus exists on a particular issue may result in electoral catastrophe, and thus there is a tendency for politicians to avoid "rocking the boat." Obviously there are exceptions to this rule, as in the case of President Truman's support of a system of national health insurance in the period following the Second World War. But, despite strong presidential lobbying, the Social Security Act was not amended to provide even limited medical assistance for the elderly and the poor until 1965. Thus, Truman's failure, which he expected, demonstrates the limited effect of presidential initiatives and the educative function of the office. At the same time, the electoral process seldom recruits, for the highest office, individuals who possess tested intellectual and leadership qualities. Those who would engage in genuine reform, from either the right or the left of the political spectrum, usually do not reach the Oval Office in the White House, or if elected, are unable to implement fully the promises made during the campaign. Presidential candidates must be "available," they must appeal to the voter's sense of what a president should be, they must seek office in years favorable to their party, but original and independent thought is ordinarily not highly valued.

Many of those presidents rated great or near great were not, as candidates, viewed as possessing the characteristics of great leaders. Furthermore, some of them entered office as minority presidents with less than fifty percent of the vote, or enjoyed no electoral mandate at all, as in the case of those who succeeded to office upon the death of their predecessor. A majority of the American voters did not vote for Woodrow Wilson in 1912; John Kennedy's margin of victory in popular votes was paper thin; while Harry S. Truman's accession to the office sent a chill down the spine of many citizens of the nation. Still, some presidents were able to abandon the safe path to election for the more dangerous course of challenging the status quo. In some cases, this proved a useful election ploy, as with Truman in 1948, or to a lesser degree Carter in 1976, and in others, it was the result of strong personal convictions. Woodrow Wilson was not physically able to seek the Democrat nomination in 1920, but he fastened the League of Nations to the party platform. Moreover, there is no doubt it would have been the cornerstone of his campaign if his illness had not prevented his bid for an unprecedented third term in office.

Presidential personality, therefore, is obviously an important ingredient with regard to presidential performance. Consequently, scholars often undertake to identify the personality traits which appear to accord with effective leadership in the White House. A recent attempt in this area is James David Barber in *The Presidential Character: Predicting Performance in the White House.* (1977) He gained national recognition when, in the aftermath of Watergate, it was noted that President Nixon's behavior was "predicted" in Barber's study.

Barber's analysis is not without flaw, but his approach is exceedingly useful insofar as it provides categories which can be employed for comparative analysis.

Barber concentrates on two variable characteristics: the amount of energy presidents invest in the office and how they feel about what they do. Do they approach their days in the manner of a human cyclone, or drift through their terms? Do they believe their political lives are happy or sad, enjoyable or discouraging? Some presidents, therefore, want success, some power, others appreciation and still others aspire to virtue. Nonetheless, some would insist that personality is less of a factor than the normal human response to follow in the paths of those who went before.

Thus, James MacGregor Burns argues, in *Presidential Government* (1965), that the first three presidents adopted dramatically different approaches to government which subsequent Chief Executives endeavored to emulate. Burns focuses on the locus of power and the role of the president within the system. He believes that some presidents vigorously govern within the constitutional system of checks and balances, still more adopt a prudent and limited style of government, and the exceptional few adhere to an egalitarian approach which is the most powerful, but also leaves the president seemingly at the mercy of shifting public moods.

Barber and Burns focus on personality, presidential style, and the administrative artistry of presidents as they attempt to alter public opinion to fit some predetermined mold, or simply stay one step ahead of events until retirement removes them from office. But those who would assess presidential leadership must not neglect the element of chance, opportunity, or circumstance. Mark Hanna's death in 1904 eliminated an individual with the capability to influence the selection of a candidate other than Taft in 1908. The death of Major Archie Butt on the *Titanic* removed from the scene a man who might have mediated the dispute between Taft and Roosevelt and thereby forestalled the split in the Republican ranks which allowed Wilson to enter the White House. At the same time, many of those whose personal qualities and command of the political structure afford an opportunity for substantial contributions are not "allowed" to do so for other reasons. Their opportunities for "greatness" are few, or they are compelled to play a role which the public does not, because of its ignorance of details, fully appreciate at the time.

It is highly unlikely, for example, that any Democratic president would have undertaken to end the diplomatic rupture with China given the fact that the party was held responsible for the "loss" of that country to the Communists in 1949. It took Richard M. Nixon, an acknowledged anti-Communist, to meet that challenge. Similarly, Theodore Roosevelt's active diplomacy with respect to the Second Moroccan Crisis in 1906 would have been compromised if his various maneuvers had been public knowledge. Indeed, Roosevelt was awarded the Nobel Peace Prize in 1906, but that award was in connection with his more public efforts to end the Russo-Japanese War of 1904–05. Yet, the Moroccan Crisis was, if anything, a more serious affair insofar as world peace was concerned.

Presidents capable of arousing both emotional and intellectual responses in an audience, on the other hand, might be handicapped by technology as to the numbers they can affect at a single time. It is interesting to speculate whether Woodrow Wilson's campaign to obtain Senate ratification of the Treaty of Versailles might not have met with greater success if he had been able to employ the resources of national radio and television networks, or if he had not fallen ill at a crucial time. Conversely, those whose style and bureaucratic expertise are well-suited to that of a "constabulary presidency," which focuses on balancing the books and the preservation of law and order, are ill-served if their term in office coincides with a period of transition in which flexibility is demanded. Warren G. Harding might have a better presidential reputation if his term in office had occurred in an earlier, less turbulent time. The intellectual baggage presidents bring to the office may also inhibit their responses, for they may not realize that what appear to be recurrent problems are, in fact, so new as to demand solutions beyond traditional remedies. Herbert Hoover was just such a president, cursed with events he could barely understand or whose impact he largely misinterpreted.

Moreover, it must not be forgotten that the office is burdened with bureaucratic inertia and tensions as well as individual desires. One of the most significant developments in the American political system is the growth of the Executive Office of the President. The centralization of important governmental functions in the Executive Office deprives the various departments of the ability to initiate decisions, thereby enhancing the opportunity for a president to exercise leadership. This centralization, therefore, makes the president appear to be more in control of events than may actually be the case. Finally, presidents who serve successive terms may demonstrate differing degrees of leadership as changes occur in the domestic or international scene.

Presidential reputations are also a result not only of their actions but the manner in which those actions are subjected to historical interpretation. Presidents may appear strong, tenacious, and purposeful in retrospect, while the judgment of their contemporaries is more severe. Harry S. Truman left office under a cloud of ridicule and Dwight D. Eisenhower was widely characterized as a do-nothing president who read western novels and played golf while others ran the country. Yet, each has undergone a process of rehabilitation and both now appear more effective than was the case at the moment they passed into private life. On the other hand, the praise and adulation occasioned by the death of Warren Harding was soon replaced by scorn and ignominy, as was also the case with Coolidge, and even Wilson to a considerable extent. Presidential leadership, therefore, is a result of personality, bureaucratic developments, historical circumstances and the interpretations of those who analyze the President's performance in office.

Nowhere is this more apparent than in the case of Theodore Roosevelt. Although some still insist that Roosevelt should be approached as any other six-year old, it is more common to assert that he undertook a more active presidency than those of his immediate predecessors. He restored the presidency, placed it in the forefront of the political scene and with the help of a large and boisterous family put it on the front page. He acted from his natural instincts, sought out new challenges, and demanded new responses if the old ones were inadequate.

Born to a life of ease and social position, he became, with the assassination of William McKinley, the youngest man ever elevated to the Presidency. He molded and interpreted public opinion, amused the press, disturbed the party bosses, delighted the country, confessed to all concerned that the White House was a "bully pulpit" and had a "simply ripping time." He loved being president, loved the power for what he could accomplish and reinstalled the Chief Executive as an active participant in every stage of the legislative process. He tried to preserve the status quo whenever possible, but if not, followed the path of least resistance towards a new order, economic and otherwise. Yet, this active president did not confront a genuine crisis which might have brought his means and ends into heroic accord, he had no war, not even a rebellion. The Panamanian adventure does not compare with Wilson's Mexican interlude, and trust busting was a pale substitute for World War One!

Roosevelt was elevated to the Presidency by an act of violence. His successor, William Howard Taft, entered the White House by virtue of apostolic succession. The son of a prominent and moderately wealthy Ohio family of jurists, Taft was Roosevelt's choice to complete his renovation of the nation and the Presidency. Yet the ideological affinity which they shared in the abstract failed in the implementation, for Taft was tempermentally unsuited for the designated role. Roosevelt broadened the powers of the presidency, but although expansive in girth, Taft was not comfortable with the larger-than-life presidential model bequeathed by his friend. He was genial, compliant, and possessed a powerful drive to be loved and appreciated, and be responsible for noteworthy legislative and administrative achievements. But he could not function n a Rooseveltian fashion. He was content to consolidate Roosevelt's achievements, to preside over a period of repose which would allow the nation time to assimilate the results of his predecessor's innovations. He was satisfied to follow the lead of the conservative faction of his party led by Senator Nelson Aldrich and ignore the liberal faction of Roosevelt and Robert La Follette.

Unfortunately for Taft, his friend left too many things undone, generated too many unfilled expectations, and generally raised the national consciousness with regard to presidential initiatives. Roosevelt's energetic approach to the nation's problems led some of the electorate to expect an active presidential program of a type Taft was unable, or unwilling to provide. Roosevelt caught the leading edge of the "Progressive" wave, but his more passive successor sank beneath the surface. Taft, therefore, was abandoned by the electorate in 1912 for the activity promised by Woodrow Wilson and his former friend and mentor Roosevelt running on a third party ticket. It should be noted, at this point, that a presidential candidate almost invariably loses the general election if opposition to his nomination is so strong and widespread as to create a chaotic convention. In 1912, the Republican Party was torn apart by a bitter struggle between Taft and Roosevelt. The Democratic conventions of 1860 and 1968 are other examples of this phenomena.

Thomas Woodrow Wilson was the first southerner elected to the Presidency after the Civil War. The son and grandson of Presbyterian ministers, he received a Ph.D. in history from Johns Hopkins University and embarked on a career in college teaching and administration. Although relatively successful, Wilson was nonetheless eager to abandon his position as President of Princeton University to become Governor of New Jersey. Wilson's achievements as governor brought him national acclaim and the Democrat presidential nomination in 1912. His appeal to "Progressive," plus the split within the Republican party caused by Theodore Roosevelt's defection, resulted in his election. Wilson, a vocal critic of congressional government, was determined to be a strong executive, dedicated to reform in the fashion of those active presidents he admired. But, Wilson, despite his triumphs, was led to over-value his own judgments, both because of his general success in life and his Presbyterian leadership concept. He neglected, while in office, to follow the advice of others who studied the same problems but with slightly different results. In short, Wilson forgot that a president remains a "political" leader, responsible to those who elected him. With a Democratic Congress and firm control of the party through the patronage at his disposal, Wilson sought to implement his grand design. Wilson achieved most of his objectives in his first two years in office, and initiated programs and policies to carry the reform process into some new areas, as in the case of the Federal Farm Loan Act (1916) and the Adamson Act (1916). Yet, while his presidential activity was rewarded, he did not receive complete public trust. When World War I broke out, opposition to his views and actions surfaced. Soon he was isolated from his critics. He felt, apparently, that leaders should not only lead, but followers should serve in strict obedience to instructions and without comment. In consequence, his demands disrupted his presidential coalition and caused the various factions to seek a less demanding taskmaster. When his pursuit of righteousness drove him to attempt to eliminate war as a factor in international relations through the League of Nations, his reach finally exceeded his grasp and his enemies combined to bring him down. Even then, Wilson might have extracted his victory, except for his reluctance to compromise his principles beyond that already forced upon him at the Paris Peace Conference. As a result the Treaty of Versailles was not ratified by the Senate. It was not that the Senate did not approve of the League, but rather that it wished to pursue a different path to the same end. Therefore, bereft of unquestioning support, he appealed directly to the people, but his plea seemed to fall upon the ears of a country interested not in nostrums, "but normalcy; not revolution but restoration." Moreover, his sudden illness late in 1919 prevented him from mobilizing those forces essential to gain Senate approval of the Treaty of Versailles.

Warren Gamaliel Harding did not ascend to Wilsonian oratorical heights, nor did he use the power at his disposal in the aggressive manner of Theodore Roosevelt. He spoke in the platitudes of turn-of-the-century rural America and firmly rejected the role of the president as the mystical embodiment of the people's will. His administration, therefore, was a shift in the temper, tempo and emphasis of government, a drastic alteration in the internal relationships of the executive branch and the role of the president. Rather than serving as the center of power, Harding, the average man personified, attempted to be a faciliator and adjudicator within his cabinet—a cabinet supposedly composed of the "best minds" in the nation. But if he established a political philosophy and a program which held sway for almost a decade, his permissive approach also allowed error and corruption to flourish. Furthermore, his cabinet consisted of mediocre as well as "best minds," and he was unable to control the former or inspire the latter. Perhaps Harding's greatest failing was that he did not desire to be the best president, but the best loved, and that was not enough. Although the accomplishments of his administration were superior to some of those who preceded him, as witness the Washington Naval Conference, the modernizing of the budget process, and general acceptance of the eight-hour work day, the problems of the nation demanded more than another "constabulary president." He might have flourished in an earlier time, as in the 1840s or 1870s, but he was clearly not equal to the challenge of the 1920s. Still, his administration was the last to rely on the cabinet to handle the affairs of the executive branch. In subsequent administrations the cabinet would be relegated to a subordinate position by ever increasing numbers of White House assistants.

Warren G. Harding and John Calvin Coolidge differed sharply in personal style, but the methods and the policies of the two administrations were similar. Coolidge not only accepted the program he inherited, he appeared more comfortable with its implications than did Harding. However, if the politics of "normalcy" was to be pursued, Coolidge was forced to modify the style of presentation. Wilson's conception of the Calvinistic doctrine of predestination required an energetic pursuit of goodness through government. For Coolidge, however, it meant to "Let well enough alone." Thus, once the most visible symbols of the Harding scandals were disposed of, that is exactly what Coolidge did. Admittedly what his administration accomplished was not insignificant; it was done with considerable efficiency, and occasionally in a forceful manner. Coolidge was successful in his resistance to the potentially disastrous MacNary-Hagen bill, supported the negotiations leading to the Pact of Paris (Kellogg-Briand Pact), extended the Civil Service merit system, and helped raise the level of competence in the Foreign Service (Rogers Act) and the federal judiciary. But the times demanded more than a custodian of the status quo, and by training and temperament Coolidge was unable to look forward or even to understand the direction in which the nation was headed. Coolidge did not seek problems to solve, he would wait for them to arrive, and, in consequence, did little to prevent the economic collapse which destroyed his successor. Yet, if the single failure of his administration was that it only attempted to embody the popular will, such was also the failure of the nation. Calvin Coolidge was what the nation professed to want, although opposition did develop in the third party candidacy of Robert La Follette in 1924. Still, his policy of drift and inaction may have contributed to the general economic collapse of 1929.

Herbert Clark Hoover entered the White House with an overwhelming electoral margin, only to be ejected from that residence by an even greater margin four years later. Hoover's confident assertion that in "no nation are the fruits of accomplishment more secure" was belied by the crash of the stock market seven months later. Hoover's progress to the presidency, like that of Coolidge, was well within a familiar American pattern: humble birth, hard work, wealth, public service and election to the nation's highest office. But he was more atypical than representative in that he left the country shortly after graduating from Stanford University in 1895 for a career as an engineer and did not return until 1920. As a result, the nation he left for remote corners of the world was vastly different from the one which greeted him with such acclaim after World War I. He returned to a nation no longer dominated by small towns, but one in which small town economics and social mores still held forth.

This philosophy contrasted sharply with Hoover's own view of "ordered liberty," which provided for a compromise between the individual's advantage and the welfare of society at large. Moreover, Hoover resolved to compensate for what he considered the inaction of his predecessors by harmonizing economic, technological, and social trends so as to improve the quality of life at home and abroad. Unfortunately, although supremely equipped to deal with prosperity, Hoover was ill-equipped to deal with the end of that prosperity. His concepts of harmony and rationality collapsed in the face of lengthening breadlines and "Hoovervilles." Nor could he rely on his cabinet for assistance, for Hoover allowed his cabinet, which was equally unprepared to deal with the crisis, little room for maneuver. His concept of the government as an umpire charting a middle course between *laissez-faire* economics and monopoly capitalism simply failed to produce results, and he failed to consider alternative solutions. Herbert Hoover left office unpopular, isolated, largely disavowed by his party and embittered by the nation's failure to appreciate his virtues. Yet, the crisis was real, and despite Hoover's confidence in his own rectitude the electorate demanded a change. Although some of his programs continued into the next administration the emphasis was different.

Franklin Delano Roosevelt appeared willing to compromise almost anything in his quest to save the nation from the economic insecurity and political instability engendered by the Depression. Unlike his rigidly doctrinaire predecessor, Roosevelt refused to conform to any consistent formulas. He was intuitive, not systematic, artful, not scientific, and innovative throughout. Born to an aristocratic family secure in its position and wealth, he was encouraged to behave in a "proper" fashion, to conduct himself in a manner befitting "a member of his class." Nonetheless, his intellectual development was uninhibited, he was not imprisoned within an ideological strait jacket as were so many young men of similar station. He was allowed to play with ideas, examine options, even entertain contradictory options, but at the same time avoid committing himself irrevocably to anything beyond faith in God and the ultimate triumph of truth and righteousness. Supremely self-confident, he refused to

President Franklin Roosevelt meeting with Prime Minister Winston Churchill in Merrakech, Morocco, January, 1943. (Courtesy of National Archives.)

invest his ego in any approach to the extent that he would be unable, if necessary, to abandon it in pursuit of another policy which promised success. Hoover carried into his personal life the mechanical qualities of his profession, and thus failed to account for human irrationality and prejudice. Roosevelt not only understood that life is a series of improvisations and accommodations which are often anything but rational and logical, he was not especially concerned with apparent inconsistencies. But, if his parents, particularly his mother and his remarkable wife Eleanor, contributed to the formation of this enormously complex personality, his presidency, indeed his political career, was to a considerable degree a restatement and improvement of that of his cousin Theodore. Franklin Roosevelt not only followed "Cousin Teddy" into various public offices, he was a conscious adherent of Theodore's stewardship theory of the presidency. A president was "bound actively and affirmatively to do all he could for the people" and it was "not only his right but his duty to do anything that the needs of the nation demanded unless such action was forbidden by the Constitution or the laws." Thus, he fastened onto the governmental structure a series of "alphabet agencies" from the AAA to the WPA which dramatically affected the economy and the shape of American society. Moreover, after Franklin D. Roosevelt, no president could claim to be a prisoner of circumstance. Rather, they were forced by his example to appear as strong, forceful shapers of events and very much in control of each and every situation.

Franklin Roosevelt, therefore, not only pointed the way to the future, but was more nearly in tune with what the United States was becoming than most of his predecessors. If he had lived, he may well have been unhappy with much that was to occur, but there is little doubt that he would not only have come to grips with those developments, but stamped them indelibly with his own peculiar seal.

It is possible, of course, that much of what he accomplished would have occurred in the natural course of events, that his successive administrations brought accelerated evolution rather than revolution to the nation. But even his most severe critics admit that he left an impressive legacy and completed the process of presidential restoration so ably begun by the "Republican Roosevelt," for he had a series of challenges to match his talents.

The history of the presidency throughout the history of the Republic is one of attempted aggrandizement of power. The examples of Thomas Jefferson, Andrew Jackson, James K. Polk and Abraham Lincoln often spurred their successors to emulate their strengths and avoid their weaknesses. Yet, few presidents until this century were able to fully utilize the potential power of the office—save in time of emergency. Strong personalities in Congress such as Henry Clay, Daniel Webster and John C. Calhoun and later the likes of Stephen A. Douglas, Charles Sumner and James G. Blaine served to inhibit many a president or otherwise restrict their viable options. Some presidents were also unable to adopt a more active approach due to developments in the society at large, such as the struggle over slavery and the recurrent cyclical depressions which disrupted the economic life of the nation throughout the 19th Century. More importantly, potentially activist presidents were inhibited by the popular perception of the president as simply a custodian of the will of Congress, in short the constabulary approach. The 20th Century, however, has witnessed a transformation in the presidency. A transformation which was, in part, the result of the effort, begun by the first Roosevelt, to secure general acceptance of the principle that the national government, particularly the president, should be activist and reformist as opposed to simply protective of the status quo.

This shift in presidential perception was accompanied by technological and institutional changes which enhanced the president's ability to strongly influence, if not control, public debate. Newspapers, increasingly subservient to national wire services, and later radio and television, afforded the Chief Executive new opportunities to manage public opinion. The development of a White House staff independent of the departmental bureaucracies allowed the development of "presidential options." In consequence, presidents assumed a dominant position in the legislative process. Presidents were no longer divorced from policy formulation in Congress, indeed they began to exert a decisive impact through the exercise of the presidential pulpit. Legislation began to emerge directly from the executive branch, and Congress became, all too often, the reluctant handmaiden of presidential initiatives rather than the creators of governmental policies.

Of course, the enactment of laws is normally followed by their gradual absorption into the mainstream of society. Therefore, intense presidential activity usually precedes a period of retrenchment and reorientation. Thus, the active presidency of Theodore Roosevelt anticipated the passive presidency of Taft, the Wilson years the politics of normalcy, associated with Harding and Coolidge, Franklin Roosevelt and Truman the relative inactivity of Eisenhower.

This is not to say that nothing of consequence occurred under the less active presidents, but instead that they were less adept at mobilizing public opinion than their skillful predecessors. Moreover, their personalities did not admit a more active role, nor did the times appear to demand renewed activity. But the presidential pulpit is a two-edged sword. Presidents, since Theodore Roosevelt, are expected to produce a seemingly endless stream of innovations, and if they do not, for whatever reason, then legislative failure and public disdain is certain. Yet, if the electorate demands intense activity, that activity produces a desire for tranquility; thus Roosevelt was replaced by Taft, Wilson by Harding, and Roosevelt, after the Truman continuation, by Eisenhower. Unfortunately, tranquility once achieved gives rise to a renewed demand for activity. Therefore, Wilson and the two Roosevelts are rated more highly than their less active successors, who are relegated to the scrap heap of history.

The challenges and responsibilities facing the United States in the 19th Century determined the type of men who would occupy the Presidency, the powers and prerogatives of that office, as well as modifying the selection process to determine the occupant of the White House. The "rise to globalism," however, so altered the Presidency that it became a new position, possessed of duties and obligations unparalleled in the nation's history. Yet, in many respects, the presidential solutions adopted to deal with these changing circumstances were one time solutions. Therefore, it has become necessary to provide new solutions with each new administration. But, if the Presidency is a much altered institution, it remains to be seen if it will survive in its present form, or undergo still more fundamental changes to face as yet unknown challenges. The effect of "instant" media coverage of each and every event affects not only a President's conduct in office, but those who would achieve that position as well. The office has survived many challenges over the decades, but its greatest threat may stem from the realization that the institution, as constituted, is too much for any one person. In the past, the individual often made the office what it was, now the reverse may well be the case!

Sources and Suggested Readings

Barber, James D., *The Presidential Character* (1977, 2nd. ed.).
Blum, John M., *Woodrow Wilson and the Politics of Morality* (1956).
Burns, James M., *Presidential Government* (1965).
Burns, James M., *Roosevelt: The Lion and the Fox* (1956).
Coletta, Paola E., *The Presidency of William Howard Taft* (1973).
Harbaugh, William H., *The Life and Times of Theodore Roosevelt* (1975).
McCoy, Donald, *Calvin Coolidge: The Quiet President* (1967).
Neustadt, Richard E., *Presidential Power* (1979).
Trani, Eugene and David L. Wilson, *The Presidency of Warren G. Harding* (1977).
Wilson, Joan H., *Herbert Hoover: Forgotten Progressive* (1975).

America's Perceptions of the Soviet Union, 1917–1945

Nelson L. Dawson
The Filson Club

America's first minister to Russia was John Quincy Adams, who presented his credentials to the Czar in 1809. Throughout the 19th century the two nations avoided conflict and for the most part enjoyed friendly relations. To most Americans, however, Russia was a vast, remote, and mysterious country which late in the 19th century acquired an ominous reputation. Some American and Western European liberals protested against Czarist tyranny because of revelations of Siberian prison camps and reports by Jewish immigrants of brutal anti-Semitism. Despite these problems, England and France allied with Russia against Germany and Austria in World War I, which began in 1914. They were joined by the United States in 1917. The Western democracies had little in common with the Czarist regime, but military necessity is the mother of strange alliances. The alliance was shaky, however, because for decades Russia had suffered from a combination of governmental weakness and revolutionary agitation. A country which had already been defeated by the upstart Japanese and threatened by a narrowly averted revolution in 1905 would have had difficulty even in ordinary times. The extraordinary emergency of war led to a revolution in March, 1917.

The moderate Provisional Government, made up of respectable Russian liberals, was welcomed by the beleaguered Allies who hoped that a reformed Russia would fight more effectively. In his war message of April, 1917, Woodrow Wilson hailed the new Russia as "a fit partner for a league of honor." Such hope, however, proved illusory. The Provisional Government continued the war at the urging of the Allies, but succeeded only in driving an exhausted people to desperation. Nicolai Lenin's communist faction of the Russian Social Democratic Workers Party, called Bolsheviks in their early history (the name comes from the Russian word for "majority"—something which they never were), skillfully exploited the crisis with intrigue, violence, and propaganda ("Peace, Land, Bread"). The hapless Provisional Government fell in November, 1917, and the Bolsheviks seized power.

The Allies were initially dismayed not because the Bolsheviks were hostile to capitalism but because they sought peace at almost any price in order to buy the time needed to consolidate their power. In the face of advancing German armies the Bolsheviks signed the Treaty of Brest-Litovsk in March,

1918, which ended Russian participation in the war at the price of major territorial concessions. The Allies, recoiling from the German 1918 spring offensive which the treaty helped make possible, felt betrayed. Some of the Allies suspected that the Bolsheviks were really German agents seeking to neutralize an enemy of the Fatherland. Continuing Soviet calls for a general European revolution after Germany's defeat, however, quickly exploded that theory.

In the spring of 1918 the British and French, alarmed by the situation in the east, requested Wilson to send American troops into Russia to help their forces safeguard Western interests. After a period of painful calculation, Wilson reluctantly assented, and American soldiers landed in northern and eastern Russia in June and July, 1918. The motivation for Wilson's action was complex. He was concerned over the possibility of German dominion over Russia and worried that stockpiled Allied war material might fall into enemy hands. Wilson was also concerned at the plight of the anti-German Czech Legion seeking escape from Russia and apprehensive about the intentions of Japanese forces in eastern Siberia and the implications of their presence for a continuation of an "Open Door" policy in the far east. But anti-Bolshevism was at least a secondary motive for Wilson who abhorred Communism and who hoped, as Daniel M. Smith has observed, that "the mere presence of Allied troops would encourage the formation of a popular democratic government and the overthrow of the Bolshevik regime."

The intervention was, however, ineffective and brief. The last American troops, having accomplished nothing positive, left Russia in April, 1920. In fact, American intervention may well have made matters worse. The scale of involvement was large enough to anger the hard-pressed Bolsheviks but far too small to affect the outcome of the Civil War. Indeed, the presence of Allied forces probably helped the Bolsheviks who were able to brand their opponents as the pawns of foreign powers. The ill-fated venture served only to confirm Lenin's suspicions and create a resentment which aggravated his hostility to Western nations.

In the immediate postwar period, the "Red Menace" replaced the "German Menace" as popular apprehension over a possible Soviet-led Communist revolution spread rapidly. Glowing reports of romantic revolutionaries like John Reed, whose book *Ten Days That Shook the World* (1919) portrayed the Bolsheviks as humanitarian idealists, were outweighed by vivid, sometimes exaggerated, reports of Communist atrocities. Such coverage of the regime was both a symptom and a cause of the 1919 American "Red Scare." Terrorist bombings, including an unsuccessful attempt on the life of Attorney General A. Mitchell Palmer, triggered a powerful government counterattack which trampled on constitutional rights. Some of the accused subversives, including anarchist Emma Goldman, were deported. The American Communist Party was bitterly hostile to democratic institutions, but it was too weak to pose a significant danger. When the escalating violence predicted by Palmer did not occur, public anxiety over the alleged Bolshevik threat subsided.

As Woodrow Wilson's "Crusade for Democracy" faded into Warren Harding's "Normalcy," American concern over Bolshevism continued to diminish. Despite the period of relative calm in the early 1920s, most Americans retained suspicions of the Soviet regime. There were, however, a number of liberals who were inclined to accept Communist propaganda at face value and to project their own aspirations for social justice onto the emerging Soviet totalitarian regime. There were also others, politically conservative for the most part, who were prepared to believe nearly any anti-Bolshevik story however absurd—there was, for example, no Soviet Bureau of Free Love! Nevertheless, the critics were closer to the truth because conditions in Russia were indeed terrible.

They could hardly be otherwise. Russia had not recovered from wartime ravages, which were augmented by revolutionary violence. The Russian civil war only added to the chronicle of misery as the Bolsheviks and their Czarist opponents sought to outdo one another in frightfulness; the people reeled under the impact of the "Red Terror" and the opposing "White Terror." Lenin's frantic efforts to revolutionize Russian society during the period of militant communism (1917–1921) only increased the difficulties. In addition to imposing rationing, compulsory labor, and confiscation of church property, the regime contributed to massive food shortages by nationalizing agricultural lands and subjecting the peasants to forcible requisitioning.

While most Americans enthusiastically supported the humanitarian efforts of the American Relief Agency to feed Russians during the famine of 1921, political developments in Russia were not reassuring. The Extraordinary Commission to Combat Counter-Revolution (the Cheka, later known as the GPU) spread terror throughout the country making it even more obvious that the dictatorship of the proletariat really meant the dictatorship of the Communist Party. Soviet rhetoric continued to urge the working classes of capitalist nations to overthrow their governments in violent Communist revolutions. The regime's hostility to religion became more evident. In early 1923, for example, the Vicar-General of the Roman Catholic Church in Russia was executed for "counter-revolutionary activity," an outrage which stirred impassioned protests from American Catholics.

There was, nevertheless, a noticeable decline of interest in Russia in the 1920s, and the number of books and articles about the Bolsheviks decreased during the decade. Isolationism in foreign affairs and lessening political interest at home caused an indifference to Europe in general and to Russia in particular. Avant-garde Americans, at odds with society, expressed their discontent in aestheticism, cynicism, and in a contemptuous indifference to politics. Radicalism was not yet as politicized as it would become in the 1930s. For many Americans, furthermore, capitalism was an overwhelming success. The prosperity of the 1920s, while uneven and shaky, was strong enough to discourage unfavorable comparisons with the Soviet regime.

By the mid-1920s some observers detected a moderate trend in Russia. In 1921 Lenin beat a tactical retreat from the rigors of militant communism when he launched the New Economic Policy (1921–1927), which incorporated some features of capitalism including the use of private property and the incentives of the profit motive. The Bolshevik victory in the civil war caused a lessening of the "Red Terror" even though the Cheka ("Our splendid Cheka," Lenin called it) continued its obsessive search for class enemies. The country began to recover from the famine. The strident appeals for world revolution were muted. By 1924, the year of Lenin's death, most European countries had diplomatically recognized the Soviet regime. Americans seemed indifferent to the bitter power struggle between Joseph Stalin and Leon Trotsky, although some expressed relief at the victory of Stalin, the "moderate" party functionary, over Trotsky, creator of the Red Army and flamboyant revolutionary.

As tensions lessened, a coalition of American liberals began urging American diplomatic recognition of Soviet Russia. Some businessmen discovered that their opposition to Communism was tempered by their hope for Russian trade. The inauguration of the New Economic Policy convinced some that the Communists were abandoning radical theory for economic realism. Russia was an underdeveloped country desperately in need of Western expertise, and by 1929 over a thousand American engineers were helping the Soviets construct their first modern industrial plants. The Ford Motor Company virtually created the Russian automotive industry; other companies, such as General Electric, were also involved in Russian business ventures. Diplomatic recognition, however, had to wait for the crisis of the Great Depression and the election of a liberal Democratic president.

The collapse of the American economy in 1929 devastated not only the pocketbooks but also the morale of many Americans. Confidence in capitalism and in American institutions was shaken, and some Americans, particularly liberal intellectuals, began to view the USSR in a more favorable light. Communist leaders were idealized as socialist reformers and the Soviet regime was perceived as progressive in comparison with the reactionary leadership of depression-ridden America. This is not to say that American intellectuals were all Communists or fellow travelers (Communist sympathizers who were not officially Party members). Some writers, impressed with the widespread pro-Soviet attitudes of the 1930s, have characterized the period as the "Red Decade." This is an oversimplification: the 1930s was not a "Red Decade," and yet it was as "Red" as any subsequent decade in American history. There clearly was, in some circles at least, an uncritical acceptance of the USSR as a socialist utopia. The irony of the situation was heightened by the simultaneous development of a pro-Soviet attitude in the U.S. and Stalinist totalitarianism in Russia.

In 1928 Stalin was firmly in control of Russia, and, having abruptly abandoned the New Economic Policy, he launched a "New Socialist Offensive." Economically the new offensive had two major features: rapid industrialization to be achieved by several successive five year plans and the forced collectivization of agriculture. Both initiatives achieved a measure of quantitative success at a fearful cost in human suffering. This was particularly true of the agricultural policy which involved the destruction of the "kulaks" (in theory wealthy exploiters but in practice including even peasants of very modest holdings). Millions were uprooted; their property was confiscated; and they were herded into collective farms where the government requisitioned most of their produce. The result was a terrible famine in 1932–33, carefully concealed by the regime, which caused widespread starvation in the rural districts. This ghastly socialist "offensive," which Adam B. Ullam has described as a "war against the nation," was made possible by Stalin's success in establishing an irresistible tyranny sustained by the power of the Red Army and the pervasive terror of the GPU, the secret police.

Soviet totalitarianism, however, was hidden from the naive gaze of most American visitors. During the great era of western tours from 1924 to 1937, hundreds of Americans, mostly intellectuals, labor leaders, and businessmen, traveled to Russia; many returned with glowing reports of a new paradise. These visitors constituted a tiny percentage of the American population, and yet their influence was important. Soviet leaders were able to reinforce the naive misconceptions of the visitors by systematic deception on a massive scale. The tours were rigidly supervised and carefully orchestrated with selective itineraries to a variety of model institutions which specialized in deluding Western visitors. The Soviets were particularly careful to conceal one of the most dreaded features of Stalin's regime, the vast network of forced labor camps later immortalized by Aleksandr Solzhenitsyn as the "Gulag Archipelago." The result was that the pilgrims had their ardent expectations confirmed, and they returned home to spread optimistic reports about Soviet successes in a variety of humanitarian enterprises.

The contemporary English writer George Orwell, himself a socialist, and later scholars as well, have noted the susceptibility of some liberal intellectuals to Soviet blandishments. Few were advocates of totalitarianism, but their liberal views, reinforced by disenchantment with the slumping capitalist system, created a "will to believe" which generated enthusiasm for the Soviet regime. The Stalinists exploited such attitudes with skillful propaganda. While Adolf Hitler revealed his barbarism in the pages of *Mein Kampf*, Stalin professed a commitment to peace, freedom, and social justice. Stalin feared the growing power of Nazi Germany and sought to make the Soviet anti-Fascism of self-interest appealing by using liberal and democratic rhetoric. The result was that many people, discouraged by the apparent impotence of the Western democracies, came to Russia as the great bulwark against the Nazi menace as well as a progressive society. So while the 1930s was not really a "Red Decade," Russia enjoyed greater respectability, particularly in liberal circles, than at any time since Wilson had hailed the Provisional Government as a "fit partner for a league of honor."

Even so, many Americans retained deep distrust of the Soviet regime. Anti-Soviet literature continued to appear throughout the period, often in popular, high circulation magazines. This literature consisted for the most part, however, of the works of defectors and prison camp escapees, disillusioned radicals, and maverick news correspondents. Most of the political pilgrims who visited Russia gave favorable reports on Soviet society. The most famous record of liberal disenchantment—*The God That Failed,* edited by Richard Crossman—was not published until 1949.

The Depression, the election of Franklin D. Roosevelt, and the change in the political climate led to American recognition of the USSR in November, 1933. Those who had hoped that recognition would bring harmony to US-USSR relations, however, were disappointed. The lure of trade with the underdeveloped USSR had long been an argument in favor of recognition and one which had gained strength during the depression. But American trade with the Soviets never came close to the predicted levels. Other factors also intruded. Although Stalin agreed to stop Communist agitation in the United States, he disclaimed responsibility for the Communist International, a propaganda agency which he manipulated at will and which, in fact, continued its American operations. Greater contact does not always lead to greater appreciation. The establishment of the American embassy in Moscow brought State Department officials into closer relations with their Soviet counterparts. Although U.S. officials argued among themselves on secondary matters, most agreed that Stalin was the absolute dictator of a totalitarian state, that the Soviet regime must be treated with caution, and that the chances of genuinely good relations with the USSR were slight. This sober estimate was not shared, however, by US Ambassador Joseph E. Davies (1936–1938), whose rose-colored views of Soviet society were more readily accepted by the congenitally optimistic Roosevelt.

What did the American people think of the Soviet Union in the 1930s? Peter G. Filene, an historian seeking a reliable generalization, can say only that the American attitude was "fickle and so self-contradictory." One can, however, perceive at least some faint guidelines. Better educated liberals were more pro-Soviet than other Americans. Anti-Soviet articles continued to appear in the religious press and in such popular magazines as *The Saturday Evening Post, American Magazine,* and the *Reader's Digest.* Liberal publications, however, such as the *New Republic* and the *Nation,* which were read by the intellectuals, viewed the USSR in a favorable light, accepting Soviet rhetoric largely at face value. An exception was the radical *Partisan Review,* which beginning in 1937 impartially denounced totalitarianism of both the Fascist and Communist varieties.

From 1928 to 1934 the Soviet regime had called for a new socialist offensive against capitalist countries. The Soviet hard line was that whoever was not with them was against them. Non-Stalinist socialists were held to be no better than Wall Street plutocrats and were, in a blatant use of smear tactics, branded "Social Fascists." Growing Nazi power, however, caused Stalin to reassess this rigid stance. Beginning in 1935 he shifted to a strategy of cooperation by ordering the Communist parties of Europe and the US to join

Soviet workman constructing a transformer for a collective farm. This kind of progress in Russia impressed many American visitors in the 1930's. (Courtesy of National Archives.)

with liberals and socialists of all persuasions (the former "Social Fascists!") in an effort to mobilize public opinion against Hitler. The characteristic vehicles for implementing this strategy were the Popular Fronts, broadly based anti-Fascist organizations which the Communists were usually able to manipulate covertly through secret financing and the placement of Party members in key behind-the-scenes positions, while permitting respected public figures to occupy the prominent but relatively powerless offices. The Popular Fronts attracted many American liberals who wished to resist the Nazis. Stalin's anti-Fascism was opportunistic. He made repeated secret overtures to an unresponsive Hitler throughout the Popular Front era. American liberals did not know this, however, and, disillusioned with French and English appeasement of Hitler, they believed Russia to be the last best hope of stopping Fascism. To foster additional support in Western democratic nations, Stalin unveiled a "democratic" Soviet constitution in 1936 which, although never implemented, helped reassure Americans.

The rise of Fascism and Stalin's Popular Front strategy, therefore, enhanced the Soviet image abroad. By 1937, however, the spectacle of the great purge trials caused growing concern over the nature of the Soviet regime. Although the Soviets had conducted trials of alleged saboteurs ("Wreckers") and counter-revolutionaries earlier, the scale of the 1936–37 public show trials (grimly immortalized in Arthur Koestler's 1941 masterpiece *Darkness at Noon*) strained the credulity even of pro-Soviet Americans. Most Americans were shocked at the spectacle of Communist Party stalwarts publicly confessing to unbelievable acts of sabotage and treason. Some desperate apologists attempted to defend the trials on the basis of the confessions, but most observers concluded that blackmail—including torture and the threat of torture—was the most likely explanation. Although some publications, such as the *Nation,* continued to defend the regime, the purge trials tarnished the Soviet image even in the eyes of former supporters. Soviet assistance to the anti-Fascist Republicans in the Spanish Civil War (1936–1939) helped reassure some Americans of Soviet progressivism, but mounting evidence of Russia's manipulation and betrayal of non-Stalinist Spanish rebels further eroded public confidence. Such exposes as *Homage to Catalonia* (1938) by George Orwell, who had himself been wounded in the Republican cause, helped to blunt the impact of Soviet propaganda. Growing disillusionment with Soviet behavior meant that although the regime continued to enjoy some support, more and more Americans adopted the view that Hitler's Germany and Stalin's Russia, for all their apparent ideological differences, shared a common totalitarian character. This view is summed up in the pungent phrase "Red Fascism." So by 1938–39 many Americans believed that the USSR, far from being a bulwark against Fascism, represented merely a variation on the totalitarian theme.

A collective farm in Russia. Many Americans were impressed by the Soviet system in the interwar years. (Courtesy of National Archives.)

These suspicions received dramatic confirmation with the announcement of a nonaggression pact between Germany and the USSR on August 23, 1939. After years of estrangement, the totalitarian powers achieved a reapproachment which marked the culmination of the cynical opportunism of an entire decade. Ostensibly a triumph of peaceful diplomacy, the pact's secret provisions divided Eastern Europe between the dictators and led directly into World War II. Hitler, freed from the threat of a two-front war, quickly launched the German blitzkrieg through Poland in September, 1939, and through France in May, 1940. World War II, long anticipated with dread, had begun. And yet the pact was also satisfactory to Stalin. It reduced the immediate danger of a German attack, offered the possibility of a protracted struggle between the capitalist nations of Europe, and enabled him to expand into Eastern Europe. In 1940 Stalin further strained the ingenuity of his American apologists by brutally attacking tiny Finland.

The pact, which was difficult for Soviet apologists in America to explain away, was clearly a public relations disaster for the USSR, but the possible advantages were too great for Stalin to pass up. And so Stalin, who never worried about discomforting his American apologists, ruthlessly shifted his policy once again. Instead of calling for an anti-Fascist crusade, the Soviets advocated pacifism and isolationism in order to gain the time needed to digest their conquered territories. Over 400 progressives had signed a public letter printed in the August 26, 1939, issue of the *Nation* which denounced the "reactionaries" who "have encouraged the fantastic falsehood that the USSR and the totalitarian states are basically alike." The Nazi-Soviet pact caused these apologists great embarrassment though most remained reluctant to admit that they had been wrong about the Soviet regime. Roosevelt finally seemed to have shed his illusions about the Soviets. In a February, 1940, speech to the American Youth Congress, he denounced the USSR as "a dictatorship as absolute as any other dictatorship in the world." The President was booed for this statemnt by some of the die-hard Soviet supporters in the audience. Soviet prestige was never lower and the Red Fascism theory never stronger in America than in the period of the non-aggression pact.

The startling success of Hitler's blitzkrieg in France upset Stalin's calculations, and destroyed his hopes for a war of attrition among the capitalist nations. For over a year England stood alone, while Stalin was content to digest his Eastern European conquests and make increasingly desperate efforts to placate the Germans. Hitler, however, had always considered the East as the primary area of expansion for his Third Reich and so, with France occupied and England apparently neutralized, he lashed out at Russia in June, 1941. Soviet armies reeled under the massive assault. A Russian collapse seemed imminent in the summer and fall of 1941. These ominous events inevitably led to a change in America's Soviet policy. Roosevelt quickly offered Russia war material under the Lend-Lease policy of aiding the enemies of Germany. Self-interest alone required that America help Russia in accordance with the Machiavellian principle that the enemy of an enemy is a friend—

if only temporarily. This step, taken in the very month of the German attack before America formally entered the war in December, 1941, began a four year era of military cooperation which did not end until August, 1945. Ironies abounded as America entered into a strange alliance with one totalitarian power in order to defeat other totalitarian powers.

Military cooperation with Russia was necessary, but it led to an unjustifiable rehabilitation of the Russia image in America, even though Stalin had done nothing to earn American gratitude. Soviet policy, needless to say, shifted again. Peace and isolationism were out; war and anti-Fascist crusades were the order of the day. The greatest factor behind the change in American attitude toward Russia was the performance of the Red Army which absorbed Hitler's attack and, with the help of Lend-Lease and "General Winter," fought the Germans to a standstill. Russian resistance was interpreted by some rebounding apologists as a vindication of the regime, and hard-pressed American leaders were less inclined to scrutinize the defects of Soviet society. In late 1942, General Douglas MacArthur asserted that the "hopes of civilization rest on the worthy banners of the courageous Russian army." During the early years of the war, this sentiment was expressed in many different ways by influential Americans, liberal and conservative.

The result was an alteration of images and a shift in popular attitudes toward the Soviet Union which proved psychologically appealing to a people anxious to believe the best of a badly needed ally. The harsh contours of a totalitarian state softened into the illusion of a "new" Russia, a progressive, dynamic society courageously resisting aggression and fighting for freedom. Perhaps the strangest of all changes was the transformation of the Soviet dictator. Stalin, *Time* magazine's Man of the Year in 1939, was depicted on the cover as a shrewd, ruthless tyrant. Stalin was Man of the Year again in 1942, but this time he appeared as a benign, almost saintly figure against the backdrop of a snowy Russian landscape. Popular culture reflected this change in a variety of ways. In 1941, Jan Valtin's searing autobiographical expose of Communism, *Out of the Night,* was third on the best seller list. In 1942, however, Joseph E. Davies's pro-Soviet *Mission to Moscow* was second on the list. Wartime films, such as "Moscow Strikes Back" (Republic, 1942) and "One Day of War—Russia 1943" (Time, 1943), presented graphic illustrations of Russian heroism. Popular music fans were treated to such songs as "You Can't Brush Off a Russian" and "Stalin Wasn't Stallin'." Popular magazines, including the traditionally conservative *Reader's Digest,* published pro-Russian articles. Even the harsh Russian weather moderated under the impact of Allied unity as depicted by Owen Lattimore, who wrote a *National Geographic* article on the charms of "sunny Siberia."

This change in the climate of opinion seems to have been a relatively spontaneous phenomenon brought about by a variety of opinion-makers, but made possible only by the circumstances of the war. The government, while anxious to promote Allied unity, did not resort to heavy-handed propaganda tactics. Pro-Soviet groups, largely silent in the grim months of the Nazi-Soviet pact, revived, but not even a sinister cabal of Communists and fellow travelers could have effected such a massive change in public opinion. Indeed, the opinion-makers had themselves been influenced by the conditions of the war and since, as Samuel Johnson once observed, "most people catch their opinions by contagion," the American people were inclined to simply follow the leader.

And yet beneath the dominant pro-Russian sentiment there was a strong anti-Soviet current which persisted throughout the war. The religious, particularly the Roman Catholic press continued to hammer away at atheistic Communism and the dangers it posed to Christian civilization. A number of respected intellectuals, such as David Dallin, Max Eastman, and William Henry Chamberlain, warned Americans against accepting popular mythology about a "new" Russia. A public opinion poll in the winter of 1944–45 showed that, while public attitudes toward Russia were improving, there remained "a hard core of distrust," with about one in three Americans clinging "stubbornly" to anti-Soviet opinions. This persistent distrust of Russia gained strength late in the war when victory became certain. Cooperation with the Soviets had been difficult even during the height of the emergency, though the public was blissfully unaware of the tensions. Apprehension over the nature of Stalin's political intentions increased, however, as the Red Army plunged into Eastern Europe.

The approaching end of the war made it necessary for the Allies to consult on matters of political as well as military significance. This necessity led to a series of wartime conferences—Teheran (November-December, 1943), Yalta (February, 1945), and Potsdam (July-August, 1945)—which had a great impact on the postwar world. With the defeat of the Axis Powers in sight, the facade of Allied unity began to crumble. The Western democracies had nothing in common with the USSR except the determination to defeat Germany. At the conferences the Allies agreed to force unconditional surrender on Germany, to establish a postwar international peace-keeping organization (the United Nations), and to continue the war against Japan (Russia was to join the struggle after Germany's defeat). But these generalities did not deal with the increasingly divisive specific issues created by the approach of victory.

By 1944–45 the ominous outlines of a Soviet East European empire were emerging. Much has been made of alleged "sell-outs" to Russia which supposedly occurred at the conferences, particularly at Yalta. It is true that Stalin was a masterful diplomat who secured maximum benefit from his ability to exploit the foibles and illusions of Winston Churchill and Franklin Roosevelt. Roosevelt was particularly naive in his casual assumption that he could deal with "Uncle Joe" Stalin much as he dealt with balky Democratic congressmen. Yet, in the last analysis, the gains made by Stalin resulted from the "configuration of forces" created by the course of military operations and not from gullibility or treason. The United States and England had nothing in Eastern Europe to give away. They extracted ambiguously phrased pledges from Stalin regarding self-determination in Eastern Europe, but they had no power short of war to guarantee the establishment of democracy. The Soviets realized these limitations and showed less and less diplomacy in stating their objectives. It is, therefore, not surprising that public opinion polls conducted later in the war began to show mounting American distrust of the USSR.

World War II was not, however, followed immediately by the Cold War. There was instead a transitional period of several years characterized by shifting currents of diplomacy before attitudes hardened and the struggle became overt. The transitional period was dominated by difficulties resulting from Western Europe's economic distress and the establishment of Communist regimes in the nations of Eastern Europe. America responded in 1947 with the Marshall Plan (named for President Harry S. Truman's Secretary of State George C. Marshall) and the Truman Doctrine. The Marshall Plan, characterized by Churchill as one of the "least sordid acts in history," was an ambitious program of economic assistance designed to help Western Europe (the USSR refused to participate) recover from the ravages of the war. The Truman Doctrine called for the containment of Soviet expansionism and expressed America's determination to help free nations resist aggression.

The immediate causes of the Cold War lie in the ending of the wartime alliance and the disappearance of the restraining presence of a common enemy. The USSR and the Western democracies did not come into direct conflict until after World War II because they were separated by a large area in Central and Eastern Europe, dominated after 1933 by a hostile Germany. In the 1930s, furthermore, America and the nations of Western Europe were struggling with the Depression while Stalin was mobilizing Russia in a massive effort at economic and social reconstruction. The wartime alliance further delayed the confrontation, but the defeat of the Fascist nations and the dramatic western expansion of the USSR as a result of the war has brought the rival blocs into an era of protracted conflict and unprecedented danger.

Sources and Suggested Readings

Caute, David, *The Fellow Travellers: A Postscript to the Enlightenment* (1973).

Feuer, Lewis, "American Travellers to the Soviet Union, 1917–1932: The Formation of a Component of New Deal Ideology," *American Quarterly,* 14(Summer, 1962), 119–49.

Filene, Peter G., *Americans and the Soviet Experiment, 1917–1933* (1967).

Hollander, Paul, *"Political Pilgrims": Travels of Western Intellectuals to the Soviet Union, China, and Cuba* (1982).

Lasch, Christopher, *The American Liberals and the Russian Revolution* (1962).

Levering, Ralph B., *American Opinion and the Russian Alliance, 1939–1945* (1976).

Maddux, Thomas R., *Years of Estrangement: American Relations with the Soviet Union, 1934–1941* (1980).

Margulies, Sylvia R., *The Pilgrimage to Russia: The Soviet Union and the Treatment of Foreigners, 1924–1937* (1968).

O'Neill, William L., *A Better World: The Great Schism: Stalinism and the American Intellectuals* (1982).

Warren, Frank A., *Liberals and Communists: The "Red Decade" Revisited* (1966).

Part II
American Economic and Social Life, 1898–1952

Nations are not always known by the politics they practice. It is often more useful in understanding a nation to understand its people and their ways than it is to know their laws. The way a people live tells us much about the way they view life, and the way they view life will determine the kinds of laws they write and the kinds of actions they will take.

The first four decades of the twentieth century saw dramatic alterations in the ways Americans lived. For those then alive, the transformations must have seemed incredible. Within the last century, the American of today can find accomplishments which eluded mankind for centuries. Man learned to fly in heavier-than-air machines; he had developed ways to send sounds through the air hundreds of miles in fractions of seconds; he learned to capture sounds on sheets of metal preserving the sounds of voices for eternity; he captured accurate images on film to leave lasting portrayals of the present. Man learned to travel faster, to build higher, and, most importantly, to share those developments with a larger segment of the population than ever before.

The development of the automobile broke, forever, the loneliness of farm life. It brought an end to the necessity of living in crowded cities. It altered social relationships, for the automobile was within the reach of almost everyone, and everyone in an automobile on the highway had a certain equality.

The development of the radio brought Americans closer together in both the immediacy of the sound and in the common language and inflections which the announcers used.

As the Americans viewed their society, some questioned the old traditions and the old ways of thinking. Newer philosophies stressed the relative nature of truth rather than its absolute values. Groups which had previously been left out of the mainstream began to demand their rightful share of the prosperity. Americans found in the new age that some could enjoy all of the benefits of the advances while all could enjoy some of them. Determining what constituted the most equitable distribution of those bounties created conflicts which tore at the very fabric of society.

The essays which follow examine the ways Americans lived, worked, played, and reacted to the new dimensions of society. More than simple observations on a complex life, these essays discuss how Americans dealt with the conflicts which created their new life.

American Women, 1898–1952

Judy Barrett Litoff
Bryant College

As the twentieth century dawned, American women could look back with pride at the achievements they had won during the past 100 years. Women played prominent roles in a number of early nineteenth-century reform movements, most notably abolitionism, temperance, and moral reform. Under the leadership of individuals like Sarah Bagley, they began the long and arduous task of improving the working conditions of the growing numbers of women who sought employment in America's burgeoning factories. At the urging of Elizabeth Cady Stanton and Lucretia Mott, they held a women's rights convention in Seneca Falls, New York, in 1848 and issued the revolutionary "Declaration of Sentiments" and "Resolutions." During the Civil War years, women were involved in a wide gamut of activities from working with the United States Sanitary Commission to acting as spies and soldiers.

The years after the Civil War witnessed the emergence of an independent women's movement with the formation of two national suffrage organizations. Educational opportunities for women continued to expand, albeit gradually. A tiny minority of women even entered prestigious professions such as medicine and law. Middle- and upper-class women saw club work take on a fresh meaning in their lives with the establishment of a number of national women's organizations, including the Women's Christian Temperance Union (1874) and the General Federation of Women's Clubs (1890).

Yet the lives of the vast majority of women had not substantially changed during the previous century. Most turn-of-the-twentieth-century women worked in their homes where they performed difficult and painstaking domestic duties. Not until the 1920s would time- and labor-saving electrical equipment be readily available to American housewives. Women who worked outside the home also faced insurmountable obstacles. While the proportion of women in the labor force had risen to 20 percent by 1900, wage-earning women were almost always forced into the least prestigious and lowest-paying jobs. Women's entry into the esteemed professions like medicine, law, and the ministry continued to be thwarted. Only the professions of teaching and nursing welcomed women.

Another area of women's lives that had not undergone substantial change by 1900 was the confining and uncomfortable clothing they were expected to wear. The Victorian dress with its emphasis on a tightly-laced corset and yards of petticoats and gowns remained standard. A typical turn-of-the-century corset was made of steel and bone and served the purpose of pushing the bust up,

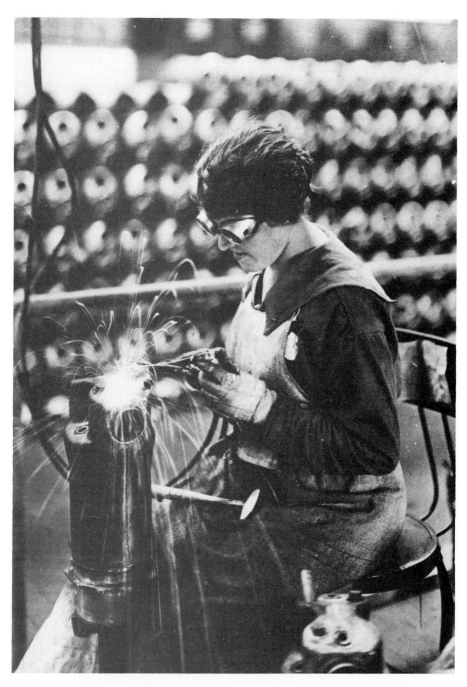

American women contributed greatly to the war effort beginning in 1917. This woman is helping to ease the chronic shell shortage on the Western front. (Courtesy of National Archives.)

the stomach in, and the rear out. The "new woman" who worked outside the home generally preferred the demure shirtwaist blouse and simple, floor length, dark skirt to the Victorian dress. However, even this pioneer continued to be hampered by confining underclothing.

Perhaps the most significant area of women's lives to be untouched by change in 1900 was their political disenfranchisement. A half century after Seneca Falls, few women were able to vote. Even the reunion of the two major suffrage organizations into the National American Woman Suffrage Association in 1890 did not make a significant difference. Interest in the federal suffrage amendment appeared to have reached a lowpoint by 1900. It had been over a decade since the issue of woman suffrage had been debated on the Senate floor. The state campaigns for suffrage also seemed to be moribund. Between 1896 and 1910, not a single state voted to enfranchise women. As politically- and socially-aware women welcomed the new century, they very much understood the work that lay ahead of them in their struggle for equality.

First on women's political agenda was their enfranchisement. Unfortunately, the original leaders of the suffrage movement, including Susan B. Anthony, Elizabeth Cady Stanton, and Lucy Stone, were now approaching their eighties, and they no longer displayed the same energy or vitality of their earlier years. Not until a new generation of suffrage leaders entered the picture around 1910 would women's enfranchisement again receive national attention.

Of course, some women did not look upon the vote as a desirable goal. A number of socially prominent women played a leading role in the antisuffrage movement. They argued that woman's place was in the home and not the rough and unsavory world of politics.

At the other end of the spectrum, many radical women viewed the vote to be, at best, an area of peripheral concern. Margaret Sanger, for example, felt that a woman's right to birth control was much more important than whether she could vote. Charlotte Perkins Gilman, the leading feminist intellectual at the turn of the century, believed that economic independence was the key to woman's advancement. Emma Goldman, anarchist, described the campaign for the vote as a "fetish." She argued that freedom came from within; not from some outward manifestation decreed by the state.

Despite the opposition, suffrage activity dramatically increased around 1910. This was largely due to the work of a small, but dedicated group of young, college-educated women. These women, several of whom had lived in England and participated in the militant wing of the British suffrage movement, were deeply disturbed about the slow, non-aggressive nature of the American campaign.

Led by Alice Paul and Lucy Burns, militant suffragists organized a giant suffrage parade in Washington, D.C., in March, 1913, to coincide with the inaugural festivities of President-elect Woodrow Wilson. Over the next several years, suffrage parades and demonstrations multiplied. At first, Paul and Burns tried to work as a committee within the National American Woman Suffrage

Association, but it soon became clear that an alliance of militant and moderate suffragists was not feasible. Thus, in 1915, the militants officially broke away from NAWSA and formed their own organization, the National Woman's Party.

Two years later, in January, 1917, the National Woman's Party began the controversial and innovative strategy of picketing the White House. They carried placards which read, "Mr. President, What Will You Do For Woman Suffrage?" and "How Long Must Women Wait For Liberty?" For the next several months, the demonstrations were tolerated with few incidents. In April 1917, however, tension mounted after American entry into World War I caused the suffragists to change their placards to read, "Kaiser Wilson," and "Democracy Should Begin at Home."

President Wilson was visibly embarrassed by the success of the suffragists at exposing the contradiction between America's democratic war aims and its undemocratic practice of denying the vote to one-half of its citizens. As might be expected, arrests of the demonstrators began in June 1917. Over the next several months, 219 women from 26 states were arrested and charged with minor infractions, such as obstructing sidewalk traffic. Imprisoned suffragists followed the example of their militant British sisters by going on hunger strikes. Newspapers across the nation prominently covered these events, further embarrassing Washington officials.

In the meantime, the National American Woman Suffrage Association experienced a new sense of vitality with the election of Carrie Chapman Catt as its president in 1915. Catt, a woman with superb organizational skills, carefully developed her "Winning Plan," aimed at coordinating all state and national efforts in behalf of the federal suffrage amendment. Under Catt's leadership, NAWSA's membership grew from one hundred thousand in 1915 to two million in 1917.

Largely because of the work of NAWSA, a number of other organizations and individuals began to support women's suffrage. Progressive reformers were often strong supporters of the vote for women. Throughout the early years of the twentieth century, these reformers worked to make the nation more democratic by supporting a variety of political changes, including the direct election of United States Senators, the initiative, the recall, and the referendum. Support for women's suffrage can be viewed as another effort by these Progressives to expand the democratic process.

Joining the suffrage bandwagon were a number of social feminist organizations whose primary concern for social reform generally took precedent over women's suffrage. Included among this group were representatives of the settlement-house movement, The Women's Christian Temperance Union, the Women's Trade Union League, and one of the last holdouts, the General Federation of Women's Clubs.

Throughout all of this activity, women's suffragists developed an elaborate argument in their defense. Although nineteenth-century suffragists most often defended the vote for women as a natural right, early twentieth-century suffragists were more likely to defend it on the grounds of expediency. The new generation of suffragists frequently argued that women deserved the vote because they were morally superior to men. Their votes would help to abolish child labor, eradicate the liquor traffic, provide for protective labor legislation, and contribute to other Progressive reforms aimed at "cleaning up" government and society. Coupled with these arguments were overtones of racism in which suffragists reminded white male voters that the women's vote would help to counteract the growing numbers of "undesirable" votes being cast by immigrants and blacks.

What finally tipped the scales in favor of women's suffrage was the admirable record of women during World War I. While the percentage of women in the labor force rose by only six percent during the nineteen months that the United States was involved in the war, there is no question that women rallied to the cause whenever possible. As early as September, 1918, President Wilson asked Congress to enact women's suffrage in gratitude for women's contributions to the war. Two years later, in August, 1920, the Nineteenth Amendment to the Constitution, granting women the vote, was ratified.

It had been a hard-won and sometimes bitter battle. Many suffragists could not help but question why it had taken them decades of toil, huge sums of money, and an untold amount of energy to secure for American women what should have rightfully been theirs all along.

The campaign for the enfranchisement of women resulted in a concrete victory in 1920. Other efforts at enhancing the position of American women were not so readily attained. Nowhere was this clearer than in the efforts to improve the lives of women employed in manufacturing.

Early twentieth-century female factory workers performed a wide variety of jobs from stripping, rolling, and packing cigars to making artificial flowers and feathers. Of the myriad industrial tasks performed by women, the needle trades contained the greatest concentration of female workers. Unfortunately, the skilled occupations of tailoring and cutting were generally reserved for male workers. Only unskilled tasks, such as finishing, tucking, basting and turning were readily available to women.

Long hours, low pay and poor working conditions typified the experiences of female garment workers. A woman sewing machine operator, who was lucky enough to find employment in a bona fide factory, could expect to work sixty hours a week and make about six dollars. Less fortunate women ended up working for subcontractors who rented cheap tenements where makeshift shops were established. These "sweatshops," as they came to be called, were notorious for their low pay and poor working conditions. Still other women worked by the piece in their own homes where they toiled longer than sixty hours a week and received much less than the six dollars earned by their factory counterparts.

Although the trade union movement, under the leadership of the American Federation of Labor, underwent dramatic expansion during the early years of the twentieth century, women rarely benefited directly from this growth. Approximately 3.3 percent of industrial wage-earning women were organized into trade unions in 1900. Around 1902, this figure began to decline, reaching a low point of 1.5 percent in 1910. One of every five industrial male wage earners belonged to a union, compared to only one of every fifteen women.

A variety of factors helps to explain why so few women were unionized during the early years of the twentieth century. Heading up this list is the fact that many semiskilled and unskilled female wage earners were ineligible for membership in the craft unions of the American Federation of Labor. Another significant factor was that most women viewed their positions in the labor force as temporary. Predominantly young, single, and of immigrant status, many female wage earners eagerly anticipated giving up factory work upon marriage.

Equally important was the fact that male trade unionists displayed only a limited commitment to recruiting women. Although the American Federation of Labor frequently called for the organization of women workers, few concrete steps were actually taken in behalf of female wage earners. Male unionists preferred to hold union meetings in saloons, where respectable young women never went. With but few exceptions, trade unionists looked upon women workers as mothers, daughters, and future wives, not as co-workers.

Even though female wage earners received only limited support from the organized labor movement, they did find an important ally among well-to-do women reformers. Two leading social feminist organizations concerned with improving the status of working women were the National Consumers' League and the Women's Trade Union League.

The National Consumers' League, founded in 1892 by Maud Nathan and Josephine Shaw Lowell, first agitated for improved working conditions among saleswomen in department stores. It worked for seats for saleswomen, as well as calling for the establishment of clean, ventilated lunch rooms. By the late 1890s, the work of the league had expanded to include a White Label campaign, whereby clothing manufacturers with good labor policies were allowed to use the NCL's label. Consumers were then urged to boycott products which did not carry the NCL's insignia. Influential until after World War I, the National Consumers' League played an important role in educating the public about the adverse conditions in America's factories.

An equally important organization was the Women's Trade Union League. Founded at an American Federation of Labor meeting in Boston in 1903 by Mary Kenney O'Sullivan and William English Walling, the WTUL was comprised of a unique coalition of women workers and well-to-do reformers, called "allies." During its first decade of existence, the League worked closely with the AFL as it strove to bring more female wage earners into trade unions. Relying largely on the financial resources and organizational skills of its "allies," the WTUL organized picnics, dances, teas, street meetings, and rallies for the purpose of promoting the value of unionism.

When almost thirty thousand New York City shirtwaist workers, the vast majority of whom were female, walked out on strike in 1909 demanding union recognition and a fifty-two hour work week, the league quickly came to the

Housewives, such as this farm woman in Nebraska, were seldom busier than during the 1930's as they struggled to "take up the slack" of the Depression. (Reproduced from the Collections of the Library of Congress.)

defense of the strikers. League members joined the picket line, posted bail for arrested strikers, protested the harsh treatment the women received at the hands of the police, and arranged numerous marches and rallies. While the city's largest clothing manufacturers refused to recognize the union, the shirtwaist uprising was significant because it was the first major woman-led and dominated strike. Two years later, when 146 shirtwaist makers were killed during the 1911 Triangle Shirtwaist Fire, the WTUL once again rallied to the aid of the workers.

In the years after 1911, the emphasis of the WTUL shifted from a focus on union organizing to working for women's suffrage and protective labor legislation. League members felt that enfranchised women would be better equipped to abolish the sweatshops, raise wages, limit hours of work, and help unionize women. Although the League had always endorsed protective labor legislation, support for such laws took on new meaning in the years after 1911. This shift represented much more than a simple change in tactics. It exemplified a new ideological orientation of the league from women as workers to women workers as women.

Many early twentieth-century women were employed in nonindustrial occupations and were therefore untouched by the efforts of organizations like the National Consumers' League and the Women's Trade Union League. Chief among these were women employed as domestic workers. In 1900, domestic service was the single most important class of women's gainful employment. Almost 30 percent of all wage-earning women were employed as household workers. Even though this figure declined to 18 percent by 1930, domestic service was a significant source of employment for women during the early years of the twentieth century. Largely unorganized and unorganizable, domestic servants frequently complained about the length and irregularity of hours, the lack of freedom, the loneliness and isolation, sexual exploitation by masters, and the general harshness of their lives. In fact, such a low status was accorded to domestic work that many women preferred lower-paying factory jobs.

Women who served as midwives also fell outside the organized labor movement. In 1910, approximately 50 percent of all births in the United States were attended by midwives. These women, most of whom were poor immigrants and blacks, remained isolated from each other during the early years of the twentieth century. Because no viable midwife association was established, the midwives found it impossible to defend themselves against accusations, emanating from the medical profession, that they were dirty, evil, ignorant, and grossly inadequate birth attendants. Due to a number of factors, their numbers rapidly declined over the next two decades. By 1930, only 15 percent of all births were attended by midwives.

Although certain occupations like midwifery were being cut off from women, other types of work offered them new employment opportunities. The most dramatic example of this was the feminization of the clerical work force. As late as 1880, only four percent of all clerical workers were female. By 1900, this figure had increased to 25 percent. In 1930, approximately 50 percent of all clerical workers were female. The rapid expansion of American business enterprises, coupled with the successful marketing of the typewriter, paved the way for women's entry into the clerical work force. Clerical work also paid better and brought a higher social status than most other jobs available to women. Because of the lack of job opportunities for women in the professions, with the exceptions of nursing and teaching, literate women turned readily to clerical work.

The decade following the passage of the Nineteenth Amendment was an era composed of false starts and contradictory currents for American women. Shortly after the suffrage amendment was ratified, Anna Howard Shaw, a prominent suffragist and minister, remarked to a younger cohort, "I am sorry for you young women who have to carry on the work for the next ten years, for suffrage was a symbol and now you have lost your symbol." Her statement did indeed prove prophetic: no solid "woman's" issue emerged during the 1920s to take the place of the vote.

Equally discouraging was the fact that only one-third of the eligible women voted in 1920. Moreover, it soon became clear that women did not vote all that differently from men. Rather than voting in a bloc, as many suffragists had predicted, women tended to vote according to their economic and social status.

Yet several areas of concern were defined as particularly women's issues. Noteworthy among these were improving the care of pregnant women and infants and the abolition of child labor. Responding in part to the pressures of the women's vote, Congress approved the Sheppard-Towner Maternity and Infancy Protection Act in 1921. This law, which remained in effect for almost eight years, provided federal funds to cooperating states for the purpose of improving maternity and infancy care and reducing the alarmingly high maternal and infant death rates. Bowing to conservative forces, chiefly the American Medical Association, who charged that the act was communist-inspired, Congress refused to extend its provisions beyond 1929. By this time, moreover, politicians were no longer worried about being punished at the polls by disgruntled women voters.

The abolishment of child labor had been a goal of many Progressives, including a number of social feminists, during the first two decades of the twentieth century. Since the United States Supreme Court had ruled that two previously enacted laws abolishing child labor were unconstitutional, reformers during the 1920s began to work for the ratification of a Child Labor Amendment. Although such an amendment was eventually passed by Congress in June, 1924, it was never ratified by three-quarters of the states. Not until the New Deal years would significant federal limitations on child labor be enacted.

Neither the Sheppard-Towner Act nor the proposed Child Labor Amendment aroused the indignation and furor of women as had the drive for their enfranchisement. The one issue that might have taken the place of suffrage, a proposed equal rights amendment, was one over which women were hopelessly and bitterly divided.

First introduced into Congress in 1923, the Equal Rights Amendment simply stated that "men and women shall have equal rights throughout the United States and every place subject to its jurisdiction." While strongly supported by the small, but well-organized, National Woman's Party, the ERA was opposed by equally significant women's groups. Prominent among these were the League of Women Voters, successor to the disbanded National

American Woman Suffrage Association, and the Women's Trade Union League.

The crux of the debate over the ERA centered around whether specially designed protective labor laws for women, which would no longer be constitutional if such an amendment were ratified, helped or hindered female workers. Early twentieth-century Progressive reformers had successfully enacted a number of state laws aimed at protecting female wage earners. Included among these were laws which limited the hours of work of women, prohibited night work, imposed weight limit provisions, and restricted the employment of pregnant women.

Organizations like the Women's Trade Union League had worked long and hard for the enactment of protective labor laws. They saw no reason to support a constitutional amendment aimed at wiping out the hard-fought for legislation. By contrast, the National Woman's Party pointed to the ways that protective labor laws discriminated against women and prohibited them from advancement within the male-dominated work world. For the next several decades, an acrimonious debate between the supporters and opponents of protective labor legislation and the ERA ensued.

It is unclear just what impact protective labor legislation had on the lives of working women. Although these laws did serve to ameliorate the worst conditions of women's work, they also served to subject women to an increasing number of restrictions. Generally speaking, with the exception of women's continued movement into clerical work, their position in the labor force inched upward only slightly from 23 percent in 1920 to 24 percent in 1930. In a few professions, such as medicine, women actually lost ground. Even the establishment of the Women's Bureau in 1920, with its broad investigatory responsibilities, did not bring about significant improvement.

As social feminists struggled to carry the Progressive impulse into the 1920s, other women ignored or were simply oblivious to the idealism of the pre-World War I era. Clearly, many young people preferred the post-war world with its emphasis on consumerism, fun, and the "new" morality. Typifying this rebellious spirit were "flappers"—young women who put merrymaking and excitement above all else. Flappers saw the "new era" in terms of short shirts, bobbed hair, make up, cigarettes, automobiles, dancing, speakeasies, and occasional triflings with premarital sex. Just how many women freely participated in these activities is open to question. If the "sexual revolution" of the 1920s had been as widespread as many have claimed, it is unlikely that generational conflicts over sexual freedom would have continued to mar family relationships to the degree they did.

The coming of the Great Depression brought with it a paradoxical message for American women. On the one hand, they were repeatedly exhorted to forego wage work in the name of family unity and jobs for man. At the same time, the harsh realities of poverty and high rates of unemployment forced many women to seek gainful employment.

Working women, particularly married, white-collar working women, were the scapegoat of the Depression. The simplest version of this scapegoating panacea called for the firing of all working women and the hiring of men in their place. After all, conventional wisdom held that most women only worked for "pin" money, or the little extras in life. Despite numerous investigations by the Women's Bureau refuting the "pin" money theory, government and business officials continued to argue that woman's place, especially during periods of depression, was in the home.

State and local governments embarked on virulent, but generally unsuccessful, campiagns to fire married women workers. During the Depression years, twenty-six states introduced bills limiting the employment of married women. Married female teachers found their positions to be particularly vulnerable. Public opinion polls across the nation revealed that an overwhelming majority of Americans were opposed to the employment of married women. At the federal level, Section 213 of the 1932 Federal Economy Act stipulated that married persons were to be the first discharged if their spouse were also employed by the federal government. In theory, there was nothing discriminatory about this law. In actuality, three-fourths of those dismissed under the act were women.

Despite these prescriptions, the proportion of women in the labor force increased slightly during the Depression decade. In 1930, women made up 24 percent of the labor force. By 1940, this figure had risen to 25 percent. However, not all women benefitted equally from even this increase. Professional women struggled to hold onto their jobs as they witnessed the proportion of women in all professional pursuits decline from 14.2 percent to 12.3 percent.

During these same years, the percentage of married women in the labor force rose by almost seven percent. In 1930, married women made up 28.9 percent of the female labor force. Ten years later, 35.5 percent of all female wage earners were married. Among black women, the figure doubled.

A number of factors propelled married women into the work force: the changing nature of the household economy, the decline of child labor, the falling birth rate, and perhaps, most importantly, economic need. Indeed, in view of the widespread poverty and unemployment of the 1930s, it is surprising that more married women did not enter the work force.

Women's relative economic strength during the Depression years was a result of several factors. First, women had been denied employment in those heavy industries, such as construction, automobiles, and steel, which were hardest hit by the Depression. Second, the areas where women were most frequently employed, the clerical and social service sectors, were the first to recover. Third, women often found employment in the new, semi-skilled jobs brought about by technological innovations.

Another development which proved beneficial to wage-earning women was the growth of the organized labor movement. The enactment of federal legislation guaranteeing the right of workers to bargain collectively and the spread

Around 1910, the organized suffrage movement was infused with new vitality as younger women took to the streets demanding the vote. (Reproduced from the Collections of the Library of Congress.)

of industrial unionism enabled large numbers of women to join unions for the first time.

Non-wage-earning women also found their lives dramatically altered as a result of the Depression. The work of housewives in physically and psychologically caring for their families became increasingly difficult as the decade wore on. Women confronted material hardships by substituting their own labor for goods and services that they had formerly purchased. Home gardening, canning, and sewing were three areas that experienced rapid growth during the 1930s. Housewives baked cakes to sell, took in laundry, established home beauty parlors, and advertised for boarders. The psychological pressures imposed upon women were equally demanding. Coping with the anxieties and loss of self-esteem of unemployed husbands was especially difficult. In fact, housewives were seldom busier than during the 1930s as they strove to "take up the slack" of the Depression.

Throughout the anguish and despair of the Depression decade, one woman stood out as a symbol of hope and confidence for others to emulate: Eleanor Roosevelt. As the prime spokesperson for women both inside and outside of government, Eleanor Roosevelt played a significant role in molding public opinion. Although she accepted the traditional belief that woman's primary responsibility was to her husband and children, she also believed that the complexities of the modern world necessitated that women participate in public affairs to protect and preserve the home.

As First Lady, she influenced her husband to appoint a significant number of women to important government offices. Most notable among these was the appointment of the first woman to a full Cabinet position: Frances Perkins as Secretary of Labor. She also guaranteed that important public women, including Mary Anderson, Mary W. Dewson, and Ellen S. Woodward, had access to the President.

Eleanor Roosevelt brought new and unique importance to the role of First Lady. Besides managing the household and overseeing ceremonial occasions, she lectured, wrote a daily newspaper column, held weekly press conferences for women journalists, made frequent radio broadcasts, lobbied assiduously for women, blacks, and the poor, and served as her husband's unofficial advisor on domestic matters. By the end of the 1930s, there could be no question that Eleanor Roosevelt was the most admired and highly-respected woman in the United States.

The outbreak of World War II produced a major, but temporary shift, in the public's attitude toward working women. No longer were women urged to forego wage work for the sake of their families and jobs for men. Government and business officials now asserted that it was woman's patriotic duty to work outside the home. Newspapers, magazines, movies, and the radio praised the woman who entered the labor force. Rose the Riveter, the highly-lauded symbol of these new workers, became a national heroine.

In response to the extraordinary demand for new workers, over six million women entered the labor force, increasing their ranks by 50 percent. The proportion of women in the entire labor force rose from 25 percent in 1940 to 36 percent in 1945. This represented a greater increase than the previous four decades combined. Married women entered the labor force in unprecedented numbers. Moreover, women over 35 made up 60 percent of this increase. No longer was the typical female wage earner in the United States young and single.

Nevertheless, discrimination against working women, particularly black and other minority women, continued. Even though their wages leaped upward, women employed in manufacturing earned only 65 percent of what men received. Faced with a critical labor shortage, many industries still refused to hire black women.

Perhaps the most difficult problem facing these new war workers was how to combine wage work with household responsibilities. Many women suffered from perpetual exhaustion as they struggled to cook, clean, and care for their families while holding down full-time jobs. Nowhere was this problem more clearly illustrated than in the grossly inadequate efforts of federal and local officials to provide child care facilities for working women. The press was filled with stories of children who were exiled to neighborhood movie houses or locked in cars parked outside defense plants while their mothers worked. Although the federal government eventually spent almost 52 million dollars on child care during the war, only a minority of children who needed it were served by public child care centers.

Part of the reason that so few concrete steps were taken to lighten the load of women war workers was that, for the most part, they were expected to give up their jobs once the war ended. While government and business leaders might encourage women to become welders, riveters, lumberjacks, and drill press operators on a temporary basis in an effort to meet wartime exigencies, there was very little support for granting female war workers a permanent position in the post-war economy.

Despite all the laurels placed upon her, Rosie the Riveter was not the typical wartime woman. Most women, even though under considerable pressure to do otherwise, remained homemakers. Like their wage-earning sisters, housewives were also expected to do their part in bringing about a victorious end to the war. They planted victory gardens and participated in a variety of volunteer activities ranging from war bond drives to Red Cross work.

Marriage rates soared as young people, uncertain about what the future would bring, rushed into matrimony. There were over one million more marriages between 1940 and 1943 than would have been expected at the pre-war rate. Emotional strains related to long separations and the exigencies of war promoted a strong desire to return to more traditional patterns of family life once the war was over. However, war-related separations provided many women with a clear view of their capabilities in what had been a man's world heretofore.

The end of World War II brought forth a loud cry for working women to withdraw from the labor force so that the 11 million returning veterans could be better assured of employment. Although some women happily left their war jobs for a more settled family existence, others were not so ready to return to the home. A study conducted by the Women's Bureau in late 1944, as the war was winding down, revealed that 75 percent of all women employed wanted to continue working. Nevertheless, women workers suffered disproportionately to their numbers as reconversion cutbacks were initiated. The proportion of women in the labor force dropped precipitously during the first two years after the war from 36 percent in 1945 to 28 percent in 1947. Even those women who remained in the labor force were often forced to shift from high-paying industrial work to semi-skilled, low-paying, dead-end jobs.

Beginning in 1947, working women began to recoup some of the losses they had experienced during the immediate post-war era, and the proportion of women in the labor force again began to rise. By 1951, women made up 31 percent of the labor force. As the decade of the 1950s wore on, this figure continued to climb. At the same time, more and more married and middle-aged women became wage earners.

Significantly, the vast majority of these working women were not perceived as a feminist threat by the male labor force. In the first place, women continued to be segregated in low-paying, semiskilled jobs. In the second place, most women who worked in the 1950s did so in order to supplement family incomes. They were not seeking careers and independence. Rather, the economic realities of family life in the post-war era, including ever-increasing rates of consumption, necessitated that many women work. Women's commitment to the family, not their rejection of it, often propelled them to seek employment as supplementary wage earners. Even as women performed routine tasks, however, many were developing a sense of pride and self-esteem in themselves as workers and individuals which would contribute to the changing self-image of women in later decades.

Largely in response to the disruptions experienced by American families during World War II, a new emphasis was placed on marriage and motherhood during the late 1940s and 1950s. From academic works, such as *Modern Woman: The Lost Sex* (1947) by sociologist Marynia Farnham and historian Ferdinand Lundberg, to popular television shows, such as "Father Knows Best," the message imparted to women was that their happiness and fulfillment depended upon their becoming dutiful wives and mothers. This back-to-the-home movement witnessed a lowering of the age at which women married and an increase in the size of families.

The ideal housewife of the 1950s lived in the suburbs where schools, stores, and trains were rarely within walking distance. She often spent hours of each day behind the wheel of a station wagon chauffering her children to school, Scout meetings, and piano lessons. Her home was equipped with every conceivable modern appliance designed to lighten her workload. Yet she spent as much time on housework as her mother had in the 1920s. With her husband away from the house for long periods each day, she found herself cut off from the mainstream, workaday world.

Women's dress styles also reflected this new emphasis on feminity. In contrast to the "mannish" clothes worn by women during World War II, the "new look" in fashion featured long, full skirts and dresses which accentuated tiny waists and well-defined bosoms. These new styles required that uncomfortable foundation garments be worn. For the first time since the early 1900s, crinolines became a standard part of woman's attire.

Clearly, American women in the 1950s still had many obstacles to overcome. Not until the emergence of the new wave of feminism in the 1960s, however, would the nation be alerted to the many inequalities which were a regular part of woman's experience.

Sources and Suggested Readings

Anderson, Karen, *Wartime Women: Sex Roles, Family Relations, and the Status of Women During World War II* (1981).

Banner, Lois W., *Women in Modern America: A Brief History* (1974).

Chafe, William H., *The American Woman: Her Changing Social, Economic and Political Role, 1920-1970* (1972).

Davis, Margery W., *Woman's Place Is At The Typewriter: Office Work and Office Workers, 1870-1930* (1982).

Dye, Nancy Schrom, *As Equals and As Sisters: Feminism, the Labor Movement, and the Women's Trade Union League of New York* (1980).

Hall, Jacquelyn Dowd, *Revolt Against Chivalry: Jessie Daniel Ames and the Women's Campaign Against Lynching* (1979).

Katzman, David M., *Seven Days a Week: Women and Domestic Service in Industrializing America* (1978).

Kessler-Harris, Alice, *Out to Work: A History of Wage-Earning Women in the United States* (1982).

Kraditor, Aileen S., *The Ideas of the Woman Suffrage Movement, 1899-1920* (1965).

Litoff, Judy Barrett, *American Midwives, 1860 to the Present* (1978).

Melosh, Barbara, *"The Physician's Hand": Work Culture and Conflict in American Nursing* (1982).

Treadwell, Mattie E., *The United States Army in World War II, Vol. VIII, The Women's Army Corps* (1954).

Ware, Susan, *Beyond Suffrage: Women in the New Deal* (1981).

Black Life in America

Gary R. Kremer
Lincoln University

The twentieth century began for black Americans much as the nineteenth ended: with themselves as the victims of racial discrimination throughout the land. Indeed, many whites interpreted the Supreme Court's sanction of segregation in the famous case of *Plessy* v. *Ferguson* (1896) as a license to harass and abuse blacks at will.

The plight of blacks was worst in the rural South, where most of their numbers remained. Even by 1910, just as the country was becoming more urban than rural, more than eighty percent of the nation's nearly ten million blacks lived in one of the former Confederate states. The vast majority of them were sharecroppers and tenant farmers who were kept economically destitute and politically powerless by whites.

No man tried harder to help southern blacks escape their poverty-laced lives than Booker T. Washington. Born a slave in Franklin County, Virginia, in 1856, Washington was educated at Hampton Normal and Agricultural Institute in his home state. Subsequently, he established a black normal school in Macon County, Alabama. The normal school, made possible by a $2,000 appropriation from the Alabama state legislature, was created to train black teachers.

Washington used his school, called Tuskegee Institute, to provide blacks with the tools necessary for upward mobility. He concentrated on teaching his students vocational skills and improved farming techniques, urging them to "cast down your bucket where you are," and make the most of a bad situation. He was aided greatly in this task by the work of George Washington Carver, who served Tuskegee from 1896 until 1943. Carver's creative genius allowed him to develop processes for extracting products from nature that previously had been unavailable to impoverished blacks. His discovery of the multiple uses of the sweet potato and the peanut were only the most publicized manifestations of his genius. His work with dyes, paints, and textiles also had far-reaching results.

Unquestionably, the work of Washington, and of his gifted young teachers such as Carver, improved the quality of life for thousands of rural southern farmers early in the twentieth century. Still, no amount of self-help could change white racism, certainly not over the short run. Washington, however, counseled patience and urged his students to forego agitation for social or political rights until after they had achieved economic self-sufficiency. Meanwhile, black life remained precarious and even cheap to Southern vigilantes

111

who had no qualms about taking the law into their own hands. For example, the lynching of blacks accused by whites of committing "crimes" reached epidemic proportions early in the 1900s. There were 214 lynchings of blacks in the first two years of the twentieth century. By the outbreak of World War I, the number of black lynchings exceeded 1100.

In the wake of this white violence, a growing number of American blacks became dissatisfied with the "accommodationist" approach of Booker T. Washington. By the time Washington died in 1915, in fact, there had emerged a new black leadership which demanded that white Americans respect the civil rights of blacks and which moved to force that respect.

W.E.B. DuBois became the best known member of that new class of leaders. In many ways, DuBois was Washington's antithesis. Born in the North in 1868, DuBois was educated in white schools where he proved himself the equal of any student, white or black. Such a background nurtured an unwillingness on his part to accept second class citizenship simply because he happened to be black. After his graduation from Harvard University in 1895 as that prestigious school's first black Ph.D., DuBois devoted his life to affirming the legitimacy of black citizens' claims to full equality before the law everywhere in America.

In 1905 DuBois gathered a group of like-minded blacks, such as the black publisher William Monroe Trotter, at a convention in Niagara Falls, Canada. He and his group, subsequently known as the Niagara Movement, issued a manifesto decrying the blatant discrimination practiced by white America and demanding its end. Four years later, the Niagara Movement joined forces with a group of whites led by Oswald Villard, grandson of abolitionist William Lloyd Garrison, to form the National Association for the Advancement of Colored People (NAACP).

The NAACP's major strategy soon became a methodical attack on the legal system of segregation. In 1915, for example, in an NAACP-argued case that came to be known as *Guinn* v. *United States,* the Supreme Court ruled that grandfather clauses in the constitutions of Maryland and Oklahoma violated the spirit of the Fifteenth Amendment to the federal constitution and were, as a result, illegal. That was the first of many NAACP victories that spanned the next forty years and ultimately resulted in the famous *Brown* v. *Board of Education* decision (1954) in which the Supreme Court declared separate educational facilities for black and whites unconstitutional.

While the NAACP fought to improve the political and civil life of the nation's blacks, another group emerged whose goal was to improve their economic condition. Acting as if it possessed a foreknowledge of the impending black exodus to the cities, the National League on Urban Conditions Among Negroes (the Urban League) organized in 1911. Its goal was to assist black urbanites to find jobs and help them to adjust to city life.

The mass movement of blacks to northern industrial centers came, of course, with increased production demands associated with World War I. When the war began in Europe in 1914, manufacturers suddenly found themselves on

W. E. B. DuBois, scholar and political activist. (Reproduced from the Collections of the Library of Congress.)

the horns of a dilemma: European demands for their goods drastically increased while their traditional source of cheap labor, European immigrants, slowed to a trickle. Their solution was to go South and recruit new workers from among the desperately poor black farm laborers who were working for 75¢ a day or less, when they were lucky enough to find a job. Perhaps as many as a million blacks left the South over the next four years.

A larger, more stable, source of income was not the only attraction for southern blacks. Racial violence still ran rampant in that region, and many blacks hoped to escape it in the North. More pointedly, a wave of patriotism washed over American blacks who reasoned that the nation's entrance in the war provided them with an opportunity to demonstrate their loyalty and commitment to the land of their birth. This patriotism manifested itself in many ways other than their wholehearted involvement in the production of war goods. Blacks invested in democracy by purchasing record numbers of Liberty Bonds, for example, and they formed self-help organizations to improve their agricultural and industrial efficiency and reduce waste. They also joined the armed forces in large numbers. Ultimately, more than 367,000 blacks served their country as members of the American Expeditionary Force and acquitted themselves well. Indeed, the ferocious fighting of the black 369th United States Infantry earned its soldiers the name of "Hell Fighters" from the Germans.

But if black Americans hoped that their wholehearted support of the war would bring them full equal rights in their homeland, they were sadly mistaken. In some ways, in fact, things only became worse for them after the war. The mass movement of blacks into the cities, for example, created extreme tension between themselves and the white people whose neighborhoods they settled in. One of the most dramatic confrontations of blacks and whites of this era occurred in East St. Louis, Illinois, in 1917. Clashes between blacks and whites of that city left perhaps as many as 40 blacks dead. Two years later, in the summer of 1919, a riot occurred in Chicago. The Windy City had become something of a Mecca to southern blacks, with its black population more than doubling between 1910 and 1920. Unfortunately, racial tensions increased proportionately. The catalyst for the 1919 Chicago riot occurred when a young black male swimming off a "Negro section" of Lake Michigan beach drifted into an area reserved for whites. Subsequently, whites pelted him with stones and the panicked youth drowned. Sporadic fighting between blacks and whites followed, escalating in intensity for the next two weeks. When it was over, 15 whites and 23 blacks lay dead and more than 500 persons were injured.

Over the remainder of the summer, riots occurred in nineteen cities, including Knoxville, Tennessee; Washington, D.C.; and Omaha, Nebraska; and racial fighting continued into the 1920s. Somehow, Americans who wistfully wanted to help President Warren G. Harding return the country to "normalcy," hoped to reverse all of the social and political trends of the prewar years. This reaction led to, among other things, a revival of hate-mongering, reactionary groups such as the Ku Klux Klan.

Originally a rural South phenomenon, the revived Klan of the twenties drew its strength from midwestern and northern cities most affected by the migration of blacks and other ethnics whom, the Klan charged, were dangerous because they were not "one hundred percent American." Klansmen saw members of their group elected to important political positions in cities as different as Indianapolis, Indiana, and Denver, Colorado. Estimates of Klan membership nationwide ranged as high as four million when the organization reached its peak by the mid-twenties.

The black response to this increased racial hostility took many forms—the NAACP, for example, intensified efforts to seek anti-lynching legislation and hundreds of groups met all over the country to protest the roughly 3500 lynchings which occurred between 1889 and 1922. Another response, however, was for blacks to look inward at themselves and their culture and to draw strength from a tradition of struggle in the face of adversity. A new wave of pride in the black past began to surface, for example, as black writers articulated feelings and thoughts which generations of blacks had shared. This trend had achieved tremendous impetus in 1915 with the establishment of the Association for the Study of Negro Life and History by Harvard-trained historian Carter G. Woodson. Woodson established and edited an important quarterly publication called the *Journal of Negro History*. Black musicians and artists, likewise, drew upon African and Afro-American traditions in the production of their works. This movement flowered particularly in the decade of the twenties when it came to be called the Harlem Renaissance, because so many of its members lived in Harlem, New York.

One of the earliest important writers of the Harlem Renaissance was Claude McKay. Born in Jamaica in the early 1890s, McKay had already won distinction for himself as a poet by the time he immigrated to the United States in 1912. But the book which brought McKay his greatest fame was a volume published in 1922 called *Harlem Shadows*. This volume, particularly selections such as "If We Must Die" revealed what well-known black historian John Hope Franklin has described as two of the "salient characteristics" of the Harlem Renaissance: "proud defiance and bitter contempt."

If we must die, let it not be like hogs
Hunted and penned in an inglorious spot,
While round us bark the mad and hungry dogs,
Making their mock at our accursed lot.
If we must die, O let us nobly die,
So that our precious blood may not be shed
In vain; then even the monsters we defy
Shall be constrained to honor us though dead!
O kinsmen! we must meet the common foe!
Though far outnumbered let us show brave,
And for their thousand blows deal one deathblow!
What though before us lies the open grave?
Like men we'll face the murderous, cowardly pack,
Pressed to the wall, dying but fighting back!

McKay added to his reputation with a novel about New York entitled *Home to Harlem* (1928).

Perhaps the man who has been most associated with the black literary movement of the 1920s was Alain Leroy Locke. Born in Philadelphia in 1885, Locke became the first black Rhodes Scholar in 1907. He began a professorial career in English and philosophy at Howard University in 1912 while continuing to work on a doctorate in philosophy at Harvard. He received the Ph.D. in 1918. Locke was a world traveler who took a great interest in the African roots of black American culture. He urged his fellow blacks to be proud of their past and to build upon their racial pride in establishing themselves as "New Negroes." His Black Renaissance classic, *The New Negro* (1925), was one of the most successful of the period's publications.

Langston Hughes was considerably younger than either McKay or Locke, but certainly no less talented. Born in Joplin, Missouri, in 1902, Hughes lived in a dozen different cities before he was 20 years old. Although he attended Columbia University for a brief time in the early twenties, he soon left the country, working at odd jobs as he traveled to, among other places, Africa. Returning to the United States in the mid-twenties, he published his first book of poems in 1926 (*The Weary Blues*). Over the next three decades, Hughes became one of the country's most prolific writers. Although primarily a poet (he published nine volumes), Hughes also wrote six novels and three collections of short stories. Additionally, he wrote numerous plays, including *Mulatto,* which played on Broadway for more than a year. And, as if all that were not enough, Hughes was also a songwriter, particularly in the musical manifestation of Black Renaissance creativity: the blues and jazz.

There was, perhaps, no more popular, and widely used, vehicle for expressing black frustration and frustration-born creativity in the early twentieth century than music. One of the earliest black musical artists of the period was Scott Joplin, born in Texarkana, Texas, about 1868. Joplin's ragtime music was a style he developed in the honky-tonks and dives of the Mississippi River towns such as St. Louis, where blacks often went to escape, at least momentarily, the effects of white racism. Creative pieces such as "The Maple Leaf Rag" and "The Entertainer" brought Joplin immortality, although the work that consumed more of his energy than any other single piece was *Treemonisha,* a serious opera which portrayed education as the key to freedom for black Americans.

Joplin's slightly younger contemporary, W.C. Handy, was born in Alabama in 1873. Handy has come to be known as the "Father of the Blues" for works such as "St. Louis Blues" (1914), "Beale Street Blues" (1916) and "Atlanta Blues" (1923). The contribution of Joplin, Handy, and many others like them was that they drew upon and legitimized Afro-American music which connected African rhythmic patterns with the experiences of black folk culture in a racist America. In so doing, they paved the way for black musicians of the twenties and thirties such as Bennie Moten, Count Basie, Charlie "Yardbird" Parker and others who led the world into the "Jazz Age."

Langston Hughes, poet, playwright and novelist. (Reproduced from the Collections of the Library of Congress.)

The desperate straits of blacks in the post-World War I era, which gave impetus to black literary and musical creativity, caused at least some Afro-Americans to despair of ever achieving equality in the United States. One of these persons was Marcus Garvey, a Jamaican-born black nationalist who dreamed of leading black Americans "back" to their homeland of Africa. Working through the medium of an organization called the Universal Negro Improvement Association, Garvey tried to establish black-owned businesses and purchased a fleet of steamships that he hoped would become the means by which Afro-Americans would escape white racism for the friendlier shores of Africa. Although Garvey attracted a following of thousands and excited the racial pride of countless others, his movement failed. Much of that failure could be attributed to the fact that the masses of American blacks were simply not ready to abandon the land of their birth. Their ancestors had lived and died struggling to eke out an existence in America; hostile though this land might be at times, it, not Africa, was still their home.

The conditions against which Garvey and others protested had some ironically positive effects for a minority of black entrepreneurs. Since racist whites refused to provide a whole host of necessary services to the black community, black businessmen found a ready-made and even captive clientele for businesses such as hair care institutes, insurance companies, building and loan associations, and burial services. Beneficiaries of this trend included persons such as Mrs. Annie Malone, a millionaire manufacturer of hair care products, and John Merrick, one of the founders of the North Carolina Mutual Life Insurance Company. Mrs. Malone, Merrick, and many others like them, in fact, helped to expand a growing and prosperous black middle class.

But a better life in America for the masses of blacks was still far off; the trials of the Great Depression were nearer at hand. The stock market crash of 1929, and the ensuing social and economic dislocation which lasted more than a decade, touched all Americans. But no single group was hurt more than the nation's black population. In fact, for many of them, the Depression had begun years before the Great Crash. The decade of the twenties was a notoriously bad time for farmers and farm laborers, white or black. A decline in markets, combined with a technological revolution in farm equipment and the advent of scientific agriculture, spelled doom for many sharecroppers and small farmers. Since the vast majority of blacks still lived in the rural South and made their living off of agriculture, they were obviously hard hit.

Many blacks simply decided to move off the land and into nearby cities, where they had hoped to find work as domestics or factory workers. Entire communities of blacks literally disappeared from the rural South during the late twenties and early thirties. Overwhelmingly, however, these black migrants were unskilled and poorly schooled, which, when combined with persistent white racism, made them eligible for only the most menial of tasks. Consequently, when the Depression hit with all of its force in the thirties, recently-urbanized blacks were the first to lose their jobs. And as the Depression deepened, many occupations that had been thought of as traditional "Negro

Jobs" were taken over by whites. Meanwhile, the black farmers and farm laborers who remained in the South were further impoverished.

Franklin Delano Roosevelt rode to the presidency of the United States in 1932 on the crest of a wave of unhappiness with his predecessor's handling of the worst economic disaster the country had ever experienced. He promised a "New Deal" for Americans, while assuring them that all they had to fear was fear itself. Unfortunately for blacks, that simply was not true.

One of Roosevelt's earliest efforts at economic recovery was the Agricultural Adjustment Act, designed to stabilize the agricultural economy by, among other things, paying farmers not to produce and facilitating their access to easy credit. But those aids for agriculture were available primarily to the *owners* of land, not to sharecroppers and tenant farmers. Fewer than one in five southern blacks engaged in agriculture in the early years of the Depression owned the land he worked. When employers suddenly discovered that crop reduction would result in cash payments, their need for farm laborers actually declined. And although the price of cotton, for example, did improve as a result of AAA actions, blacks rarely enjoyed anything approaching an equal share in the benefits of this price increase. Likewise, the "easy credit" available to owners of land was not within the reach of persons who could not provide substantial collateral, usually a first mortgage on property owned. In short, the very governmental actions taken to stabilize agricultural production in the country ended up further victimizing large numbers of black sharecroppers and tenant farmers.

Urban blacks, North or South, found Depression-era life little better than did their rural counterparts. New Deal legislation which established minimum wage laws did not cover many occupations, such as domestic service, dominated by blacks. Moreover, white employers forced to pay a minimum wage often hired white workers when they could no longer employ blacks at cheaper rates. "Makework" programs such as WPA and PWA put many unemployed blacks to work building schools, hospitals, bridges, and other public facilities, but the number of blacks obtaining employment in this way was a small fraction of the number which needed it.

The black response to the Depression was as varied as the white response: some protested their situation, some went so far as to call for a fundamental movement away from the economic system of capitalism, and many simply tightened their belts and adjusted as best they could. One of the immediate results of the Depression was the emergence of a radical group which coalesced around the dynamic leadership of an unemployed black man in Detroit named Elijah Poole, who later took the name Elijah Muhammad. Muhammad, whose followers became known as Black Muslims, preached a message that explained all the problems of blacks in terms of hundreds of years of white racist oppression. He called upon his followers to reject everything in their lives that could be identified with white culture, including religion, food, even the names given them by their ancestral masters. In the place of this poisonous, evil white culture, Elijah Muhammad urged a search for and adoption of the pre-slavery roots of African life and customs. The foundation of these "roots" was an adherence to an erroneous interpretation of Islamic religion which identified the Caucasian race as evil incarnate—the Christian Devil.

While Elijah Muhammad's movement was gaining followers, particularly in the urban North, other black leaders mounted alternative forms of protest. Socialists A. Philip Randolph and Chandler Owen used the medium of their magazine *Messenger* to encourage blacks to abandon support of Roosevelt in favor of advocating a turn toward socialism.

Perhaps the most immediately successful response, however, was that taken by men such as Robert C. Weaver and William C. Hastie. Their approach was two-pronged: first of all, they reminded administration officials that the 1932 election was the first in American history in which black voters overwhelmingly supported a Democratic presidential candidate. With blacks becoming increasingly concentrated in urban areas they had become potential "swing votes" in crucial areas. Secondly, Weaver, Hastie, and others appealed to the conscience of persons who had the President's ear—his wife Eleanor, for example, and his trusted advisor Harold Ickes. It was Ickes, in fact, who was most responsible for the creation of an informal "Black Cabinet" of advisors, which included Weaver, Hastie, Robert L. Vann, Eugene Kinckle Jones, Lawrence A. Oxley, William J. Trent, Edgar Brown, Frank S. Horne, and Mary McLeod Bethune. The efforts of these persons were responsible for increasing black participation in New Deal programs during the late 1930s.

Not unrelated to the efforts of the Black Cabinet was the intensified fight in the courts against racial injustice. The NAACP led this fight, continuing a long tradition which it had begun in 1915. The most important case it became involved in during the decade of the thirties began when a young black student tried to gain admission to the University of Missouri Law School in 1936. The student, Lloyd Gaines, a graduate of the all-black Lincoln University of Missouri, filed a lawsuit against the state when he was denied admission to Missouri's only public school of law. No one denied that the sole reason for rejecting Gaines's application was race, a policy that was supported by state law. But Gaines and his NAACP lawyers contended that the refusal to admit him to the law school constituted a violation of the 14th Amendment clause which promised all citizens the equal protection of the laws. By 1938, the case wound its way to the United States Supreme Court and that body ruled that either the State of Missouri had to open the university's school of law to blacks or that it had to provide truly "equal but separate" facilities for them. The recalcitrant state steadfastly refused to open its white institution to blacks and the state legislature quickly appropriated money to establish a Lincoln University Law School. The real significance of the case, however, was that it established the principle that separate educational facilities had to be truly equal. Over the next 16 years, NAACP attorneys continuously pointed to the fact that separate schools were always inferior and discriminatory. By 1954, the Supreme Court, in the case of *Brown* v. *Board of Edu-*

cation, was ready to take the next logical step, declaring that separate educational facilities were inherently unequal and, therefore, unconstitutional.

But if the Gaines case promised change in a not-too-distant future, events in Europe and the Far East brought more immediate alterations in the daily lives of America's blacks. World War II, of course, ended the Depression, accomplishing in a few months what Roosevelt's New Deal failed to do in nearly a decade. Like the Great War of a quarter-century earlier, this conflict also brought jobs for unemployed blacks and prompted another great wave of migration to the urban industrial centers of the North. Perhaps a third of a million blacks made the move during the war years.

The war, however, provided something equally important, if less tangible: it offered Americans the opportunity to see the logical end product of racism, in all of its odiousness. When Adolph Hitler talked about exterminating people simply because of the accident of their birth, many persons began to realize that the sophistication of mid-twentieth century western civilization could not tolerate racism, even in its more benign, but still destructive American form. For millions, then, the war became not only a battle against depotism, but against bigotry as well.

Victory against the Axis powers required the utilization of all of America's resources, not just those of its white citizens. And black freedom fighters at home and abroad were quick to join the battle. The War Department's policy toward black recruits was to enlist them into the military services in proportion to their percentage of the total population. Additionally, and unfortunately, the Department also decreed that black G.I.'s would serve in segregated units, a policy which only served to diminish black morale. Ultimately, approximately one million black men and women joined the military forces.

On the home front, blacks were discriminated against in obtaining jobs related to war production which were funded by the Federal Government. Black leader A. Philip Randolph, founder of the United Brotherhood of Sleeping Car Porters, was particularly incensed and in 1941 he began to lay the groundwork for a March on Washington by 100,000 blacks to protest industry's stance on hiring blacks. The politically sensitive Roosevelt realized the negative effects to be incurred by such a confrontation and ultimately he capitulated. On June 25, 1941, he issued Executive Order No. 8802, designed to eliminate racial discrimination in industries operating under federal government defense contracts. In addition, Roosevelt created a watchdog committee (the Committee on Fair Employment Practices) to insure compliance with Executive Order 8802. Black optimism heightened as the country witnessed tangible evidences of the Chief Executive's efforts to improve equality of opportunity for blacks.

That optimism was further heightened by actions taken by Roosevelt's successor, Harry S. Truman. Although a product of a former slave state, and the son of a woman who never forgave the North for its "mistreatment" of the South, Truman was deeply troubled by the gap between America's promise of "life, liberty and the pursuit of happiness" for all its citizens and the nation's abject failure to fulfill that promise. Equally important, with the war's end, he saw his country lead the effort to establish a United Nations, whose "Universal Declaration of Human Rights" opened with the proclamation that "All human beings are born free and equal in dignity and human rights."

Truman decided he must do something to narrow the gap between promise and reality. In 1946, a year which saw six blacks lynched by whites, the President appointed a committee on Civil Rights, charged with the responsibility of investigating the status of black Americans and recommending remedial legislation. One year later, the Truman committee proposed a set of resolutions aimed at the elimination of discrimination based upon race.

It was one thing for the President to support his committee's recommendations; quite another to see those recommendations turned into laws, particularly with a Congress heavily influenced by southern Democrats.

But Truman made at least symbolic efforts: he became the first president to address a meeting of the NAACP, and in his 1948 State of the Union message he proclaimed the country's chief goal to be that of securing "fully the essential human rights of [all] our citizens." Later that same year he took action that did not require Congressional approval: he issued an executive order abolishing segregation in the armed forces.

The changes in race relations that occurred in the generation after the Second World War, of course, would cause those changes that occurred during the Truman years to seem almost trivial. But they were not. The Truman era was a real turning point, in fact, the culmination of a combination of changes that had been occurring since the century began. Organized opposition to white racism from both blacks and whites had been chipping away at segregation and discrimination in the courts and in legislatures for more than three decades, and that opposition was beginning to mesh with a growing sensitivity to the sufferings heaped upon blacks by whites. When that sensitivity reached the apex of American power—the Whitehouse itself—the fall of the old order could be only a matter of time. The road to the revolution of the fifties and sixties was well-paved.

Sources and Suggested Readings

Barbeau, Arthur E., and Florette Henri, *The Unknown Soldiers: Black American Troops in World War I* (1974).
Berman, William C., *The Politics of Civil Rights in the Truman Administration* (1970).
Franklin, John Hope, *From Slavery to Freedom: A History of Negro Americans* (5th ed., 1980).
Huggins, Nathan I., *Harlem Renaissance* (1973).
Jackson, Kenneth T., *The Ku Klux Klan in the City, 1915–1930* (1967).
Lee, Ulysses, *The Employment of Negro Troops* (1966).
Logan, Royford W., *The Betrayal of the Negro: From Rutherford B. Hayes to Woodrow Wilson* (1965).
———, and Michael R. Winston, *Dictionary of American Negro Bibliography* (1982).
Myrdal, Gunner, *An American Dilemma* (1944).
Wolters, Raymond, *Negroes and the Great Depression* (1970).

Picking and Grooving:
The Rise of an American
Popular Music

David C. Smith
University of Maine—Orono

Although it is probable that all cultures have popular expressions of their emotions of love, hate, territory, anxiety, and other personal feelings, without a means of demonstrating these feelings, others can seldom detect the depth of the emotion. Occasionally the statements of conquerors or the upper classes are a source of knowledge. Examples are the statements of Caesar that the British covered themselves with blue paint, or at a later time, the surviving portions of street cries that occur in classical and medieval music. Why the British tribes chose blue, or how the street cries actually sounded simply eludes us today. A third example is that most nursery rhymes were apparently created for a much different purpose than to entertain children, or so it is thought. Many of them may have been political statements which have been transformed over time.

These losses of reality will never be true again. Since the invention of the radio and phonograph, it has been possible to know what makes up the popular culture of groups. The joining of these two inventions, which occurred early in the 1920s, has meant that we know more about that period than any other before, but it also meant at the time that an incredible transfer and fertilization of knowledge affected the people living in that period. In the United States, and to a considerable extent in the western world, the result was a mass cultural experience which by the end of World War II had begun to wipe out regional differences. It produced a democratic culture, easily learned and readily usable by nearly everyone within the culture.

These technical innovations, radio and phonograph, did not occur spontaneously. Our species has always attempted to speed the movement of knowledge over distance, and the radio is a logical output of earlier efforts with semaphore flags, lights, heliographs, and the telegraph. The radio simply extended the distance, and, because signals were transmitted without wires, the movement occurred at the speed of light, producing virtually simultaneous reception. The phonograph, in a similar way, came from the wish to reproduce music through mechanical means. Mechanical instruments, often utilizing keyboards, had been known since the late eighteenth century, and great composers wrote music for such mechanical instruments. By the end of the nineteenth century, primitive music boxes activated by coins produced music in bars, saloons, and in the homes of the wealthy. The invention of the phonograph by Thomas Edison simply made the transmission less expensive and, therefore, available to more people for individual use.

A music of the people also existed and probably always had. We are able to observe bits and pieces of that music when we study the role played by such musical groups as the Hutchinson Family of Vermont. In the pre-Civil War period, this group and others similar, travelled the United States, singing songs which were well known to their audience. One of the famous songs was "Resin the Bow", used by the Hutchinson group as a campaign song for Abraham Lincoln. Other campaign songs in wide use after 1820 are examples of popular culture. "Tippecanoe and Tyler Too," "Roll the Ball Along," and "Van, Van, He's A Used Up Man" were all catch phrases sung in political and popular songs. Between political campaigns such songs were sung with other words and became part of the standard knowledge of many people.

Development of this sort of music led to a stereotyped and relatively static form of entertainment, the minstrel show. An interlocuter, his end men (or straight men), and a background chorus produced standard humor and music on a stage. Although usually blackfaced, occasionally the minstrel show was played in white face, or other stage makeup. The way one differed from another was in the "olio" acts, performed singly or in small groups, usually in front of the curtain, while scenery was changed or the group within took an intermission from their performance. Here individuals could show their own skills and widen the extent of the entertainment.

Minstrel shows travelled from place to place and might be described as a form of predominantly rural popular culture. These shows developed production methods which allowed liberal use of local talents (in the olio bits), as well as standardized sets and stage directions. Published dialogues were provided for amateurs wishing either to put on their own versions or to participate with the travelling group.

Urban citizens tended to focus on another type of stylized entertainment, the vaudeville show. Vaudeville was essentially a theatrical presentation which primarily featured olio acts, strung together by a master of ceremonies who filled the time between scene shifting and other intervals. The types of acts, and the place that they appeared on the bill were standardized, so that if an emergency intervened a similar act could be inserted without disturbing the flow of the music, the jokes, or even, in some cases, a primitive story line. This sort of entertainment leaned heavily on ethnic humor and stereotypes. The stage Irishman, Jew, Black, farmer's daughter, or other well known types were the strength of vaudeville. Music in small groups or from the pit band, tended to be stylized as well.

The virtue of all these forms of entertainment were that the audience knew what was coming, in general, and it could indulge stereotyped attitudes, racial misgivings, and super patriotism without thinking much about it. Minstrel shows, travelling entertainments such as the Hutchinson Family, and the larger city vaudeville theaters knew their customers, and seldom trifled with their wishes.

Bessie Smith on stage before a radio audience. (Reproduced from the Collections of the Library of Congress.)

Not everyone accepted these dictates, of course. In black communities, in the South, and in northern cities, a less rigid music, often only constrained by the availability of instruments and frequently using as themes black victories over whites or moanful analyses of white success, became an underground music for the oppressed group. For white rural Americans, vestiges of Elizabethan music, often played on antique instruments, tuned and keyed differently and sung with plaintive voices in styles probably similar to those of their Elizabethan forbears, continued to be popular. The strength of this genre of music was the use of balladic forms, well known through repetitive singing, chanting or declamation. Both forms of music also featured dancing, either singly as a way of interpreting the music or in groups. Examples of these musical forms would be the ballad "Barbara Allen," dances such as the contra and the cakewalk, and the song "Rye Whiskey," sung all over the United States.

These forms of popular music apparently did not change much from about 1870 to 1905 or so. Cheaper paper and better methods of printing combined with higher literacy rates to extend the audiences somewhat, but that is all. One off-shoot produced by both blacks and whites, ragtime music, most often played on the piano, did become increasingly difficult and technical, but this was due in part to the development of the mechanical piano. Soon formal orchestras were playing this music as well, because the various parts could be taken by different instruments, and played slowly, or rhythmically, the music also lent itself to dance interpretation as well.

Centers of the more traditional music are fairly well known, even before the days of the phonograph and radio. New Orleans, the Gulf Coast, and the river boats of the Mississippi featured black music, both jazz and the blues. All of the music was apparently called blues, because of the sliding tones used in attacking new phrases, as well as the content of the lyrics. Tempo was not the distinguishing feature. Jazz, a black slang word originally meaning sexual intercourse, became associated with the music as a way of disparaging it and its listeners. Especially good performers of this music were known in a fairly wide area. Such trumpeters as Buddy Bolden pioneered a piercing style of playing utilizing many high grace notes. Early pianists developed individual styles as well. Bolden and others fronted orchestras available for dancing. A professional style of music was born, and professional performers were widely recognized for their abilities to perform to this style. Gradually some forms of this music appeared in upper Mississippi Valley cities such as Kansas City, and Chicago, as black performers moved north, as their audiences had moved before them.

Fewer changes were noted in the white music. Some copying of black styles of playing, at least on individual instruments such as the guitar and banjo, as well as a more bluesy styles of vocal began to transform the music somewhat. Purer forms retained their styles of playing and singing in the more remote areas of the Appalachian mountains. In some of the larger urban centers, such as Nashville, Knoxville, Birmingham, Atlanta, and Memphis, the two forms of popular music influenced each other. The color line tended to be observed for political or economic reasons, but the two types of musicians knew each others styles well, even if the mixed band or orchestra was very unusual. In the Southwest, both forms were also invaded, to some degree, by Mexican or Spanish sounds. The instrumentation of all three types was similar, so the cross-fertilization was relatively easy. Without stretching the terms very much, the popular music which resulted, on the eve of World War I in the United States, was a music which could be termed white blues, black blues, or even Mexican blues. A creative performer and composer, such as Ferdinand "Jelly Roll" Morton, used all of these strains, as well as his classical training, to produce his musical expressions. The minstrel show and the vaudeville theatre were still active, but cross fertilization of these types seldom occurred before the radio provided the catalyst.

Radio came into wide spread use during the First World War, primarily in the U.S. Navy. At first utilizing continuous wave transmission, broken by a key to send coded messages, radio soon turned to sound broadcasting. After the war the Radio Corporation of America (RCA) was formed to manufacture instruments and do research on ways of inexpensive transmission. Experimental stations (the first was KDKA in Pittsburgh) began to provide programming, mostly orchestra music, but soon speeches, discussions, lectures, and political analysis were offered between the musical pieces. At first few were able to hear the broadcasts, but as the radio receivers became less expensive more and more people bought them. With wider audiences, the programming became less experimental.

Invented in the early 1890s, the phonograph had a similar history. Originally expensive, a toy of the rich, the recordings available (whether cylinders, or soon on disc) consisted primarily of orchestral music, of speeches, and declamations. Methods of recording were crude, and this sort of material was transcribed and sent out with relatively little change. A voice at the beginning or end of a record nearly always identified the performer and the song. Once the phonograph became less expensive, record makers began to seek other forms of material to produce. Politics, news, discussions were of little use. So phonograph records soon began to offer more popular music, humorous bits, and vaudeville acts. Increasingly this was music which appealed to larger and larger groups of potential purchasers.

Another trend of American life that was encouraged by the World War was the well known propensity of Americans to move about. Southerners, both black and white, fled a South overcome with the ravages of the boll weevil and the appearance of man made fabrics. People moved to cities, both north and south, everywhere in the U.S., looking for employment. Inevitably they took their music with them. Homesickness, a desire to return to another, and in memory a better life, the wish to retain childhood, or a desire to attack the horrors of the new life into which one had been forced—all these now became the stuff of which the music was made, along with the older forms and styles so well known after years of repetition.

These three facets of American life coincided in the 1920s. That period of change and modernity also retained a profound desire to return to the world before the war. Harding did speak for most Americans when he wished to return to "normalcy." The radio, the phonograph, and a displaced people combined to make possible a retention of some of that past, even in the new world, and a tremendous boom resulted in radios (RCA was the most active and most successful stock in the '20s), and phonographs (everyone had their Victor with the picture of a dog listening to "His Masters Voice,"). White and black blues musicians found that fortune loomed for those who could provide the appropriate sounds, both vocal and instrumental, for radio and phonograph owners to play over the over again. Each playing, no matter where, could provide income for the performers, the manufacturers, and promotional personnel associated with the industry. Nostalgia, and a return to the known, was provided for the listeners. Everyone benefitted.

There were many musicians available to record the necessary music. On the jazz side, since most of the recording facilities were in the North (New York, Chicago, and Richmond, Indiana), the early recordings were primarily the work of white bands playing black music. The Original Dixieland Jazz Band, made up of New Orleans whites, had a tremendous success, both with their records and their appearances in New York and London. They played an adulterated, and somewhat slapstick version of the music, most particularly in their hit record, "Barnyard Blues," or as it was sometimes known, "Livery Stable Blues." The group was made up of excellent musicians, however, and it overcame the fad nature of their parodies. Another white group, also made up of excellent musicians, the New Orleans Rhythmn Kings, set standards with its recordings. The Kings even experimented with mixed racial recordings, as when the great jazz composer, Jelly Roll Morton, sat in for a recording session of several of his own compositions.

Black musicians also began to perform widely. Such remarkable talents as King Oliver with his Creole Jazz Band, and Jelly Roll Morton and his group, usually called the Red Hot Peppers, recorded some exquisite pearls of timbre, color, and melodic line. Duke Ellington took an extraordinary writing talent from Washington to New York and established a band which set standards for performances, along with revolutionizing the style of the music through his compositions. Oliver's band soon broke up, but members of the group led by his second trumpeter, Louis Armstrong, began to make both in groups, and individually, records of the highest artistic quality. Jazz became the music of the urban masses. Yet nearly all the bands were segregated by race, and their audiences were often segregated as well.

Recording companies began to produce "race" records, blatantly advertised for their proposed racial customers, which had lyrics designed to appeal to specific customers. Today we listen to the music for the virtuosity of the artists, and the technical ability of the composers, but in their own time, this music spoke to hopes, dreams, and stereotyped visions of the record purchasers. When Bessie Smith sang, "Ticket Agent, Ease Your Window Down,"

Duke Ellington at the piano. (Reproduced from the Collections of the Library of Congress.)

she spoke to the hopes of millions of blacks who thought of leaving the South for the North. And when she recorded "Empty Bed Blues," the sexual desires of the young were graphically portrayed. When Johnny Dodds recorded "Rent Party Blues," he was describing tenement life, and, when Jelly Roll Morton recorded "Smoke House Blues," and others played "Buck Town Stomp," they were performing for persons who lived in the segregated parts of town. Often the words were encoded, so blacks knew the meaning, but whites, "ofays" as they were called in black jargon, were outside the pale. Whites such as Bix Beiderbecke, and Mezz Messrow, along with a few others, crossed the color line, to play black music, and become part of the black world, which the music described, but they were accepted as musicians, not as pale versions of their friends. This music spoke for the broad urban underclass, with its stories of rent difficulties, street relationships, sexual life, the numbers game, violence, and oppression. "If Beale Street Could Talk," was the first line of W. C. Handy's "Beale Street Blues." Although some may look back at the Jazz Age and equate the music with Clyde McCoys "Sugar Blues," the real people's music lay in the writing and performance of such numbers as "Harlem Air Shaft," "I'm the Winin' Boy," and "That's Why I'm Black and Blue," all recorded originally in the 1920s.

A similar pattern was true of the white blues music played by rural southerners. As early as 1922 Eck Robertson recorded old time fiddle tunes for New York producers. Southern string bands, such as Gid Tanner and the Skillet Lickers, provided typical white southern music, some of it with a racial overtone, for record buyers, still mainly living in the South. However, the same revolution which drove blacks to the cities, did the same thing for their white underclass cousins. Their desires for music led the record companies to trade in old time southern music (still performed and recorded, but in smaller numbers) for music which played on the nostalgia and homesickness of the transplanted whites. Vernon Delmore (a trained operatic tenor) reacquired his accent and recorded "Birmingham Jail" and "The Wreck of the Old Ninety-Seven." But it was a white railroader, who had learned his music travelling through the countryside on the trains, listening and talking to blacks, Mexicans, whites, and mixed bloods, who created the revolution in country music. Jimmy Rogers only recorded 110 numbers from 1927 to his untimely death in 1933, but in that time he created modern country white blues. His first number, "Sleep Baby Sleep," was innocuous enough, but he soon became famous for his series of Blue Yodels (with their remarkable subtitles such as "T for Texas," "California Blues," and "The Women Make A Fool Out Of Me"), as well as his songs of the old South. Records like "Mississippi Delta Blues," "Brakeman's Blues," "Mule Skinner Blues," "Away Out on the Mountain," and perhaps his most remarkable tug at the heartstrings of those far from home, "Waiting for a Train," were among the most successful records ever made. In this last example, the singer is not only a thousand miles away from home, waiting for a train, he is waiting without money to jump a freight.

Rogers' success led the record companies to scour the South, looking for similar artists and materials. They found the Carter family in the Clinch

Mountain Valley in Tennessee, and discovered Bill Monroe, who played a particular kind of Appalachian music, called Bluegrass. Monroe's music was propelled by his mandolin and a voice nearly as clear as a classical countertenor. Others came from Alabama, Texas, the Carolinas, Mississippi, and all over the South, and they went north to record their songs of unrequited love; of men forced by circumstances into the cities, the mines and the mills; the romantic tanglement created by these situations; and above all, a homesickness for a land that may never have been but which remained vividly in the heads of all who dreamed of the past. This sort of music has been a staple of country music ever since, and Bobby Bare's great song, "Detroit City," is a first cousin to "Waiting for A Train."

Three music producers were instrumental in bringing these different musical voices to the phonograph records of America. The first was RCA, with its chief artist and repertoire man, Ralph Peer, who went to the South to do on site recordings, both of whites and blacks. The Carter Family and Jimmy Rogers were both discovered by Peer. He and his groups of technicians would travel to a location, and record all the musicians who appeared in the hopes of finding another like Rogers. Those test recordings played today, often by artists never heard of again, bring an authentic voice of this time as their recordings have become available again from specialty houses. RCA also recorded many black orchestras playing their weird and wonderful versions of the more sophisticated urban music they were purchasing for their own phonographs. Mechanical wind-up versions, which took no electricity, were available in the poorest homes in the nation. As a method of recreation, these instruments were sometimes the only visible evidence of the industrial changes that had occurred to more affluent members of the same society.

The second of the two forces in this revolution was the Okeh/Gennett record company, recording in Richmond, Indiana. Readily accessible from Chicago, musicians, both black and white, could go to the Okeh studios and with a day's work, perhaps make it into the big time. For a half dozen years, until the recording equipment improved and became more costly, these studios were a sort of Mecca to those recording hopefuls.

The third force, the Paramount Record Company, led by its entrepreneur, Mayo Williams, was even more original. It specialized in mail order sales, and the founding personnel were associated with a furniture store. Hoping to sell furniture suites to the whites and blacks who had moved to the northern cities, Paramount gave away phonograph records and phonographs to purchasers. Rather than pay for well known artists, it recorded little known performers and sold the records very inexpensively. Such performers as Blind Blake, Blind Lemon Jefferson, Sippi Wallace, Bessie Smith, along with dozens of others recorded through the decade of the 1920s for Paramount. This music was a more earthy, often sexually oriented music, but it was the authentic music of a people faced with great economic and social problems. Both Sears Roebuck and Montgomery Ward used the same sales methods, and although they were more apt to purchase the rights to well known artists from RCA, they were not above recording these artists under pseudonyms. These records, from the mail order houses, and Paramount, were not made to last. They were inexpensive, 39¢ each or three for a dollar, usually, and wore out quickly. Their reproduction today is often tinny, scratchy, but through the static, one hears again some of the voices of the 1920s.

There were tremendous amounts of money to be made from the marriage of the record company and the radio. For that reason technical advances changed this world very very rapidly. From the home made radio of the early 1920s, it was short step to the large transmitters, and well organized programming of the latter part of the decade. By World War II, radio dominated popular entertainment. Ordinary people relied on the radio for information of every sort.

This reliance was enhanced by the creation of some very large stations with clear channel designed to blanket whole areas of the country. WSM in Nashville, WCKY in Cincinnati, WGN in Chicago, WLW in New Orleans, KWKH in Shreveport, WGY in Schenectady, WWVA in Wheeling were the very largest stations. Extremely powerful stations located across the river form Del Rio, Texas, were licensed by Mexico. These stations, radiating their signal from 200,000 watt transmitters (later cut to 100,000) were U.S. stations in disguise. Monsters such as XEAF and XERA broadcast signals which could be heard all over the East and Midwest. Small children, listening on their radios, could fantasize that they would be in those stations producing the music they were already attempting at home.

Radio began to rely on regular broadcasting to attract audiences. The Grand Old Opry in Nashville, the National Barn Dance from Chicago, The Wheeling Jamboree, and the Hayride from Shreveport were examples. The Hayride was a sort of minor league of country music—when you made it big there, then you could appear on the Opry. These stations made their living out of advertising, and sponsors offered by mail everything from a thousand day old baby chicks to a replica of the Last Supper. For other programming these stations, and their northern counterparts, began to rely on other tried and true entertainment forms. Vaudeville artists (especially singing or talking acts) found themselves in great demand. The best of these performers transformed their vaudeville acts into sophisticated stereotypical performances sure to please listeners. Perhaps the greatest of these performers were Jack Benny, Fred Allen, Fibber McGee and Molly, and Edgar Bergen with his ventriloquist's dummies. The vaudeville method which used a number of short well programmed acts was carried over by Ed Wynn and others to radio versions of the vaudeville stage.

In music several country music groups began to take the spotlight, as they also began to program a complete show including a country dance or two, on through a waltz, a song of unrequited love, and the standard sacred music with which these shows always ended. Bob Wills, perhaps the most famous of these entrepreneurs, combined the Texan, Mexican, country, jazz motifs in an extraordinarily successful orchestra, called the Light Crust Doughboys (named for their sponsor's motto) and later the Texas Playboys. The Carter Family, staying with the music of their youth, simply transferred it to a New York studio, from which their sponsors brought them into the homes of many. Other groups were led by Bradley Kincaid, "The Kentucky Hummingbird," and Roy Acuff. Their very sophisticated western swing cousins, The Sons of the Pioneers, were also known to millions of listeners. Many people purchased their records to listen to during the time they were not on the air. In both the 1932 and 1936 national campaigns, country music was used to great effect by Franklin D. Roosevelt's organizers to promote his views. One only has to listen to such campaign songs as "White House Blues" (1932), "Bread Line Blues" (1932), "No Depression in Heaven" (1932), or the exuberant "Franklin D. Roosevelt's Back Again" (1936) to know how the rural southerners were voting, wherever they lived.

The ability to put this music into the homes of every American also meant that new artists emerged, playing regional versions of similar music. Two examples, both from Canada, illustrate this point very well. Wulf Carter, better known as Montana Slim, and Hank Snow, who fronted one of the best country bands ever to perform, the Rainbow Ranch Boys, simply illustrate how this music had become North American, not southern by the mid-thirties. The same thing was true of black music, although to a much lesser degree. With the depression the race record came to and end, as sales dropped out of sight. Those black musicians who survived had to be prepared to cater especially to the white audiences that remained. Louis Armstrong remained popular by playing not only stereotyped music such as "Shine," but he also survived by using the stereotypes of black people held by many whites along with his tremendous ability to market his unique style. It depended ultimately on a sophisticated form of stereotyped racism. In exchange for this Armstrong often performed brilliant choruses of jazz in the most banal surroundings. "A Ding Dong Daddy From Dumas" and "Shine" are just two of perhaps a thousand such recordings. On the musical stage Eubie Blake and Noble Sissle played to a white audience as well as a smaller black one with their show *Black Birds of 1928* and songs such as "Bandanna Days" and "Pickaninny Blues."

Duke Ellington and Fats Waller played an increasingly brilliant and sophisticated music to uptown pub crawlers in New York, and took the music on the road for whites to dance to, but most of the jazz of the 1930s was white, although it retained its hot and urban quality to a considerable degree. Many of the best of the black musicians, Coleman Hawkins, Buck Clayton, and others, found that they could still make their music, and their recordings in Paris and Amsterdam. Much black music, therefore, survived the depression across the Atlantic.

Just as the music became more sophisticated while appealing to a wider and wider taste, technical innovations in the industry increased remarkably as well. Recording was made simpler, and the reproduction became much better. Acoustical recordings gave way to electrical recordings. This meant that the bass tones in particular was less muddy and clearer. Microphones reproduced better approximations of actual tones, and the jazz and country blues of the early 1930s approached a real fidelity. Longer playing recordings were available, although a true long playing record would not appear until after World War II. But, during the war, V-disks made for reproduction to the armed forces, heralded the changes of the postwar world. In addition it became cheaper to reproduce recordings, and by the end of the era, companies were experimenting with nearly unbreakable plastic in place of the old lacquer waxed disks so easy to drop and destroy. Radio receivers were easier to operate, with push button dialing of favorite stations. For those Americans who did not yet have electricity, the batter radio brought music, jazz and white blues, along with news, farm reports, and other items to farmers across the land. Although everyone dreaded "when the juice ran out," anyone, no matter where they were, could listen to the Dempsey-Carpentier fight, the World Series, the musical broadcasts from the Metropolitan, or more likely the National Barn Dance, or the Rainbow Room of Rockefeller Center where one might hear Duke Ellington, Tommy Dorsey, or Benny Goodman. A truely popular culture had been created and dominated the country. The marriage of the phonograph and the wireless, along with population changes had made it possible, perhaps even necessary.

Sources and Suggested Readings

Birdwhistell, Terry L., "WHAS Radio and the Development of Broadcasting in Kentucky, 1922–1932," *Kentucky Historical Society Register,* Autumn, 1981.

DeMeglio, John E., *Vaudeville, USA.* Popular Press, Bowling Green, Kentucky, 1973.

*Robert Dixon and John Goodrich, *Recording the Blues,* Stein and Day, 1970.

Finkelstein, Sidney, *Jazz: A Peoples Music,* Citadel, 1948.

Laurie, Joe, *From Vaude to Video.*

Lomax, John A., *Mr. Jelly Lord,* Grove Press, 1950.

Malone, Bill, *Country Music, U.S.A.,* University of Texas, 1968, paperback, 1975.

Porterfield, Nolan, *Jimmie Rodgers, The Life and Times of Americas Blue Yodeller* University of Illinois, 1979.

Toll, Robert C., *Blacking Up: The Minstrel Show in Nineteenth Century America,* Oxford, 1974.

Townsend, Charles R., *San Antonio Rose: The Life of Bob Wills,* University of Illinois, 1976.

Wik, Reynold, "The Radio in Rural America in the 1920s," *Agricultural History,* October, 1981.

Williams, Roger, *Sing A Sad Song: The Life of Hank Williams,* revised edition, Illinois, 1981.

Those who wish to listen to the music should seek out Bill Malone, ed., *The Smithsonian Collection of the History of Country Music.*

Time-Life Books, Giants of Jazz.

Folkways, *History of Classic Jazz.*

J. R. Lomax and Jelly Roll Morton. *The Library of Congress Recordings.* (The last two sets are out of print, but appear in many libraries, nonetheless.)

* = paperback

The Rolling Revolution:
The Ascendancy of the Automobile

Larry D. Lankton
Michigan Technological University

Americans "vote" their beliefs and desires not only behind drawn curtains at a polling place, but in the marketplace. To a considerable degree, people really are what they own; their lives are greatly shaped by their material possessions. In choosing which goods to purchase and which to leave on the shelves, consumers render judgments on alternate ways to live. Sometimes, however, consumers get far more than they originally bargained for. This was certainly the case early in this century, when many Americans opted for a new-fangled transportation device: the automobile. The stunning, rapid success of the automobile demonstrated that the long-range effects of technological change can be difficult to predict or control. While solving some old problems, the automobile created a host of new ones.

The automobile seduced the public. It was more than just a utilitarian, self-propelled vehicle. It was a rolling revolution, a four-wheeled instrument of political, social, economic and environmental change. Between the mid-1890s and the Great Depression of the 1930s, the automobile evolved from an experimental, underpowered, rickety "horseless carriage" into a powerful, reliable, comfortable and easy-to-drive machine. It went from being the toy of mechanical tinkerers to being the prized, indispensable possession of the masses—one they would be loath to part with, even during the Depression's economic deprivation. By 1930, 26 million cars were registered in America, about two cars for every eleven people. Such a high degree of automobility was neither automatically nor easily achieved in such a short time. As millions of Americans voted in favor of the automobile by purchasing one, consciously or not they also bought a great many ancillary changes in American society.

The early 20th century motorcar capped the 19th century Industrial Revolution. The automobile was not an invention in the strict sense of the word, and not the dream or product of any one individual, group, company, or nation. Many hands on both sides of the Atlantic worked on the development of the motorcar, which represented the convergence of numerous technologies. The idea of a self-propelled road machine predated the 1890s by many years, yet only in that decade did conditions finally encourage large-scale experimentation and innovation.

Nascent auto makers staked their success on both the strengths and weaknesses of an American society that had already undergone a great deal of industrialization since the American Revolution. They counted on Americans believing in progress and on their being receptive, not resistant, to still more change. They counted on an already mobile people wanting even more mobility in the form of a vehicle that seemingly embodied liberty, freedom and privacy. The auto would be the socially acceptable slave; it would serve at the beck and call of its master. It would take people when and where they wanted to go and take them door-to-door. Auto makers also counted on Americans wanting a vehicle that promised a quick-fix to well-known urban and rural problems.

In the 19th century, American cities had grown tremendously in population but not in physical size. As a result, they were highly congested and densely populated. The motorcar, more than fixed streetcar lines, promised to allow the urban population to push farther outward and spread itself more thinly over a wider area. It would create more commuters—persons with a foot in each of two worlds, individuals who worked in the city and then retreated nightly in their cars to suburbia's semirural environment of fresh air, trees, grass and single-family homes. The automobile would also ease the terrible traffic in city streets already choked with pedestrians, bicyclists, horse-drawn vehicles and electric streetcars running on fixed tracks. A horseless carriage would be half as long as a horse and carriage, so it would bemore maneuverable, more tractable and easier to park. It would also be a great deal cleaner. Irony of ironies, Americans initially saw the motorcar as a boon to environmental fastidiousness and public health. Any gases spewing from its tailpipe paled in comparison to the vast quantities of manure and urine contributed to the city scene by horses, and a disabled car pulled over to a curb was far less a health menace than a dead horse, left by a teamster where it dropped and attacked by a squadron of flies.

Problems were different in rural America. Americans have traditionally had an idealized view of rural life. Farmers supposedly lived a dignified, wholesome existence, because they worked for themselves at their own pace, provided life-sustaining food for others, and toiled amidst the bounties and beauties of nature. In reality, however, farmers worked hard and long, often for relatively little reward, and in isolation. For the population stranded in the countryside, agrarianism lost much of its luster as other Americans benefitted from amenities, amusements and technological advances, such as electrical lighting, that were slow in reaching the farm. The automobile did not promise heaven-on-earth to farm families, but it did promise easier access to town, less isolation, and a greater chance for the good things of life. In addition, cousins of the automobile—at first trucks and later tractors—promised the farmer an economic gain by lessening the costs of growing and shipping produce.

Problems and weaknesses in urban and rural America and in existing transportation systems thus opened the way for the motorcar. The road to automobility was also paved, however, by important strengths already exhibited by American industry and the economy. The automobile could not have been so enormously successful if other industries had not pioneered in developing power plants, materials, and manufacturing techniques. And it could not have

Ford Motor Company workers utilize assembly line techniques as they make ready another Model-T. (Courtesy of the Henry Ford Museum, The Edison Institute.)

been sold in such great numbers if the distribution of wealth, although far from ideal, had not been at least sufficient to allow millions of families to pay for and operate their first cars.

Automobile production owed major technological debts to numerous inventors and industries. It followed a trail blazed in the previous century by manufacturers of such goods as cotton textiles, firearms, clocks, watches, locks, engines, business machines and bicycles. It was indebted to the rise of the factory system, to mechanization, and to mass-production. Before the advent of the automobile, the American economy already had torn down traditional methods of craft and home production and had replaced them with an industrial regime centered on large-scale corporations and factories. Within factory walls, industries mass-produced specialized products, which they sold across broad markets.

Industries made these products by machine rather than by hand. They made them using laborers or "machine tenders," rather than highly skilled craftsmen. And to keep the factory system humming, managers subjected laborers to a stringent discipline. The factory, an intricate mechanism, functioned smoothly and profitably only if the workers knew their place—and were there day after day. Thus, before the automobile, American consumers were already accustomed to buying machine-made goods, and workers had been prepared to tend machines in a manufacturing system that emphasized the division of labor and broke down the manufacturing of an object into numerous simple tasks that unskilled or semiskilled workers could perform with the aid of machines.

American industry provided the early auto makers with the materials, components and manufacturing capabilities that they needed, with machine-tools, steel, rubber, glass, wood-products, leather goods, textiles, paints, lubricants and fuels. Several industries in particular directly contributed to putting Americans on wheels. The builders of steam engines, electrical motors and especially gasoline engines provided early auto makers with the choice of three different power plants. In the late 1890s and early 1900s, all three—gas, steam and electricity—powered practical and commercially successful vehicles. A German, Nicholas Otto, had invented the four-stroke internal combustion engine in 1878. Originally conceived of as a stationary engine for driving machinery, the Otto engine became central to the rapid diffusion of the car because manufacturers could modify it for the specific purpose of powering a vehicle. They made it a reliable, serviceable powerplant with a favorable horsepower-to-weight ratio and a long touring range. Improvements in gas-engine technology made cars more desirable, while they also made steamers and electrics first obsolete, and then extinct.

The carriage and wagon industries provided early auto builders with essential components, such as wheels and bodies. These industries did more than serve as parts suppliers, however. Many manufacturers turned their facilities from the production of horse-drawn to horseless carriages. Since the early motorcars were very much buggy-like in their design, this transformation was not that difficult to achieve. A notable case was the Studebaker firm of South Bend, Indiana. Prior to building automobiles, Studebaker was the largest producer of horse-drawn vehicles in the world.

Bicycle makers, too, proved important advance men for the motorcar. With the advent of the low-wheeled, chain-driven safety bicycle, the two-wheeler became very popular in the late 1880s and 1890s. Mass-producing bicycles gave manufacturers skills that later transferred to the auto industry, such as the ability to produce millions of precision ball bearings. Out of the ranks of bicycle makers came parts suppliers and important early auto builders, such as the Pope Manufacturing Company of Hartford, Connecticut. Just as important, the bicycle craze of the 1890s had heightened Americans' desire to get out on better roadways. Bicyclists led auto owners in lobbying for the extension and improvement of the American road network, which was woefully inadequate and poorly surfaced at the turn of the century. Much improvement was necessary to make auto touring both practicable and pleasurable.

In the first two decades of the 20th century, America adopted the automobile faster than any other nation. This represented quite a turnaround, because in the 1890s this country had lagged behind Europe—especially Germany and France—in automobile development. Thanks to the work of individuals such as Karl Benz and Gottlieb Daimler, the early European motorcars were technically superior to their U.S. counterparts. Americans wisely kept abreast of European advances, and yet they pushed ahead with their own ideas. As a consequence, auto development here was neither subservient to nor dependent upon foreign practices. Americans felt free to go their own way, to develop their own style of automobiles, and to create a distinct industry of their own, soon the largest in the world.

The American auto industry prior to 1910 was radically different from today's. It was not dominated by a few giant corporations; instead hundreds of small firms produced motorcars, at least briefly. Mechanics, machinists, engineers, wagon builders, bike builders and engine manufacturers entered the competition, principally in New England and in the Midwest. When experimentation and development produced a road-worthy vehicle, the next step was the production of a standard model for sale. Here, Charles and Frank Duryea, the Pope Manufacturing Company, and Francis and Freehan Stanley were some who led the way. By 1896–97, consumers, albeit in limited areas, could already choose from several gasline- electric- and steam-powered automobiles offered for sale, and by 1900 U.S. auto makers turned out 4,192 units.

The ranks of early motorcar companies swelled for a variety of reasons. First, the car had not yet advanced so far in its mechanical refinements that a neophyte could not readily comprehend its rudimentary technology and set himself up as an expert. Secondly, it took little capital to enter the business. While more mature industries ran highly mechanized factories, the young auto industry was still characterized by innumerable small shops. Auto builders conserved capital by not investing heavily in tooling and extensive physical plants. They jobbed-out parts production and assembled automobiles from purchased components, using traditional bench-building techniques. At stationary work platforms, teams of men added parts to a chassis until they had a complete automobile. Capital requirements were further lessened by auto makers buying their parts on credit, and then selling their finished products for cash before the bills came due. A great stimulus to the proliferation of manufacturers was the fact that in the United States for about twenty years the demand for automobiles outstripped the industry's production capacity.

By 1900 Americans predicted a great future for the automobile, and popular interest ran high, even on the part of those who, for the time being, could not afford one. Auto makers staged races that tested mechanical improvements and garnered public attention. Long-distance tours or endurance runs proved even more important in capturing the public's eye. By running hundreds of miles over extremely poor roads, all under the light of journalistic scrutiny that soon turned to acclaim, the motorcar proved its mettle. An automobile press quicky established itself, with the founding before 1900 of *Horseless*

Age, Motocycle, and *Motor Age,* and automobile shows, commercial events in cities and at county fairs, became popular.

Early enthusiasts banded together in automobile clubs for the purposes of sharing the fun, lobbying for better roads, and nipping in the bud any anti-automobile sentiment from government officials and others. Actually, little such opposition surfaced. Governments did create speed limits and ultimately required auto registration and driver licensing, but these were more to ease the diffusion of the automobile, rather than to check or discourage its use. The most outspoken opponents of the motorcar, not surprisingly, were those with vested interests in rival modes of transportation directly threatened by the new competition. The auto's greatest detractors, perhaps, were horse breeders and livery stable owners.

America's chief contribution to the automobile lay not with any singular technical improvement, but with the production of millions of cars priced within reach of the masses. While European auto makers early in this century continued to produce a "better" automobile, it nevertheless remained costly except for the well-to-do. In the United States, once companies had begun to saturate the upper-class market with expensive vehicles, many sought an expanded market among middle-class buyers, both urban and rural. Some cars produced for this new market about 1905 to 1910 were indeed cheap, in all senses of the word. They were inexpensive, but also poorly designed and made. They were underpowered, technically-retarded throwbacks to motorized buggies. They ran with multiple-cylinder, water-cooled engines mounted out front under a hood. They came equipped with fenders, running boards, tops, electric lights, and better brakes, controls, transmissions and wheels. The future was particularly bright indeed for the manufacturer who could produce a high-quality, modern auto for the mass market. Of the many who tried, the man who did it first and best was Henry Ford, the single most important figure in the ascendancy of the American automobile. His vehicle, which he rode to fame and fortune, and which America rode into its new "car culture," was the Model T. The Ford Motor Company sold 15 million of them between 1908 and 1927.

Henry Ford, born in 1863, became one of the most famous Americans of the early 20th century. He was a legend throughout the world, a figure admired alike, and paradoxically, by middle-class Americans, Russian communists, and Adolph Hitler. Unfortunately, Ford the man proved distinctly inferior to Ford the legendary hero, and he was cursed with living too long. History would be far kinder to Henry Ford, had he died in 1917 instead of 1947. In his advanced years he engaged in all sorts of quirky, questionable behavior. He went from being the champion of the average man and a symbol of independence and change, to being an intolerant, anti-Semitic, anti-union, strong-willed and yet doddering old man who wielded unparalleled power over an industrial empire. Ford abused this power and nearly carried his once-invincible company to ruin. But tarnished reputation or not, Henry Ford died a giant, because he was the uncommon man who put the common man on wheels

Taking a drive in a touring car was a popular Sunday activity in early twentieth century America. (Courtesy of the Henry Ford Museum, The Edison Institute.)

by following a brilliant two-stage program. First, for over a decade he concentrated on refining the designs and engineering of his automobiles. Then, when he had the automobile he wanted, he switched from working on the product itself to working on its production.

Prior to 1908, Ford's automotive career was nothing out of the ordinary. A mechanic, machinist and practically-trained mechanical engineer, Ford built his first gas-powered buggy, his quadricycle, in 1896. Other experimental cars followed, and then Ford moved into production. His first companies failed, and by 1903 he was already into his third, this one dubbed the Ford Motor Company. Between 1903 and the introduction of the Model T in 1908, the company produced eight other models. In the main, Ford produced these early models in typical fashion. The company had limited production facilities and relied on outside suppliers for the parts assembled into a car.

In developing new models, Henry Ford was searching for a "universal" car, not a limousine or a sportster, but a well-built, utilitarian vehicle, reasonably priced, that would be reliable over the nation's poor roads. It would be light yet strong, capable of attaining sufficient speed and yet not overpowered. Ford feared that "breakneck velocities" might spook more timid buyers. His car would be large enough for the family, easy and safe to drive and simple to maintain. When Ford arrived at the Model T, he made a bold decision. Convinced it was the car Americans would and should want if priced right, he essentially froze product development and turned to production problems. In 1909–1910, to meet short-term needs and to reach long-term goals, the Ford Motor Company temporarily *raised* the price of the Model T to help acquire the capital necessary to build a new factory at Highland Park, just outside Detroit. Within this factory, improved manufacturing techniques hastened auto production and thus lowered unit costs. By mass-producing many more of its own components, and by achieving economies of scale in making large purchases of needed materials, Ford planned to cut significantly the price of the Model T and to drive up demand for this product.

The scheme worked. The Model T touring car that sold for $950 in 1908 cost only $360 in 1916. By 1913–14, the Ford Motor Company produced 1,000 cars per day, and more cars per week than the entire American auto industry had produced per year in 1900. By the early 1920s, the Model T captured as much as 56 per cent of the annual new-car market at home, and over half the vehicles on the road across the world were Model T's. Ford's production of the "Tin Lizzie" peaked in 1923, when it manufactured 1.7 million units.

The automobile revolution was truly a double-edged sword. The auto industry's product profoundly affected the social history of the American people and the face of our environment; and the *making* of that product greatly altered the way Americans worked. Ford's Highland Park plant not only provided the most important automobile in history; it also provided the foremost symbol of modern American technology: the moving assembly line.

For the technical achievement of mass-producing the Model T, Henry Ford unquestionably took (and has been given) too much personal credit. Others within the company—managers, engineers, and tool makers—worked out many of the details. Also, the Ford Motor Company borrowed ideas and practices already found elsewhere. The diffusion of the inexpensive, easy-to-service Model T depended upon the use of interchangeable parts, machine-made components so identical in size that they could be swapped one for another and assembled virtually at random, without any hand-filing or special fitting. The mechanical ideal of interchangeability was well over a century old, and several industries had already worked to realize it, beginning with the firearms industry. Thus Ford and other auto makers did not have to invent the idea of using precision gages, jigs, fixtures and specialized tooling to machine parts to close tolerances.

Nor was Ford the first to streamline production processes, to exert strong managerial control over the shop floor, or to turn to a highly rationalized system of production. The Ford Motor Company was not the first to emphasize efficiency and time-savings, or to scrutinize workers' movements with stopwatches. It was not the first to concern itself with materials-handling problems. Over a hundred years before, Oliver Evans had automated flour production by moving grain up and across mills using screw-augers and conveyors; and the meat packing industry had already pioneered in the "disassembly line," where animal carcasses hooked to overhead conveyors were pulled past workers who took off the appropriate cuts. Yet credit should go where credit is due. The problem of taking an animal apart to make a consumer's dinner was infinitely easier than Ford's problem: the putting together of 5,000 parts to make a consumer's car. Ford borrowed ideas and techniques. But the company modified them, applied them to more complex tasks, carried them further than they had been carried before and added new wrinkles of its own. Chief among them was the moving, endless-chain assembly line, constantly in motion. Ford turned to assembly line production in 1913–14. The company first tried the technique in assembling magnetos, then quickly applied it to engines, other components and to the final assembly of the entire automobile.

Strict discipline and repetitions, monotonous labor came together on the assembly line. The main idea was to divide the work of assembly into a series of simple jobs; to keep the worker as stationary as possible, bringing parts and tools to within easy reach; and to have the work move by the laborer at a rate slow enough for the simple task to be completed and yet as fast as possible. Under the old system of bench-building a magneto, a worker assembled the entire unit, from start to finish, in about 20 minutes. By dividing the operation into about 30 simple steps that required little thought or motion, each done by a different individual standing beside a chain-driven assembly line of convenient height, Ford cut magneto assembly time to only five minutes. The same technique cut engine assembly from ten hours to six, and chassis assembly from 12.5 hours to 1.5. The economic benefits derived from such time-savings and productivity increases were obvious. But the production system was not without serious flaws and problems, many unresolved even today.

Ford management, to keep the line moving, "could not for a moment consider allowing the men to have their own way." They had to enforce "utmost discipline" to avoid "utmost confusion." Adapting humans to serve as such unthinking extensions of the machinery exacted a toll and led to labor problems, particularly labor turnover. Turnover at Highland Park was widespread. To assure that 14,000 workers would be at their stations daily, Ford had to hire 53,000 people a year. To check the problem, and to buy labor stability and greater contentment, in 1914 Ford voluntarily cut the workday from nine to eight hours and instituted a wage and bonus system that raised laborers' earnings to $5.00 per day, about twice the norm for industrial workers. The $5 day attracted great publicity and many job applicants. The next year the company had to hire only 6,500 new employees. Still, even if higher earnings lessened workers' objections to the assembly line routine, much criticism of the technology continued, criticism condemning the technology as deadly monotonous, uninspiring and unfulfilling, stultifying and—in short—dehumanizing.

Henry Ford did not long have a monopoly on the complex auto factory equipped with assembly lines. Within the American auto industry, this innovation quickly spread to other well-capitalized manufacturers. The Highland Park plant and the Model T raised the stakes involved in car manufacturing and changed the complexion of the entire industry. The numerous, small-scale producers that dominated the early auto era fell by the wayside when they could no longer compete, when they could not make a good, yet inexpensive, product. Advantage shifted to the giant car companies that could achieve economies of scale through mass production, that could support expensive product development and heavy advertising campaigns. In a Darwinian-like test of survival, only the large and strong could ride out any significant economic downturns, such as the one occurring shortly after the First World War, and the Depression following the Crash of 1929.

The year that saw the introduction of the Model T—1908—also saw the formation of General Motors. While Henry Ford put all his hopes into one product, William C. Durant took General Motors down a different road altogether. Durant was a man who hedged his bets. Unsure of what cars the public would want tomorrow, he had General Motors obtain controlling interests in a variety of automotive firms. Many of these were weak and siphoned off the profits of General Motors' more profitable endeavors. Also, Billy Durant, masterful at creating new organizations, proved incapable of managing them well. As a consequence, General Motors was by no means an overnight success. Nevertheless, it survived a very rough beginning and during its Durant-era began to overtake Ford and became the industrial leader in the 1920s, because of important corporate reorganizations and the leadership and managerial skills of its president after 1923, Alfred P. Sloan, Jr. While Henry Ford stubbornly stuck with his Model T for far too long, Sloan's General Motors rode to the top by building better Chevrolets, Buicks, Cadillacs and other types—targeted at different, more diverse markets—and by creating innovative sales and marketing techniques.

General Motors, Ford and Chrysler prevailed while many others failed. Competition in the marketplace, even for the giants, became particularly keen during and after the 1920s when the middle-class market for new cars became saturated, and when a large stock of used cars threatened new car sales. The giants (often following the lead of General Motors) held on or strengthened their positions by more broadly offering automobiles on credit, instead of demanding cash. They heavily advertised their vehicles nationwide. They introduced "planned obsolescence" and yearly model changes to stimulate further the buying impulse. And they offered still better products, having all-enclosed steel bodies, electric starters, V-8 engines and automatic transmissions. By the time of the Depression, the auto industry was the largest in the nation and the bellwether of the national economy. Seemingly forevermore, the nation's fortunes would rise and fall with the combined fortunes of only a few giant car corporations.

In adopting the automobile, then, Americans voted into power industrial corporations—auto manufacturers as well as steel and oil companies—that would have great sway in the future over national economic affairs. They voted for mass-production techniques and the assembly line. These were bearers of a higher standard of living, because industrial wages rose while the prices of goods fell. But they also created dead-end and monotonous labor. In numerous ways, the rise of the automobile failed to live up to early promises, while it simultaneously created unexpected problems.

The car was to be the inexpensive, quick-fix for urban and rural transportation problems; automobility was to be less costly, for example, than the construction of mass transit systems. But the direct and indirect costs of reshaping our environment and our social institutions to accommodate the automobile have been enormous. The auto age started an endless race in which street, highway and bridge construction has attempted to keep pace with the growing number of automobiles on the road. Usually, American roads have lost this race, despite huge infusions of money. Americans have paid a high direct cost to purchase, maintain, insure and operate their cars, and they have also paid higher gasoline and other taxes needed to support road construction and maintenance, to erect traffic controls and to hire larger, motorized police forces. With so many Americans in favor of the automobile, and with so many economic resources applied to meet the needs of automobility, little surplus remained for building or maintaining mass transit systems, which withered or died. This left American travellers overwhelmingly dependent on the car, which as is now well understood, makes inefficient use of non-renewable petroleum resources. The automobile was offered to eliminate urban congestion, but the traffic jam in American cities has not gone away, despite the piercing of urban neighborhoods by interstate highways and the construction of beltways. The motorcar was to be more tractable, predictable and safer than the horse, and yet fatal automobile accidents claimed 32,000 victims annually by 1930, and the figures would get worse. The automobile was to clean up the environment, yet its exhaust gases finally came to be recognized as a major pollutant and health menace.

The car accelerated the sprawling of suburbia and the accompanying decline of the inner city. At untold, incalculable cost, it caused wholesale realignments of small businesses, stores, schools, hospitals and churches—institutions that were forced to move as the people moved. It gave more people the opportunity to escape to the countryside, to visit such wonders as our national parks, and then it threatened to despoil these natural retreats with asphalt, concrete and over-visitation. It seemingly gave us a motel and gas station at every crossroad, and a billboard on every hill.

With access to the automobile, Americans not only changed where they lived, but how. It brought families together, and yet split them apart. It created the Sunday drive, where the family drove aimlessly about, just for the sake of it, and it encouraged vacationing, travelling long distances with kids and luggage in tow. At the same time, the automobile gave individuals, and particularly the young, a chance to get away on their own. Ultimately it created the youth-dominated subculture of cruisers, those who parade their cars up and down the main drags of American cities, large and small. The automobile also served as the mobile bedroom. Adolescents, having driven beyond the reaches of parental authority, could reach out for each other in darkened backseats, perhaps at a drive-in theatre, yet another symbol of our car culture.

The automobile also led Americans toward conspicuous consumption. It was something people had to have, the cost be damned. In purchasing automobiles, many Americans first became used to buying on credit and living in debt. Americans chose their cars to serve not only as transporters, but as travelling signs of status, as symbols of what they were and how much they made. Being seduced by advertising to buy on credit the latest assembly line product— whether it was a car, a refrigerator, a washing machine or a television—became the American consumers' way of life.

It may be impossible to overstate the importance of the automobile in shaping modern American culture, just as it is perhaps impossible to weigh, fairly, its benefits against its costs. Particularly since the 1960s, the automobile and the auto industry have served as whipping-boys for many historians and social critics, who have seen them as the roots of many evils in contemporary America. Through the application of hindsight, it is obvious that achieving automobility entailed a massive reordering of American society, that many of the automobile's promises were illusory and that many of the changes it wrought were wasteful and destructive. Yet it is also clear that most Americans adapted to these changes as they came about, even if they did not outrightly desire or favor them. And it is clear that Americans' fondness for their automobiles still runs deep—even if they are now stamped "Made in Japan" instead of "Made in Detroit"—and that they will not soon be willing to give them up.

Sources and Suggested Readings

Arnold, Horace L. and Fay L. Faurote, *Ford Methods and the Ford Shops* (1916, reprinted).

Belasco, Warren James, *Americans on the Road: From Autocamp to Motel, 1910–1945* (1979).

Chandler, Alfred D., ed., *Giant Enterprise: Ford, General Motors, and the Automobile Industry* (1964).

Flink, James J., *America Adopts the Automobile, 1895–1910* (1970).

———, *The Car Culture* (1975).

Foster, Mark S., *From Streetcar to Superhighway: American City Planners and Urban Transportation, 1900–1940* (1981).

Lewis, David L., ed., "The Automobile and American Culture," *Michigan Quarterly Review* (1980).

Meyer, Stephen, *The Five Dollar Day: Labor Management and Social Control in the Ford Motor Company, 1908–1921* (1981).

Nevins, Allan, and Frank Ernest Hill, *Ford: The Times, The Man, The Company, 1863–1915* (1957, the first of three volumes on Ford).

Rae, John B., *The American Automobile: A Brief History* (1965).

Rose, Mark H., *Interstate: Express Highway Politics, 1941–1956* (1979).

Rothschild, Emma, *Paradise Lost: The Decline of the Auto-Industrial Age* (1973).

Wik, Reynold M., *Henry Ford and Grass-Roots America* (1973).

The New Deal: A Conservative Challenge to Laissez-faire

Donald L. Zelman
Tarleton State University

The Great Depression of the 1930s caught most Americans by surprise. The previous decade seemed so prosperous. In the 1920s industry was producing at a record rate; employment was high; and many Americans were dazzled by the prospect of owning new homes, cars, and countless luxury items. Most people were confident that the good times would continue.

Yet before the twenties were over the nation had entered the worst economic depression of its history. Thousands of banks failed; factories shut down; people lost their homes; and farmers were thrown off their land. The number of unemployed increased drastically. In early 1929 one and a half million Americans were out of work. A year later that number rose to four million, and by 1933 nearly thirteen million Americans, almost a quarter of the labor force, were jobless.

What had happened? Why the economic collapse? The underlying cause was that the 1920s economy was never as sound as it appeared. Certainly there were people who enjoyed great wealth, but the vast majority of Americans did not earn large incomes. For example, American farmers, who represented more than 40% of the nation's population, suffered through one of the worst decades in American agricultural history. Urban laborers, while enjoying high employment, found that their paychecks did not stretch far beyond the purchase of daily necessities. These rural and urban dwellers, though earning low incomes, still bought homes and cars and enough gadgets to keep America's factories busy, but they made these purchases only because businessmen extended credit. However, as the bills mounted, consumers used up their credit. By 1926 the buying spree was sharply reduced and factories had to stockpile their products. As profits declined companies were forced to cut wages and then lay off workers. As the farmers and workers sunk to the level of economic casualties, there were fewer consumers for the nation's products. A downward spiralling cycle was created.

Before mid-1929 much of the nation did not realize the serious nature of these economic problems. The people were blinded by a false sense of optimism that was fed by advertising and the optimistic statements of boosters. One area especially guilty of this was the widely watched stock market in New York. The stock market had serious problems. Financial mismanagement, unethical dealings, and a decline in stock earnings—caused by the slowing of the economy—undercut confidence in the market. Stockholders panicked and rushed to sell their stocks. The panic selling caused a drastic drop in stock values, and the market collapsed. This was a rude awakening for the overly naive. Optimism vanished as people recognized that the economy was in trouble. The Great Depression was underway.

After the crash, many came forward with plans which they believed would bring economic recovery. The plans were varied and complex, but for purposes of simplification they can be placed into two distinct categories, *liberal* economics and *conservative* economics. These two ideas vied for support in the Congress for much of the next dozen years.

Liberals argued for government action. They wanted the federal government to pour money into the economy through a variety of methods, including relief programs or by hiring people to perform useful public work. They believed that government money in the hands of the people would stimulate buying and the economy would eventually be restored. The government projects would be paid for through deficit spending. This meant the government would establish programs now and pay for them later through future taxes.

Big business and other conservative groups did not agree with these proposals. They opposed deficit spending partly because they were convinced that a strong economy required a balanced budget (the government should not spend more than it took in each year) and also because they feared they would have to pay most of the taxes. Equally important, many conservatives did not feel that the government should be in the business of employing the jobless or of providing relief, for, they believed, this could cause people to come to rely on the government and thereby lose the desire to do things for themselves. If jobs and welfare are needed, the conservatives concluded, businessmen and other private citizens should provide them.

President Herbert Hoover was a staunch supporter of this conservative point of view. Because he was a self-made man, Hoover was convinced that even when times were difficult people could pull themselves up if they had the ambition and initiative. If the government stepped in to help people, Hoover believed, they would lose their strength of character. As his method of dealing with the depression, then, Hoover asked business to refrain from firing workers or cutting wages. For the unemployed he recommended charity from private or community relief agencies.

These policies did not work. Business and the charities were overwhelmed by the depression. Only a fortunate few workers suffered no cut in income. The rest either had their wages, their hours, or both reduced, or they were simply laid off. When they turned to charities for relief, only meager benefits or no aid at all was available.

Unable to find new jobs or adequate relief, the unemployed survived as best they could. They used up their savings, borrowed from friends and family, and begged the grocer and landlord for credit. Eventually many could no longer pay rent or provide decent meals for their families. This meant some had to sleep on park benches or under bridges. Others built shacks on vacant lots out of whatever scraps of material they could find. They rummaged for food in garbage cans or dumps, or they walked from house to house seeking to work for a meal or begging for a handout. Many, including over a million young people, took to the road, traveling aimlessly from place to place. Most Americans did not suffer this badly, but there was growing fear that anyone could be next. As the fear grew, people realized that Hoover's programs were not working.

Hoover's programs failed partly because his philosophy about the relationship between government and the citizen had not changed as America changed. The President's philosophy was a product of the 19th century when America was largely a rural nation. In a rural setting people could assume much responsibility for themselves, and government played a limited role. However, as individuals moved to the cities, they became dependent on people they did not know or control. They therefore turned to government to provide regulations which assured that the products they ate and used were safe, reliable, and reasonably priced and that their employers provided decent wages, as well as safe and healthy working conditions.

Urban society needs government to care for its members during times of economic adversity. Individuals cannot always be expected to find work when unemployment is high. Charities cannot provide adequate care when the applications for aid overwhelm their resources. Only the government has the means to provide sufficient jobs or relief benefits. Further, society as a whole benefits when government assumes this social obligation. A large unemployed work force adversely affects everyone in society, since a rise in joblessness means less money in circulation. When government pours money into the economy in the form of welfare or wages, it gets money into circulation and helps stimulate recovery.

Hoover's reluctance to accept this new role for government hampered his efforts to curb the depression and its attendant misery. He became a hated man, the object of ridicule and scorn. Therefore, when the people went to the polls in November, 1932, Hoover suffered a resounding defeat.

Ironically, Governor Franklin Delano Roosevelt of New York, the man who now replaced Hoover in the White House, shared many of his predecessor's conservative attitudes regarding government's proper role. The two men differed, however, over their willingness to alter their philosophies. Hoover was reluctant to change course. Roosevelt, on the other hand, was much more pragmatic, meaning he was willing to experiment with new ideas when the need arose.

When Roosevelt became president on March 4, 1933, the economy was at its lowest point. Farm incomes had dropped seventy percent since 1929; the national income had been cut by more than half; bank failures wiped out nearly nine million savings accounts; and over thirteen million Americans were out of work. The people were understandably frightened. The new President sought to reassure the nation in his Inaugural Address when he said, "the only thing we have to fear is fear itself." He made clear he had a plan to tackle the eco-

A New Deal poster offering some hope to the victims of the Great Depression. (Reproduced from the Collections of the Library of Congress.)

nomic problems, and he expected that through national discipline and sacrifice the economy would recover.

Actually, Roosevelt did not have a specific plan. The New Deal, the name given Roosevelt's administration, would, over the next six years, take the country in several directions. Yet, before the depression was over, the administration's programs achieved three major goals.

First, Roosevelt strengthened the nation's financial institutions (such as banks and investment firms). He did this by enforcing regulations and creating agencies to curb many of the unethical practices that led to the financial problems of the past.

Second, the New Deal diminished the imbalance that plagued the national economy. To aid those who had suffered hardship in the twenties, Roosevelt's administration gave top priority to restoring the buying power of the nation's farmers, laborers, small businessmen, minorities, and even its youth.

Finally, the government provided services and relief to groups in society that had long been neglected. Federal works programs and relief funds aided the unemployed, while providing projects that have benefitted later generations; rural areas that once knew only the kerosene lamp were furnished with government generated electricity; a social security program extended economic security to the aged during their retirement years; and the American minority communities, once the nation's outcasts, were included in New Deal relief programs and, in some cases, helped shape New Deal policy.

Such changes did not come easily. Every step met strong opposition. Big businessmen, industrialists, and other conservatives were greatly worried about the new president and his programs. They were convinced the new expanded role assumed by government meant that Roosevelt was leading the country into socialism or worse.

These critics were wrong. Roosevelt was not out to change the nation's economic system, nor was he intent on redistributing the wealth. Some of his most significant programs were aimed at helping big business and big agriculture, for he felt that they could help turn the economy around. He also helped the poor, but his welfare programs served mainly to relieve their suffering not to increase significantly their wealth or power. Finally, Roosevelt did not expand the role of government to the extent that his critics charged. Throughout his administration there were tremendous pressures on the president to move the government boldly into all phases of the economy. Roosevelt, however, moved cautiously, careful not to over-extend the powers of government.

The first measure Roosevelt sent to Congress illustrates his caution and his support for private enterprise. At issue was the national banking crisis. With so many banks failing many people told the president that he should nationalize the banks, that is take them out of private hands and turn them over to the government. Roosevelt did not agree. He sent to Congress his Emergency Bank Bill which kept the banks in private hands. It also helped weak banks reorganize and offered government loans and support to assure that national banks would remain strong. Roosevelt chose the banking issue as a focus for his first report to the people over the radio—the famous Fireside Chats. A few months later the New Deal strengthened the banks even more when it established the Federal Deposit Insurance Corporation (FDIC). This agency still provides federal guarantees for savings accounts up to established limits.

Moving cautiously as he did, the president saved the private banking system and restored the people's faith in it. He did the same for other financial institutions by establishing legislation and agencies, such as the Securities and Exchange Commission, which prevented financial firms from engaging in stock fraud, over issue of securities, and other activities that contributed to the Great Depression.

Just as Roosevelt resisted pressure to move the government extensively into the financial sector, he also moved slowly when urged to pour government money into the economy to stimulate spending. However, it soon became apparent that action was needed. The economy needed people to spend, and this was possible only if money was put into circulation, not taken out. Realizing this, Roosevelt began to change directions, although he remained careful not to move too far too fast.

His first few steps were aimed at restoring the purchasing power of the nation's farmers and businessmen. Both groups suffered from over-production which kept the prices they received for their commodities low. In an effort to reduce production the New Deal in 1933 established the Agricultural Adjustment Act (AAA) for farmers and the National Industrial Recovery Act (NIRA) for business. The AAA paid farmers a subsidy to take land out of production and to kill a portion of their livestock. The funds for the subsidy came not from the government but from taxes levied on industries that processed agricultural products. These taxes were eventually passed on to the consumers in the form of higher prices.

The NIRA, in an effort to diminish the surplus of manufactured goods, encouraged industrialists to develop behavior codes for their industries. The codes regulated the amount of goods a company could produce, assigned markets, set prices, and in other ways controlled production. The NIRA also provided benefits for labor. Its codes established minimum wages and maximum hours of work, and, even more important, its Section 7(a) granted to labor the right to chose a union and to bargain collectively with employers.

The two programs achieved their primary goal: they brought a decline in agricultural and business production and a rise in prices. Such success, however, mainly benefitted large farmers and major industrialists and were harmful to the poor. For example, migrant workers, white and black share-croppers, and tenant farmers were pushed aside by the AAA when land was taken out of production. Labor, despite its gains under the NIRA, found that companies frequently violated the labor codes. Consumers paid more dearly for needed commodities as prices rose. Meanwhile, the unemployed felt betrayed. While many were ill-clothed and ill-fed, the AAA, in 1933 alone, encouraged farmers to plow under 10.4 million acres of cotton and to slaughter 220,000 sows and six million pigs. When the Supreme Court ruled major portions of the AAA and the NIRA unconstitutional, many people breathed a sigh of relief.

Caddo, Oklahoma, 1938; A town suffering from the Depression in the heart of the Dust Bowl. (Reproduced from the Collections of the Library of Congress.)

The New Deal also established the Public Works Administration (PWA) in 1933. The PWA was established to build public works projects as a means of "priming the pump," through releasing government dollars into the economy to stimulate spending. The PWA eventually established some 35,000 public works projects, poured over four and a quarter billion dollars into the economy, and, in the process, helped to stimulate a temporary economic recovery.

While the New Deal established programs to aid the producing farmers and businessmen, Roosevelt and the Congress did not neglect the poor. They were particularly concerned with the plight of the rural poor, and much legislation was aimed at improving the quality of their lives. The New Deal established federal loans that enabled farmers to refinance mortgages on their homes and land and thus keep them in their own hands. The Rural Electrification Administration (REA) was created in 1935 to generate and distribute electricity to isolated rural areas not served by private power. The most impressive program of all, however, was the Tennessee Valley Authority (TVA), established by Congress in May, 1933, to aid the impoverished Tennessee Valley.

This public corporation built dams to control floods and to generate hydroelectric power; it reclaimed and reforested land; and it produced nitrogen fertilizers and explosives. The agency also engaged in various social projects. It cooperated with state and local agencies in establishing social programs; it educated farmers regarding new agricultural techniques; and it even sponsored bookmobiles to bring traveling libraries to the area's citizens. The TVA has been judged to be the New Deal's most successful agency. It significantly improved the massive Tennessee Valley area, and, because of its success, it has served as a model for similar projects elsewhere.

Roosevelt's programs for the poor were aimed at urban dwellers as well as rural. The New Deal provided federal loans so people could keep their homes; there were public housing projects for people who previously lived in slums; a surplus commodities program provided surplus agricultural products for people who could not afford to feed themselves; and for those who suffered because of inadequate incomes, the New Deal sponsored two types of relief programs: one provided direct relief; the other offered the people work, with relief coming in the form of wages.

The president did not favor direct relief. He feared it could lower people's morale, rob them of their dignity, and cause them to become dependent on government. He much preferred that the government put people to work, and he set up public works projects for that purpose. Yet the president recognized that the sick, the young, the aged, and others were unable to work and deserved assistance. His direct relief programs were therefore aimed primarily at this group. Benefits were small, usually just enough to provide daily existence. However, there were few restrictions on eligibility. New Deal regulations allowed no discrimination because of religion, race, sex, political affiliation, or national origin. Even citizenship was not a requirement, and many aliens were found on direct relief agency rolls.

Eligibility was more restricted on public works programs, including requirements of citizenship. There were few restrictions on types of skills, however, for there were projects for both blue and white collar workers. The types of projects frequently depended on the needs of the area where the project was established. Projects could not compete with private industry, nor could the tasks involve expensive materials, since most of the funds were expected to go toward wages. The wages themselves amounted to more than a person could obtain from direct relief, but, in an effort to get workers to take private employment when possible, the New Deal paid less than private companies.

The New Deal eventually established five major agencies which conducted public works projects. The first one created was the Civilian Conservation Corps (CCC). This agency combined Roosevelt's interest in conservation with his concern for the four million unemployed young people. The CCC took young men between the ages of eighteen and twenty-five and put them to work in wilderness areas. Under the supervision of military personnel they engaged in such conservation projects as planting trees, clearing trails, and building bridges, dams, and reservoirs. The boys also spent time attending educational classes.

The remaining agencies, the Federal Emergency Relief Administration (FERA), the Civil Works Administration (CWA), the aforementioned PWA, and the Works Progress Administration (WPA), were aimed primarily at adults. These agencies were established for varying reasons, but their works programs were basically the same. Laborers constructed bridges, terraced lands, and built roads. The FERA hired teachers to conduct adult reading and writing classes and to run nursery schools. PWA employees constructed such projects as the Triborough Bridge in New York City, a sewer system in Chicago, and two new aircraft carriers. The CWA, for its part, built or improved 40,000 schools, over 3,500 playgrounds and athletic fields, and one thousand airports. It also hired artists and writers and employed 50,000 teachers to keep rural schools open and to teach adult education classes in the cities.

The WPA was the most extensive of the public works agencies. It was created in 1935 as part of the Emergency Relief Appropriation Act, a measure which provided for the largest government peacetime appropriation in history, five billion dollars. The WPA developed many of the same blue collar projects as the previous works programs, building or improving more than 2,500 hospitals, 5,900 school buildings, 1,000 airport landing fields, and nearly 13,000 playgrounds. The WPA also had an extensive program for white collar workers, many of whom were put to work promoting and preserving America's cultural heritage. Under the Federal Theatre, Arts, Music and Writers Projects, actors, artists, musicians, composers, and writers were hired to ply their crafts. Musicians and actors performed before audiences in areas that had never seen live performances; art, drama, and music lessons were given free to interested students; artists painted murals on buildings; and writers toured states and localities, digging up and publishing for posterity all but forgotten historical incidents and folklore. The WPA encouraged creativity, and several young, talented writers, artists, and composers got their start by working for the WPA.

157

There is little dispute over the good accomplished by the various public works agencies. They gave people jobs and money to spend. The workers could now buy food and clothing and pay their rent. Merchants also benefitted as sales increased. It was not just the economic benefits that were important, however. The public works projects themselves provided city and countryside with services that ranged from construction projects to educational and cultural ventures. Had it not been for the relief agencies, many of these services would have been a long time in coming, or they might never have come at all.

The successes of the programs, however, were countered by their own failings. The programs were not large enough to hire all the eligible unemployed, nor did they pay the workers enough to end the depression. Many historians now realize that had the works programs provided full employment and had they paid high wages, the amount of money poured into the economy might well have stimulated complete economic recovery. Roosevelt, however, did not move in this direction. He could not totally shake his conviction that the government should avoid going deeply into debt; he therefore felt that more extensive programs would be too costly. In addition, after the first few months, the Congress became less ready to spend. The president also was convinced that high-paying works programs would entice workers to government employment and create a permanent class of government dependents. Such concerns worked against improving the programs and, indeed, played a crucial role in the early termination of the CWA.

By 1935 the New Deal's record was mixed. The economy had improved, unemployment was down; and misery had abated somewhat, thanks to the various federal relief programs. Yet all was not well. The depression continued, as production, employment, and wages remained below pre-depression levels. Overall, most Americans approved of their president's efforts; yet there were powerful critics who constantly reminded the nation of New Deal's failures and what they perceived to be its flaws.

Conservatives, particularly businessmen, continued to argue that the government had grown too large, spent too much money, and moved into areas where it did not belong. These criticisms angered Roosevelt, but they failed to attract wide support, for most Americans approved of the direction the New Deal was taking. What most worried the president was the growing clamour from the left, that is, from movements which demanded greater governmental intervention. The greatest challenge to Roosevelt's presidency appeared to come from the Union Party, comprised of the followers of the three most influential critics of the New Deal, Father Charles Coughlin, Dr. Francis Townsend, and Senator Huey "Kingfish" Long of Louisiana.

Father Coughlin attacked the New Deal on a variety of issues. He was particularly critical of the AAA for plowing under crops and killing livestock. He delivered his harangues on his weekly radio program that attracted the largest audience of any show then on the air. Dr. Townsend appealed to the elderly with his plan to give $200 a month to every citizen over the age of sixty. In addition, substantial and widespread support went to Senator Long's

"Share Our Wealth" movement. Long advocated that the government lay heavy taxes on the wealthy and use the proceeds to furnish each family a homestead allowance of $2,000, an annual income of $5,000, and a free college education. The Union Party threatened to take significant support away from Roosevelt in the 1936 Presidential election, even after Long was assassinated in 1935.

To counter the threat to his presidency Roosevelt went on the offensive. He set out to "steal Long's thunder" by moving the New Deal toward the left. He began in the spring and summer of 19335 to strike at business and to pass social programs that brought many of his former followers back into the fold. This new presidential offensive is referred to by historians as the Second New Deal.

The attacks on business were motivated in part by business criticism of the New Deal. If they won't cooperate with government, Roosevelt said, then government will "cut the giants down to size." The administration passed several measures to achieve that goal, including: legislation that drove inefficient holding companies out of business; a tax bill that placed heavy taxes on excessive business profits, and a major labor bill. This bill, the National Labor Relations or Wagner Act (NLRA), replaced the NIRA's Section 7(a) which was invalidated when the Supreme Court ruled the NIRA unconstitutional. The NLRA gave labor what it had sought for decades—the right to form unions and, if necessary, to strike against their employers.

These measures all worked against the interests of the business community. The major thrust of the Second New Deal, however, was not anti-business; rather it was to put more emphasis on programs that eased the plight of those who had suffered longest: this included the unemployed, the aged, and the rural poor. Part of the motivation for this emphasis was political, but there was also a humanitarian side to Roosevelt as well, reinforced by the influence of his wife, Eleanor. Called the conscience of the New Deal, Eleanor Roosevelt constantly reminded her husband about his duty to help the poor, minorities, women, and others who were not politically powerful. One of the great persons in American history, Eleanor Roosevelt played a major role in influencing many of the president's social decisions.

The Emergency Relief Appropriation Act of 1935 was a key part of the New Deal's humanitarian thrust. Two of the funded agencies have already been discussed, the WPA and the REA. Two other ERAA agencies reflected Roosevelt's concern for the victims of the depression, the National Youth Administration (NYA) and the Resettlement Administration (RA). The NYA placed unemployed young people between the ages of sixteen and twenty-five on work-relief programs and provided part-time work for students seeking to finish high school and college. The RA took farm families who lived on depleted land and resettled them on more productive acres. It also extended loans to farmers who could not get credit elsewhere.

The RA was an illustration of the New Deal's continued commitment to rural America. That commitment was furthered in 1937 with the establishment of the Farm Security Administration (FSA). The FSA absorbed the RA and continued to relocate families; it also provided share-croppers and tenant farmers with loans so they could purchase their own land, livestock, supplies and equipment. The FSA also established migratory labor camps. The camps significantly eased the plight of some migratory workers, one of the most abused groups on the American depression scene.

Of all the social programs established by the Second New Deal, the Social Security Act has been the most beneficial over the longest period of time. Established in 1935 in response to the popularity of the Townsend plan to provide funds for the elderly, the act created an insurance system for the aged. This was not a government handout. A fund was established through a required wage tax levied on most of the nation's workers and their employers. When employees reach retirement age, they draw monthly benefits from the fund in proportion to what they contribute during their working years. The federal government participates only as the administrator of the fund, although it does provide matching funds to states to care for eligible recipients who are unable to care for themselves. Other aspects of Social Security included employment insurance, medical schools, and aid for the blind and handicapped.

The Social Security Act did not cover several classes of workers, including many who most needed security, such as farm laborers and domestics. Yet the act was a bold departure from the government's hands-off role of the past. Today, millions of retired workers enjoy at least a degree of economic security, thanks to the Social Security plan.

The Second New Deal's social programs brought back much of Roosevelt's support and he won a landslide victory in the 1936 election. Yet the New Deal remained intact for only two more years, to be replaced by preparations for war. The two years did not bring many major accomplishments. Roosevelt did get a second labor bill through Congress that set minimum wages and maximum working hours for labor. He also established a Second AAA that paid farmers to store their surplus commodities until the prices rose.

The president, however, suffered serious reversals. Angered when the Supreme Court ruled some of his earlier legislation unconstitutional, Roosevelt tried to control the Court by asking for a law that would allow him to appoint additional justices who would see things his way. The court packing plan angered both liberals and conservatives who felt the president was tampering with the Constitution. The bill was defeated.

The President also tried once again to balance the budget. He was never very comfortable with deficit spending. Therefore, in 1937, when he felt confident that the economy was on the path to recovery, drastic cutbacks were ordered in government spending, including a fifty percent cut in the WPA budget. The results were a disaster. Roosevelt had misjudged the nation's economic health, and the withdrawal of government funds sent the economy into a tailspin. This forced the president to return to deficit spending, and billions of dollars were again poured into the WPA, the CCC, and other agencies in an effort to achieve recovery. The process took over two years.

It was apparent that the New Deal had not ended the depression. The economy had not revived to the extent that it could survive without government aid. The president deserves some blame for this. His desire to achieve a balanced budget prevented him from pouring enough government money into the economy to stimulate a strong recovery. Recovery did come eventually. Ironically it was due to massive federal spending, for when the nation entered the Second World War the government poured billions of dollars into defense. As the money went into the hands of industrialists and farmers, soldiers and defense workers, the renewed spending spree that resulted created a strong economic foundation, and the Great Depression was over. Full employment was finally achieved.

Was the New Deal a failure? The answer depends on the definition of its purpose. It was not a revolutionary program. A revolution in political terms means a fundamental change. The New Deal brought no such thing. For the most part people held the same economic and political status after the depression was over that they had when the depression began; there was little shifting of wealth and power. However, the New Deal's legislation did strengthen the nation's financial institutions; its welfare programs enabled millions of Americans to survive the nation's worst economic collapse with their dignity intact; and, particularly important, the New Deal renewed people's confidence in their financial and political institutions. Much credit for this must go to the president. His goal was not to change the system; it was to strengthen it. He recognized that to achieve this end the government and the citizen had to work together. The citizen could no longer be expected to travel alone. In a very real sense, laissez-faire economics could never return, as governmental responsibility in a time of difficulty was accepted by nearly everyone. Only in that sense was the Roosevelt New Deal a revolution—a fundamental change in attitude.

Sources nd Suggested Readings

Bennett, David H., *Demagugues in the Depression* (1969).
Bird, Caroline, *The Invisible Scar* (1966).
Burns, James McGregor, *Roosevelt: The Lion and the Fox* (1956).
Conkin, Paul, *The New Deal* (1967).
Freidel, Frank B., *Franklin D. Roosevelt,* 4 vols. (1952–1973).
Hoffman, Abraham, *Unwanted Mexican Americans in the Great Depression: Repatriation Pressures, 1929–1939* (1974).
Leuchtenburg, William E., *Franklin D. Roosevelt and the New Deal, 1932–1940* (1963).
O'Connor, Francis V., *The New Deal Art Projects* (1972).
Rosenman, Samuel I., *Working With Roosevelt* (1952).
Schlesinger, Jr., Arthur M., *The Age of Roosevelt,* 3 vols. (1957–1960).
Sitkoff, Harvard, *A New Deal for Blacks* (1978).
Stein, Walter J., *California and the Dust Bowl Migration* (1973).
Steinbeck, John, *The Grapes of Wrath* (1968).
Terkel, Studs, *Hard Times: An Oral History of the Great Depression* (1970).

The Evolution of the American Mind

Jane Stephens
Southeast Missouri State University

On the evening of December 31, 1899, J. Pierpont Morgan, America's most powerful businessman, sat in his big brownstone house at the corner of Madison and Thirty-sixth Street in New York City, playing solitaire and contemplating the vast business opportunities in his future. Not far away in a hospital in White Plains, New York, Margaret Sanger was working on a new job as a nurse-probationer, still grieving over what she considered the unnecessary death of her forty-nine-year-old mother, who had given birth to eighteen children.

Halfway across the country in Terre Haute, Indiana, Eugene V. Debs, a tall, gaunt man who had served a prison term as a labor agitator, was considering the desperate plight of millions of immigrant workers whose only hope, he firmly believed, lay in public ownership of railroads, mines, and utilities.

Back in New York, Theodore Roosevelt was having a "bully" time as governor and was contemplating his political alternatives. Should he seek re-election as governor, a cabinet position with the sure-to-be nominated McKinley, or run for vice-president? His decision proved to be crucial for the new century, but, then, Morgan, Sanger and Debs would each, in totally different ways, also stamp indelible footprints in twentieth century America.

As the new century dawned, there was an exciting new pulse in America. The belief in supernaturalism was slowly being eroded by the advances in the natural sciences. Geological studies such as those of Charles Lyell had questioned the belief in the seven-day creation of the universe. Then Charles Darwin's theories in organic evolution launched the attack. His work challenged the supernatural belief that man was created by God in His image. If organic evolution was true, then man had not descended from angels but rather had ascended from a simpler organism. Where did an all-wise, all beneficent Creator fit into this scheme?

Indeed, God's hand in disease and death had also been struck a blow by new discoveries in bacteriology. The universe was found to be much more complicated than the old Newtonian concept. Research in astronomy broke down the simplistic views of a stable solar system. Then in 1905 Albert Einstein demolished what remained of the old belief in an easily understood universe with his *Special Theory of Relativity* followed by his *General Theory* in 1916. For centuries educated Americans had believed in a mechanistic universe, the mysteries of which could be unraveled by a study of natural laws and the application of common sense. But, according to Einstein, the universe was not composed simply of physical bodies moving about in an ocean of an invisible gaseous element known as ether, where earthly laws were immutable. In fact, absolutes dissolved in Einstein's newly discovered universe, and *relativity* became a word that most Americans discussed even if they did not comprehend. The fixed universe of the 19th century was replaced with a world of flux in the new century. Strict determinism was superseded by what Charles Pierce referred to as the "calculus of probabilities."

What was the impact of this new wave of thinking on society? Suddenly there was hope for reforming society's ills. Conservative Social Darwinism had advocated "survival of the fittest" and laissez faire. Human society should rely on natural evolution just as nature was bound to do. Each person must stand alone. It is instructive that a popular song of the 1880s was titled "Paddle Your Own Canoe." Government must not meddle but should restrict itself to maintaining order, preventing crime, and protecting property.

But this philosophy had ignored an extremely important element of humanity, said Lester Frank Ward. Whereas plants and animals might simply evolve as Darwin said, humanity had been given a unique possession—a mind.

> When a well-clothed philosopher on a bitter winter's night sits in a warm room well lighted for his purpose and writes on paper with pen and ink, in the arbitrary characters of a highly developed language, the statement that civilization is the result of natural laws and that man's duty is to let nature alone . . . he simply ignores every circumstance of his existence and deliberately closes his eyes to every fact within the range of faculties. (*Mind,* October 1884).

If Ward successfully attacked determinism, it was William James who rang its death knell. In 1907 James published *Pragmatism,* a short work that explained a new philosophy that the American public was searching for as an explanation for recent scientific discoveries. People were not passive beings manipulated beyond their control by nature, declared James. Each individual was a center of spontaneity, a unique being in his own way and capable of making the universe different from what it was before he was a part of it. Pragmatism was trying "to interpret each notion by tracing its practical consequences." If an idea worked, it was truth; if it did not, it should be tossed aside. This approach, said James, opened up new possibilities. Gather facts, he said, think, be ready to risk, and in this process, there was the hope for a world created by man to his own advantages. These ideas were to be basic concepts in the new disciplines of sociology and psychology, and even older disciplines like history and government were substantially changed by pragmatism.

Once the deterministic philosophy was effectively damaged, powerful reform efforts emerged, and by the time the United States entered World War I in 1917, the American middle class had not only accepted the possibility of change but demanded it. Progressives, supported by the middle class, transformed city governments, insisted on a larger participation in government with initiatives, recalls, referendums, direct primaries, and direct election of United States senators. They questioned the existence of monopolies, insisted that

William James, an American pioneer in the field of Psychology. (Reproduced from the Collection of the Library of Congress.)

national regulatory agencies be created to oversee business enterprise, enacted legislation for improved working conditions, reformed the financial system, attempted to tax the rich, and lowered the tariff in some areas. Slums had been invaded by social workers and even America's drinking habits were not safe from attack.

These reform efforts, known generally as Progressivism, followed on the heels of America's successful endeavor to become a world power. When Spain was defeated in 1898, the United States emerged with an overseas empire to match its role in the world economy. The United States led the world in production of manufactured goods. Perhaps it was inevitable that the same stirrings that resulted in an attempt to reform America would be applied to our new interest overseas. If life in America was subject to improvement, could not the world be greatly improved by our influence? In fact, there was an even broader base of support for this overseas venture. Conservative businessmen who were reluctant to support reform legislation at home recognized the benefits of American influence abroad. They, like most Americans, accepted without questioning that exporting reform was synonymous with exporting the American way of life; therefore, there was no conflict with expanding American capitalism in advance of American democracy. Who cared whether business, the flag, the military, or a version of the United States Constitution came first? The goals were the same for all.

In addition to the expansionist motives of reformers and corporate interests there was a genuine missionary zeal which was coupled with strong nationalism in early 20th century America. A few years earlier, Josiah Strong had expressed the connection between these: "It is manifest," he had declared, "that the Anglo-Saxon holds in his hands the destinies of mankind, and it is evident that the United States is to become the home of this race, the principal seat of his power, the great center of his influence." To the voice of Strong were added the voices of Alfred Thayer Mahan, Brooks Adams, and Theodore Roosevelt. Force based upon naval power was the real hope for world peace declared Mahan. People of the world were divided between the civilized and the backward, proclaimed Roosevelt, and the civilized peoples like those in the United States had a moral obligation to assist the backward peoples such as in the Philippine Islands. "Our wealth and our power have given us a place of influence among the nations of the world," he stated, "but world-wide influence and power mean more than dollars or social, intellectual, or industrial supremacy. They involve a responsibility for the moral welfare of others which cannot be evaded." Brooks Adams preached an inexorable drive to the west in *The Law of Civilization and Decay* and with the concept that the United States did not need to give up the reins of power in *America's Economic Supremacy*. These widely read books provided intellectual support for the activist theories of Mahan and Roosevelt. John Hay, friend of all of these people, served as an activist Secretary of State to promote this new ideal of empire.

America's adventures into Chinese, Japanese, Russian, African affairs, and especially our intervention in the affairs of our Latin neighbors in the early

20th century, were somehow related to what Americans conceived as a God-given destiny.

The impact of this new way of thinking took on dramatic meaning after August, 1914. The outbreak of war in Europe shocked and haunted Americans. Liberals saw the resort to arms as a regression for world civilization, but even they were sharply divided over what America's role should be. Some, like Robert La Follette and William Jennings Bryan, opposed any American involvement and were convinced that munitions-makers and bankers had manipulated the entire catastrophe for vulgar gains. Others such as Roosevelt saw in the conflict a struggle between right and wrong. "Right" was defined as the democratic side of Britain and France; "wrong", as that of autocratic Germany's invasion of Belgium, her commitment of atrocities, and her use of such weapons as poison gas and the submarine. No one, or at least no one in authority, saw the war as resulting from economic and social problems of assimilation of the industrial and democratic revolutions. To do so would have called too much into question.

President Wilson, torn between the two accepted arguments, first urged neutrality "in thought as well as in action." But the American bias for the "mother country," combined with a great deal of allied propaganda as well as Germany's blundering showmanship, brought America into the war against the Central Powers. The "world must be made safe for democracy" Wilson declared, and in another instance, "right is more precious than peace." Even this decision was substantially challenged by those with different perceptions.

In making the world safe for democracy, sacrifices, therefore, were needed in America's own democratic system. Dissenters were not tolerated. Eugene V. Debs and other socialist leaders received long prison terms for criticizing the war effort. "When a nation is at war, many things that might be said in time of peace are such a hindrance to its efforts that their utterance will not be endured as long as men fight. . . ," said Justice Oliver Wendell Holmes, in a famous comment. Debs's view was "while there is a single person in prison, I am not free." But those views were swept away in the demand for conformity.

Not only was free speech crippled during the eighteen months of American involvement but so was the American movement for reform. When Wilson returned home from Europe in 1919 with his hard-fought-for Treaty of Versailles, the American people were disillusioned with their efforts which had achieved so little. Enthusiasm for extensive domestic reform and world involvement gradually eroded as most of the prewar problems remained. America was tired of causes and was ready for "normalcy." The electorate demanded a return to easier views of personal culpability for failure to achieve.

To middle class, Protestant, white America "normalcy" implied a return to what was deemed traditional in America. The war left a legacy of distaste for many things foreign. This distaste was combined with a genuine fear about the worldwide impact of the Russian Revolution of 1917. Many Americans became convinced that communists (the term was used almost interchangeably with socialists, anarchists and radicals, and had been since the late 1870s) were plotting an overthrow of the American economic system. They also believed that the means of overthrow would be radically-controlled labor unions. The steel strike of 1919, with its violence, the demands of those who wished to pursue the unfinished agenda of progressivism, and a growing nativism led to further public and governmental repression. The result was deportation of aliens and other undesirables, lynch mobs in many areas, mob violence against radicals, and intolerance on the part of the American public as demonstrated by immigration restriction laws and a rebirth of the Ku Klux Klan.

Traditional America which feared not just communism but any change, had more with which to concern itself than alien radicals and other harbingers of doom. The industrial and urban revolutions wrought many changes in American society. In the economy, the individual enterpriser had been supplanted by the giant corporation in which the individual found himself a cog in a power structure beyond his comprehension, let alone his control. When a majority of Americans chose to live not on farms but in cities, as they had by the 1920s, they left behind the security of extended families and the face-to-face associations offered by small communities. The 1920 census marks the first time that over fifty per cent of Americans did not live in rural America.

The isolated country life of family, church and community, occasionally supplemented by "homespun" events such as quilting bees and church suppers, and elevated by Chautauqua and Lyceum speeches, came under attack by social upheavals brought on by automobiles, movies, radios, vacuum cleaners and the concepts of Freud and other thinkers. The mass culture became urban and cosmopolitan as the countryside motored into the city and saw Hollywood-produced movies or listened to radio advertisements of new consumer-oriented goods. The new American was a clearer type but even more frightening to his parents generation.

Young people and women were especially changed by the new culture. The young distrusted the generation that led them into a world war. They poured over the literary works of Dos Passos, Hemingway, Faulkner, Cather and Lewis, and tended to share their disillusionment. They danced to the new jazz music, idolized sex gods and goddesses of Hollywood, and discovered that "sex and automobiles went well together." The glory of military adventure that had been handed down from the Civil War and the one hundred days' ruckus with Spain had dissipated in the wake of World War I. Idealism was replaced by bitterness, or at least confusion, as the veterans returned to Main Street to find a country hardly touched by the horror of war. Jobs had been taken by those who stayed home and the postwar recession caused widespread unemployment. Parents believed that the whipped up energies and destroyed idealism of youth should somehow be replaced by a revived Victorian innocence and morality. If the problems were not difficult enough, the returning soldiers were also confronted with a defeated Treaty of Versailles, prohibition, and war profits. The nearest thing to a solution seemed to be "an air of naughty alcoholic sophistication and a pose of Bohemian immorality."

Sigmund Freud, a major force in shaping the American mind in the 20th century. (Reproduced from the collections of the Library of Congress.)

The Victorian stereotype of the proper lady, who was swathed from chin to toes in cloth and who knew her proper sphere as she reigned over her kitchen and parlor, had been largely replaced by the image of women war workers, women voters and professional workers. Having abandoned the armor of corsets, women now wore knee-length dresses, smoked, drank and discussed Margaret Sanger's latest efforts to legalize birth control. Few read Freud, but most knew of the implication of Freudian thought, freer sexual attitudes. In addition, the sexual freedom enjoyed by the heroines of F. Scott Fitzgerald, Edna St. Vincent Millay and D. H. Lawrence was not overlooked by American women who were tasting the fruits of economic independence.

The climax of the battle waged by traditional Americans against the new culture occurred in Dayton, Tennessee, in 1925. Fundamentalist Protestants believed that the teaching of Darwin's theory of evolution in public schools was undermining Christianity, and this fact alone, could explain the "flaming youth" of the decade. Other states had previously outlawed the teaching of evolution when Tennessee joined the ranks by securing passage of legislation which made it illegal to teach "any theory that denies the story of the divine creation of man as taught in the Bible. . . ."

John T. Scopes, a local school teacher of biology, agreed to challenge the law with the backing of the American Civil Liberties Union, an organization which rural America came to equate with urban ethnic minorities, especially Jews. William Jennings Bryan, a fundamentalist who was practically an American folk hero by this time, arrived in Dayton to lead the prosecution in what he proclaimed would be a "duel to the death." Bryan was pitted against Clarence Darrow, a "big city" lawyer. When Bryan took the stand he was mercilessly pilloried by Darrow, and although Scopes was found guilty, America felt embarrassed for Bryan who died soon after the ordeal.

While more traditional Americans were attacking evolution, foreigners and blacks, modern science continued to introduce bases for further change. One scientist who had a great impact on 20th century American thinking was Sigmund Freud. In the late 19th century, Freud had discovered that many of his patients could be cured by talking freely about their intimate fears and experiences. This discovery of the "talking cure" led him to a recognition of the concept of the unconscious mind, and to the belief that psychoanalysis (the act of talking and interpreting the words and dreams of the subject) could release pressures and fears which struggled in the unconscious. Then persons could be truly free. Freud believed that the most powerful of all forces were those which originated in the body as instinctual drives. Human personality was best described as a battlefield, said Freud, where reason struggled constantly against primitive passions. Freud never advocated that this struggle justified sexual license, but American movies and magazines introduced the sex theme as a major part of popular culture. Americans had believed historically that individuals had a natural right to happiness, and this belief may have accounted for Freud's popularity.

The popularity of Freud was a part of a national optimism which the nation fervently clung to in spite of the postwar social upheaval. Technology had conquered time and space. Opportunities seemed endless. Businessmen were no longer viewed as conservative money-makers. They were daring innovators. "The man who builds a factory builds a temple," proclaimed Calvin Coolidge, and "the man who works there worships there." Henry Ford became the American symbol of the creative individual who achieved status through his own efforts and even Jesus Christ was described as a successful businessman by Bruce Barton in his book, *The Man Nobody Knows,* (1925). Religion and business were also blended in Charles Sheldon's *In His Steps* (1898) in which he pictured an American community where every person committed himself to act in every situation as Christ would have done.

"The business of the United States is business," declared President Calvin Coolidge, and the booming new industries, widespread construction of new offices, the soaring market for Florida real estate and rising Wall Street stocks and bonds attested to his statement. Voters elected president Herbert Hoover in 1928 believing as he did in "rugged individualism." This phrase was the key to the old American dream, and in his book *American Individualism* (1922), Hoover emphasized that hard work, thrift and morality were the prerequisites to success.

This optimism was smashed by the Great Depression which began in 1929. Even before this crisis, however, American writers had been critical of the American system. Sinclair Lewis mimicked small town boredom and the greed of American businessmen in *Main Street* and *Babbitt.* H. L. Mencken spoofed the values of middle class America in his description of the "booboisie." A sophisticated iconoclasm could be found in the pages of slick periodicals like *The New Yorker* and *Vanity Fair.* Mencken and others began *The American Mercury* to discuss the world that they wished to replace *The Sahara of the Beau Arts* perceived by these sophisticates. As the depression deepened, other voices of pessimism were added. Reinhold Niebuhr, a religious leader, wrote "the middle-class paradise which we built on this continent, and which repeated its zenith no later than 1929, will be in decay before the half-century mark is rounded."

All the wisdom of American businessmen combined proved inadequate to heal the nation's wounds. Factories closed, unemployed millions walked the streets and waited in bread lines, farmers could not meet their mortgage payments, banks failed, and depositors lost lifetime savings. Many thought the apocalypse was imminent. Some believed this was simply just deserts. Other Americans looked to the government for help.

President Hoover, convinced that the depression stemmed from the effects of the World War in Europe, did not see changes in the domestic economy as the solution. "Prosperity was just around the corner" and "rugged individualism" could still prevail. The little technical displacements would soon pass. But as the situation worsened the American people demanded relief, jobs, protection for their savings, increased prices for their crops, and reform.

For most Americans President Hoover's philosophy of "rugged individualism" did not survive the crisis. Instead the American people turned to Franklin Delano Roosevelt, a pragmatist, who promised to fight the depression as though a foreign foe had invaded the land. His New Deal policies irreversibly changed the role of American government as a social interdependence began to supersede traditional individualism. His goal of providing work and security for Americans implied an enlarged function for the state. Hoover had hoped for the elimination of poverty through actions of private business in cooperation with the government. Roosevelt believed the abolition of poverty could only come by using governmental power to aid directly those being threatened by the economic system. Whereas liberty was earlier defined as freedom from governmental restraint, Roosevelt held that "We have come to a clear realization of the fact that true individual freedom cannot exist without economic security and independence." In the efforts to achieve "economic security" the government embarked on a new role and established the precedent that in times of disaster, the government must come to the aid of the distressed people. In spite of this new governmental role and the New Deal experiments with control and regulation, the basic capitalistic framework of America survived. Roosevelt had no plans to destroy American capitalism. In the introduction to his book *Looking Forward* (1933), he stated: "The plans we make during the present emergency, . . . may show the way to a more permanent safeguarding of our social and economic life, to the end that we may in a large measure avoid the terrible cycle of prosperity crumbling into depression."

While Americans were dealing with the Great Depression at home, Europe resorted to more drastic measures. Eventually the totalitarian regimes of Benito Mussolini and Adolf Hitler began threatening world peace, and the United States was determined not to become involved in another mire in Europe. Fearful of repeating the mistakes of preWorld War I, Congress passed a series of Neutrality Acts. The spirit of isolationism that defeated Wilson's Treaty of Versailles and pervaded the American mind during the 1920s, was strengthened by the fascist dictatorships of the 1930s. Americans generally believed that the entry into World War I had been a tragic error brought on by munitions profits and British propaganda. Roosevelt's most difficult task was in convincing the American public that it must abandon isolationism and throw its support against the fascist aggressors. This was not actually achieved until the United States was attacked at Pearl Harbor in 1941.

Public opinion began to change with the fall of France and became even more uneasy as battered Britain pleaded for aid through the summer of 1940. Only the illusion of neutrality remained once Congress passed the Lend-Lease Act to supply arms to the Allies. Convoys, "shoot-on-sight" orders, and other acts further eroded isolationism. Nevertheless most Americans were still struggling to avoid war when Japan bombed Pearl Harbor.

World War II was to some degree a repetition of World War I, but with considerable magnification. Twelve million Americans were required in contrast to the five million in the former war. The first war had increased the national debt by twenty-four billion dollars; the second, 220 billion. Dissent was not a popular cause during World War II and there was not a united effort to suppress criticism, as most Americans felt fascism had to be suppressed.

The war's most important result was to awaken in America the realization that isolation in world affairs was no longer an alternative. Toward the end of the war Roosevelt pursued a plan for a United Nations similar to Wilson's rejected League, but in 1945 there was relatively little opposition. The horrors of Hiroshima had awakened a fear in many Americans that called for drastic commitments to the maintenance of peace. Victory over the fascist nations had only been achieved through an alliance with Soviet Russia, and America realized immediately after the war that the power vacuum created by the collapse of the axis powers was quickly being filled by Soviet Communism. Senator Arthur H. Vandenberg, an isolationist before December 1941, stated that his "convictions regarding international cooperation and collective security for peace took firm hold on the afternoon of the Pearl Harbor attack." Other Americans surrendered their dream of noninvolvement and embraced collective security arrangements such as the North Atlantic Treaty Organization. While there was support for President Truman's policy of containing communist expansion within its present limits, there was also anxiety and dismay. When communism was perceived to be spreading, Americans became aware of another war, potentially more deadly than that just won.

The Cold War created so many questions without answers that a near paranoia gripped the American mind. A witch hunt which exceeded the Red Scare of 1919–1920 was energized by radicals to the Right like Senators William Jenner and Joseph McCarthy and supported by political opportunists such as Representative Richard Nixon. Who was to blame for the failure to stop communism? These politicos jumped at the opportunity to pin the blame on Democrats supposed to be "soft on communism."

After several years of such fear and intolerance, the American moral sense eventually prevailed. Joseph N. Welch, counsel for the Army during the McCarthy-Army hearings, expressed what America came to feel: "The two principal emotions now in evidence in this country are fear and hate, and fear and hate when fanned to white heat are frightening to me, and anyone who fans these emotions . . . may be doing this country a disservice. . . . It is not necessary for us to live in fright and terror. . . . It seems to me that in this lovely land of ours there is no problem we cannot solve, no menace we cannot meet, nor is it in any sense necessary that we surrender or impair our beautiful freedoms."

By 1952 Americans were apparently as tired of containment and accusations of disloyalty as they had been of world involvement and reform during the early century. Rather than turning to another era of "normalcy," they turned to what might be termed "complacency." Dwight D. Eisenhower's election was symbolic of this new attitude. He promised to find a solution to the Korean conflict, lower taxes, curb inflation, reduce the federal deficit, but, at the same time, he pledged not to neglect such social issues as social security and federal aid to education. "There is . . . ," Eisenhower stated, "a middle way between untrammeled freedom of the individual and the demands for the welfare of the whole Nation. This way must avoid government by bureaucracy as carefully as it avoids neglect of the helpless." At mid-twentieth century Americans were still unsure whether they preferred "rugged individualism" or a "welfare state." Eisenhower's election may have indicated that, in fact, they sought both.

Sources and Suggested Readings

Blake, Nelson Manfred, *A History of American Life and Thought,* 1971.

Conkin, Paul and John Higham, *New Directions in American Intellectual History,* 1977.

Curti, Merle, *Growth of American Thought,* 1981.

Faulkner, William, *Light in August,* 1932.

Gabriel, Ralph Henry, *The Course of American Democratic Thought,* 1956.

Horton, Rod W. and Herbert W. Edwards, *Backgrounds of American Literary Thought,* 1967.

Kennedy, David M. and Paul A. Robinson, *Social Thought in America and Europe,* 1970.

Lewis, Sinclair, *Babbitt,* 1922.

Farland, C. K., *The Modern American Tradition: Readings in Intellectual History,* 1972.

Nash, Roderick, *The Nervous Generation: American Thought, 1917–1930,* 1970.

Persons, Stow, *American Minds: A History of Ideas,* 1975.

Sinclair, Upton, *The Jungle,* 1906.

Steinbeck, John, *The Grapes of Wrath,* 1939.

Wolfe, Thomas, *You Can't Go Home Again,* 1940.

Zoll, Donald Atwell, *The Twentieth Century Mind,* 1967.

Americans at Play, 1898–1952

Jeffrey T. Sammons

University of Houston, Central Campus

Sports and recreational activity are pervasive elements in American life. Their impact on the economy continues to amaze observers. By 1972 the leisure-time market accounted for a total expenditure of $100 billion—a figure in excess of national defense costs. In 1982 the money spent on athletics and recreation approximated $262 billion, $41 billion more than the defense budget. Sports seem to be equally important to America's political and social life. Some would argue that Americans elect their politicians, fight their wars, judge their minorities, and raise their children based on values extracted from the world of sports. It is no accident that we hear coaches, sportswriters, generals, politicians, and businessmen saying in unison, that a man must be physically and psychologically "tough" to succeed, that he must be clean cut, loyal, and obedient, that he must "take his lumps" without a wimper or an excuse. Their advice, if heeded, has been accepted by many as a prescription for success. Consequently, sports standards and the American way appear virtually synonymous.

Many scholars agree that the 1890s represented the take-off point for modern sports. At that time changes in attitudes toward play spawned the world of sports we know today. An activist, aggressive mood overtook America then and profoundly affected the nation's development and character. A craze for sports and out-of-door recreation stood as an indicator of the change. The legacy of the 1890s, however, has clouded the fact that athletics and leisure activities were once taboo and carried little value and importance.

Colonial Americans, especially in puritanical New England, considered most amusements counterproductive, if not threats to their survival. By the time of the American Revolution, an ideology known as Republicanism, combined with Puritanism to reinforce the traditional repulsion for game playing. Puritans and Republicans shared the belief that amusements belonged to the decadent and oppressive monarchies of Europe. In the nineteenth century evangelical Protestantism exerted its influence to limit the growth of sports. With it, a vast network of voluntary associations emerged to promote a common morality. More often than not the associations agreed on strict Sabbatarian rules (Sunday as a day of worship and rest) and laws against gambling, "riotous" amusements and drinking. Moreover, the Protestant work ethic and the American quest for wealth militated against the pursuit of pleasure. Americans had not yet learned that sports and wealth were not mutually exclusive.

This is not to say that there were not amusements and leisure events, there were. In fact the 1820s and 1830s heralded a remarkable growth in the entertainment industry. Still the prevailing ideology before 1850 stood firmly in opposition to recreation. Not long after the mid-century mark, incipient forces had gathered, presaging a great change in attitudes toward leisure. Concern about morality and health figured prominently in the new outlook. But the concern with health had far larger implications. The physical state of Americans was relative. An America which prided itself on its accomplishments could not live with an image of "a pasty-faced, narrow chested, spindle-shanked, dwarded race—a mere walking manikin to advertise the last cut of fashionable tailor." The example of England and of continental Europe seemed to indicate the value of out-of-door exercise and play. For, young America in 1850 had not yet learned to play in the modern sense. The sporting state of affairs led one English observer to declare, "To roll balls in a tenpin alley by gaslight or to drive a fast trotting horse in a light wagon along a very bad and very dusty road seems the Alpha and Omega of sport in the United States." Others put down American recreation as "chewing, smoking, drinking, and reckless driving."

Concerned observers and critics alike found their most convincing evidence in the inability of American pugilists to best their British counterparts, in the ultimate sporting proof of character, strength, skill, and courage. Indeed the battle for world athletic supremacy, before the revival of the Olympic Games in 1896, was waged almost entirely in the ring. After the Civil War Americans began to close the "muscle gap." The legendary "Boston Strongboy" John L. Sullivan played a large role. Yet even he could do no better than draw with Charlie Mitchell in 1882. Not until 1894 with "Gentleman" Jim Corbett's knock out of Mitchell, could America claim undisputed possession of the World's Heavyweight Championship. Corbett's victory symbolized a tremendous transformation in American sports.

By the 1890s a rage for competitive athletics and for outdoor activities swept across the nation. It was part of a much larger "master impulse" which seized the American people and reshaped their thought, action, and being in the ensuing years. Theodore Roosevelt, captured the essence of this impelling force in a 1899 speech "The Strenuous Life." Roosevelt commanded his audience to "boldly face the life of strife . . . for it is only through strife, through hard and dangerous endeavor, that we shall ultimately win the goal of true national greatness." His words reflected a new activist mood, characterized most by an aggressive nationalism. Accompanying it were: a new upbeat and martial music, a marked change in the condition of women, a rekindled interest in nature, and last, but not least, a boom in sports and recreation.

Not surprisingly, sports which appealed to tastes for speed or violence accelerated greatly in the 1890s. The most popular sport of all was bicycling. Primarily social and recreational, it was truly one of the crazes of the age, as figures clearly show. The number of "bikes" jumped from one million in 1893 to seven million in 1900. Other forms of racing and basketball also satisfied the desire for speed. As for violence, football and boxing filled the bill.

Oddly enough, the nation's colleges led the new aggressive athletic movement. Once the centers of cerebral development, theology, and conservatism; their obsession with football made them theaters of organized combat. Football promoted a combative team spirit, which became virtually synonymous with college spirit and soon athletic prowess became a major determinant of institutional status.

Yale University cultivated the game of football and under Walter Camp's leadership developed it into a big business by 1890. Football's popularity and commercial success were threatened in 1900, however, by mounting injuries to players, an increase in the number of deaths, and the tendency to violate standards of fair play. Long a subject of debate, in 1905 the sport stood on the brink of abolition. In an editorial that year, the *New York Times* labeled the game "The Homicidal Pastime." *The Times* reported that nineteen boys had been killed in the fall alone, in a sport promoted as healthy exercise. The paper called for new rules, administered by university authorities. It found deliberate injury and the "insane" rooting of the crowd, prime causes of the problem.

The controversy had reached such a level, that in 1905 President Theodore Roosevelt, a leading proponent and symbol of the rigorous life ordered the colleges to cleanse the sport. Roosevelt's admonition was moral in tone and addressed foul play as much as brutality. The latter reason exposed an American dilemma, the fear and enjoyment of aggression. Thus American attitudes toward football demonstrated a forceful need to define, limit, and conventionalize the symbolism of violence in sports.

A rules committee met that year and addressed the problems of the game. In 1906 it announced sweeping rules changes to govern play on the field and to revamp the organizational structure of the game. Perhaps the most revolutionary of the changes was the forward pass rule, designed to open up the game and reduce brutal power play. Still a large number of deaths occurred, once again compelling the rules committee to take quick action. In 1910 it abolished interlocking blocking and liberalized the forward pass by permitting the ball to cross the line of scrimmage at any point.

Gradually, the rule changes ushered in the "modern" game of football. The new game which featured craft and field maneuver would get its impetus from the West and most noticeably at the hands of two second-generation immigrant boys attending little known Notre Dame. They were the legendary Knute Rockne and Gus Dorais. In 1913 these clever athletes unleashed an aerial attack against Army which led to a stunning victory and a revolution in the game, as coaches everywhere experimented with the forward pass. More than this, the success of Notre Dame and its new stock players was symbolic. For the second-generation boy, football now seemed a means to social mobility. Lads lacking the necessary finances believed that college was now accessible.

Only prize fighting, among the spectacles of the 1890s and 1900s grew as rapidly as football in mass appeal. Although most states still outlawed professional pugilism, it drew large and increasingly respectable audiences. The unsavory reputation declined tremendously after 1892, when "Gentleman Jim" Corbett displayed an "artful" technique in defeating John L. Sullivan, who had, in his own right, brought boxing out of the backwoods and into urban athletic clubs.

Just as brains had allegedly replaced brawn in football, Corbett's victory signified to many "a triumph of youth, skill, agility, intelligence, and good generalship over age, lack of science, and brute force." Prize fighting, like football, seemed to capture the spirit of the age. In an era dominated by competition in politics and business, boxing rose in popular esteem by reducing the values of American society to a pair of gladiators meeting in the ring in the "truest test of man." Yet there was another apeal to boxing—it was also an escape, a return to primal man. The growth of industry and the quickened pace of urbanization subordinated people to the control of the machine and the time clock. Consequently, individual achievement was overwhelmed by an increasingly collective society. Prize fighting gave the appearance of reversing this process by glorifying boxers who had risen above the masses.

Prize fighting during the 1890s and early 1900s never totally shed the stigma which it carried from England. Consequently the sport suffered from an ambivalent public and found itself often subject to judicial whim and shifting reform movements. When the spirit of reform swept the East at the end of nineteenth and beginning of the twentieth centuries, many states tightened the reins on boxing, by enacting specific legislation to prohibit it. At the same time, the wild and somewhat lawless states of Nevada and California became havens for championship fights. Soon, the success of prize fighting in the West won adherents in the East and the public's desire to see fights led states to reconsider prohibitions on the sport. Consequently, some states proposed the idea of strict government regulation as a middle ground between outright prohibition and unfettered legalization. By the 1920s statutory regulation found widespread acceptance and replaced prohibitory laws. The so-called Walker Law of 1921, named for its sponsor, James "Beau Jimmy" Walker, then New York State assemblyman, became the "Magna Carta" of prize fighting. The law marked a watershed event in the history of the sport. While state officials knew that strict regulation would not end gambling, rioting, and "fixed" and collusive matches, it might "insure a measure of decorum." An activity once classed with bear baiting, cock fighting and bull fighting found sanctuary and sanction in law.

Of all the games, baseball maintained its supremacy at both the professional and sandlot levels. Despite its lack of sensational growth, Americans still held a special affection for baseball. As early as the 1850s people were calling it the national pastime. This belief in the Americanness of baseball had evolved into a formal mythology or ideology by the turn of the twentieth century. The myth asserted that baseball was an uniquely American sport, developed in the country along with other basic rural institutions. It promoted baseball as a transportable frontier institution, which could supply the "decadent" and "unAmerican" cities with the best of America's traditional values. Such belief reflected a long standing anti-urban feeling held by many Americans. The city was a den of iniquity, mysterious, unhealthy, and the haven of immigrants. Thus something as American and as good as baseball had to be a product of rural America. The myth persisted despite the fact that baseball games were played in the cities, by urban boys, and were controlled by entrepreneurs and urban politicians.

There were opponents, however, who irritated Americans by insisting that baseball evolved from rounders, a British game, played by girls. What could be worse for a "muscle flexing" world power than to have its national sport called a "girls game?" In 1905 Albert G. Spalding, once a fine pitcher, club owner, and founder of the sporting goods house bearing his name, initiated a movement to prove that baseball was an indigenous sport and not a derivative of rounders. He established a blue ribbon commission, which announced in 1907 that baseball had its origins in the United States and the first scheme for playing it was devised by Abner Doubleday in Cooperstown, New York, in 1839. Despite a public controversy over the lack of evidence, baseball officials accepted the findings.

If anyone is to be credited with the invention of the modern game, he was Alexander Cartwright. A plaque at the sight of the first organized game, Elysian Fields in Hoboken, New Jersey, outlined his contribution:

> 'Father of modern Baseball', Set bases 90 feet apart. Established 9 innings as game and 9 players as team. Organized the Knickerbockers Baseball Club of New York in 1845. Carried baseball to Pacific Coast and Hawaii in Pioneer days.

Nonetheless, in 1939 the founding of the National Baseball Museum and Hall of Fame in Cooperstown memorialized the "inventor," the "original site" and the game. Recently, Doubleday's place in baseball lore has been shaken, but Cooperstown's position remains secure as baseball officials maintain that it is the symbolic birthplace of the game and befits the pastoral image of the sport.

By the early 1900s professional baseball teams flourished in nearly every major city, at a time when the other major sports, boxing and horseracing, were functions under severe legal and social constraints. Football was still property of the colleges and universities. More importantly, baseball became America's representative mass institution. Some disturbing features, however, characterized the role. The national pastime increasingly reflected mainstream, middle-class, white Anglo-Saxon America, and set the tone for other sports. Consequently blacks, Indians, ethnics and women found dwindling opportunities in athletics. Perhaps the experience of blacks most clearly demonstrated the development.

Race relations in sports around the turn of the century often reflected and occasionally initiated trends in the larger society. Segregation and discrimination in sport also reveal the shallowness of the myths that abound in athletics and the larger realm. Contrary to myth, the evidence indicates that there has not been slow but steady progress in the elimination of racial discrimination in sport, nor has athletic competition since the late nineteenth century been essentially democratic. Prior to the acceptance of Social Darwinism and the hardening of discrimination, white America tolerated and in some instances encouraged athletic competition among the races. During this time blacks participated freely in and excelled at horse racing. The most outstanding jockey of his day was Isaac Murphy, a black man, who rode 3 winners in the Kentucky Derby. But by the turn of the century black jockeys were a rarity.

At the same time, whites allowed some black participation in baseball. Brothers, Moses and Welday Walker, both played for the Toledo Mudhens of the American Association, a major league in the 1880s, but an incident occurred which served as the pivotal event in fixing black-white relations in American sports for more than half a century. When the Chicago White Stockings went to Toledo in 1887, Adrian "Cap" Anson, refused to take the field until the Walkers were banished. The Walkers did not play and in less than a week they were gone from baseball entirely. Anson's actions were not isolated, but represented a hatred of blacks fanned by politicians in the South such as James K. Vardaman and "Pitchfork" Ben Tillman. In the North there was a distinct departure from the abolitionist spirit resulting in a betrayal of blacks as the two regions attempted reconciliation. The United States Supreme Court confirmed the national sentiment in a series of decisions upholding segregation and discrimination from 1875 to 1898. Of course, *Plessy* v. *Ferguson* in 1896, established the doctrine of "separate but equal" and ensured second class citizenship for blacks.

Whatever the sport, the "color line" became increasingly difficult to cross. The Afro-American athlete was called "a growing menace" and symbol of "a black rise against white supremacy." Whites no longer wanted to watch blacks dominate athletic encounters or to even have them participate. Individuals such as the great bicyclist Marshall Taylor at the turn of the century and Jack Johnson, heavyweight boxing champion of the world from 1908 to 1915, were exceptions. They were allowed to participate and excel because their economic value to sports magnates and officials outweighed racial considerations. To be sure, both men suffered extreme persecution and hardship for their success in areas reserved for whites. Consequently many black athletes resorted to or found themselves reduced to entertaining whites who paid to watch the "darkies" clown around. Others, not willing to submit to such humiliating displays formed serious barnstorming teams.

In 1910, Beauregard F. Moseley who had promoted a successful all black team in Chicago, called together a group of black baseball officials from throughout the Midwest and South to organize a National Negro Baseball League. Moseley's plans and goals reflected a more widespread concern among blacks for self-help and race pride to counter the exclusionary practices of white America in baseball and the larger society. The venture suffered from a lack of financial support and never advanced beyond the planning stage. Early in 1920, Rube Foster, one of baseball's great pitchers and a resourceful promoter, revived Moseley's plan for a black baseball league. In that year, he and five managers of other Midwestern teams devised a scheme. With Foster as the first President of the National Negro Baseball League, black baseball enjoyed a decade of prosperity.

The Indian athletic experience, while on a much smaller scale, is also quite revealing. The story of the legendary Jim Thorpe and the "athletic boys" at Carlisle Indian School provide a tale of triumph, tragedy, and victimization. In 1879 an idealistic army captain, Richard Henry Pratt, with Interior Department help, founded Carlisle in Western Pennsylvania. The school's purpose was to remove Indian youths from the reservations and bring them into the American mainstream through education, practical experience, and athletics—especially football. Pratt knew the appeal of football and valued the attention it would draw among a wide variety of Americans.

Carlisle fielded some of the best football teams in America and Thorpe gained recognition as the world's greatest athlete. His victories in the pentathlon and decathlon at the 1912 Stockholm Olympics confirmed public opinion. Thorpe's career highlighted the ups and downs of the conspicuous two decade role of the Indian athletic presence. Ironically, success for him and others fostered their demise. In 1903 Pratt was removed from his job. Shortly thereafter Glen "Pop" Warner returned as head football coach. As a result the school became more military and football grew into a big business. Worst of all, the players had become professional. Reports of payoffs, uneven discipline, drinking, and a decline in educational standards invited a congressional investigation in 1914. The school closed in 1918. Carlisle and its Indian athletes were products of a system that the government had tired of. The bureaucratic trend toward mainstreaming Indians had passed. Many hoped that the problem would fade away.

Thorpe like many of the other athletic boys, left Carlisle unprepared for life outside of sports. Stripped of his gold medals in 1913 for violation of the amateur code, he found the stigma impossible to shake. "Big Jim" bounced from one unsuccessful venture to another and died in 1953 a poor and broken man. In 1982, after a protracted struggle by family and friends, his gold medals were returned.

The problems of blacks and Indians in sports pale in comparison to those of women. With them, the major issue has not been a matter of competing against white men, but of competing at all. Men have traditionally promoted sports as natural for males but unnatural for females. For athletics promote belligerent attitudes and competitive spirits which are fine in men, but detrimental to "feminine health and attractiveness." Atavistic notions about sport as ritual, as man's last sanctum provided even more justification for excluding women. In some primitive societies, the witnessing of ritual or play by a female might result in her death. In modern society, death is replaced by the loss of reputation or femininity. Male insecurity also plays a role. When men profess to protect women from something harmful at worst and unladylike at best, they often really fear female success and change.

No doubt, in the late 1890s and early 1900s, women's participation in sport was dominated by Victorian attitudes. Their activities were relatively few in number and included: croquet, archery, cycling, bowling, tennis, and golf. Clothing, in the form of high heeled boots, heavy hats, and suffocatingly tight whalebone corsets, greatly restricted movement. Those who did play were gentlewomen, who performed without acquiring an "indelicate sweat." These games, perhaps more than anything, facilitated the opportunity for respectable social encounters. In an age of puritanical sexual morality, they gave men and women something to do together.

Even advocates of athletics for women, prescribed severely limited participation. The extremely influential, Dr. Dudley Sargent, Physical Director at Harvard University, did much to establish the acceptable guidelines, in a 1906 address before the Public School Physical Training Society. Sargent warned, "In physical education women should not be expected to excel in physical exercise which is adapted to men." He cited, as off limits, football, ice hockey, basketball, boxing, pole valuting, and heavy gymnastics. Moreover, Sargent not only determined the appropriate games for women, but also their nature. According to Sargent, athletics for women were to be recreational and not competitive, because "competition emphasizes qualities that are . . . unnecessary and undesirable in women."

Many female physical educators subscribed to the views of Sargent and themselves retarded the advance of women in competitive athletics. Yet, by the second decade of the twentieth century, a distinct deterioration of external control over morality helped women in their sports push. How? Urbanization had brought with it a dissolution of moral authority which formerly resided in the family and small community. Consequently, the individual gained more say in his or her behavioral norms. Women's individualization and independence increased as they spent more time outside the home and on jobs. Economic participation directly related to social independence, consequently women pressed for entry into the sports arena.

By the second decade of the twentieth century the nature of women's sports had undergone considerable change. The number of activities increased greatly as did their vigor and danger. So noticeable was the shift that in 1914 the *New York Times* pondered, "How far and into what unexplored fields the ambitions of 'the new woman' will lead her is a question that appears to have no answer." The answer was: a growth of organized competition accompanied by national and international tournaments for most sports. In fact women won the right to compete in the 1916 Berlin Olympic Games, before they were cancelled. Perhaps even more significant was that participants in women's sports no longer came primarily from the upper class.

The take off in women's sports was quickly followed by an unprecedented boom in male spectator sports. An unsettling war, promoted as necessary for democracy and freedom, and also as a proving ground for masculinity, fell far short of its ideals. Disillusioned, Americans looked to the gridiron, prize ring, and baseball diamond for heroes. Before the war there had been popular excitement about spectator sports, but the intensity was unparalleled in the 1920s.

The twenties created an obvious need for heroes. The rampant materialism, wealth, and luxury coupled with the seemingly uncontrollable change in moral standards, must have made Americans feel uneasy and a bit guilty. The athletic field symbolized the strenuous life where real men ruled. Before the disillusionment could be lifted and the past restored, however; a purgative or cleansing event was needed. It came in 1919 with the "Black Sox" scandal— a throwing of the World Series by the Chicago White Sox to the Cincinnati Redlegs. There had long been excessive gambling and shadiness surrounding the game of baseball. Owners were deeply concerned about the image of the "national pastime" and the effect of that image on fan confidence and support. Since 1900 baseball had sought bright, educated disciplined well-mannered athletes who could play brainy ball, project a wholesome image, and attract middle-class fans. The eight players accused of throwing the 1919 World Series did not fit the sanitized mold. All eight were poorly educated, working-class men from the rural South or the immigrant cities.

The "Black Sox" scandal came at a time when many old-stock Americans worried about the future of the country. Baseball, that great national institution, which many believed represented the finest American values, was revealed to be corrupt. Thus if baseball was bad then America had to be. Consequently, Judge Kenesaw Mountain Landis, the newly appointed commissioner of baseball, summarily banned the eight "Black Sox," even after they had been acquitted in a court of law. Thus, Landis emerged as an ethical hero who had "redeemed" baseball from the sins of the "Black Sox." Under Landis's strict leadership baseball regained its stature as the finest and noblest mass American institution.

Yet, diversion from the problems of the past came from a unlikely source, but one who fit the spirit and mood of the times—George Herman Ruth, "the Babe." Born of humble origins in Baltimore, Maryland, Ruth was a gargantuan man-child prone to excesses. His crude behavior, alcoholic exploits, and enormous sexual appetite should have been contradictory to the carefully cultivated image of baseball. Instead, with proper press screening, the fans received information which excited more interest than outrage. Beyond this, his anti-heroic qualities, flouting of authority, and carousing endeared him to a public which had grown tired of the Victorian repression. Most of all, his incredible hitting exploits made him seem superhuman. In 1920, Ruth hit 54 home runs, 25 more than the record setting 29 he had hit in 1919. In every 11.7 times at bat he hit a home run. According to Benjamin Rader, "With nothing but his bat, Ruth revolutionized the National Game of baseball." Moreover, Ruth was the living embodiment of the American success dream— living proof that the lone individual could still rise from poverty and obscurity to fortune and fame. His popularity also brought about a broader foundation for baseball's appeal.

From a business perspective, sports in the twenties had never done better. In 1926, for example the National and American Leagues recorded a paid attendance of about 5,000,000. In the same year, football reached its first million dollar gate from one game when Army and Navy played at Soldier Field in Chicago before 110,000 people. Approximately 15,000,000 spectators attended college football games, with $30,000 000 paid in admissions. Horse racing, once nearly fiscally dead drew some 7,000,000 fans in 1926. While baseball held sway outdoors, boxing ranked first as the greatest indoor spectacle. Tex Rickard, boxing promotor *par excellence* clearly understood and openly announced that boxing was "big business and getting bigger all the time." As the first man to arrange a million dollar gate in 1921, when Jack Dempsey fought Georges Carpentier, he spoke with authority. More than a promoter and master of "ballyhoo" or "hype," Rickard helped to create an image of honesty in the sport. Rickard unlike others before him did not hesitate to use women in the process. He often boasted, "Women have given us insurance for the future of boxing . . . , here in the Garden we do not think much of a fight unless it draws women."

Women not only watched, but also made tremendous strides in the sports business. According to Stephanie Twin, "Competitive female athletics blossomed in the 1920s and 1930s." In tennis, swimming, ice skating, and golf top female competitors gained celebrity status. They were praised for their skills and copied in advertising. Indeed the commercialization of women, especially their bodies helped to open competitive athletics to women as opportunists used sex to sell sports.

The two most notable female athletes of the time were Gertrude Ederle and Mildred "Babe" Didrikson. In 1926 Ederle became the first woman to swim the English Channel. Her time eclipsed the male record by over two hours and shook traditional notions of female capacity. Didrikson won two gold medals at the 1932 Olympic Games and was also an All-American basketball star and golfing champion. The *Associated Press* named her Woman Athlete of the Century in 1950. Her growth in athletics came in part from employer sponsored industrial leagues, which served as important promoters of competitive female athletics. By 1935, with a few exceptions a "play for play's sake" strategy and the Great Depression severely limited women's sports.

Men also expressed concern that commercialism was contaminating the "sporting" quality of athletics. That which is now referred to as the "Golden Age" of sports was considered by many contemporaries the "Fat or Crooked Age" of sports. It seemed, the more urbanization and technology closed or corrupted the possibilities for "the strenuous life," the more men vainly sought the elusive manly mystique. Probably more than anyone else Charles Lindburgh, personified the heroic individual. In 1927, Lindy's solo flight over the Atlantic signaled the triumph of man over nature. Within days the public made the "Lone Eagle" *the* national hero.

The world of sports turned to golf for its ideal hero and uncontaminated sportsman—Robert T. "Bobby" Jones. As an amateur golfer, Jones won 13 national titles. He climaxed his short golfing career in 1929 with the Grand Slam—The American Open and Amateur and the British Open and Amateur. After his feat, Jones received a New York ticker-tape parade not unlike those for conquering warriors. Conservative, modest and clean-cut, Jones personified the American image. Above all else, the public loved his amateur status.

The departure of Jones and other athletic heroes by 1930, coupled with the staggering economic crisis, dimmed the American spirit and brought on a malaise which clearly showed in the world of sports. Lou Gehrig could not fill Babe Ruth's shoes as a popular force, Red Grange never satisfied the fans' expectations as a professional football player, and the boxing world stood on the brink of disaster when Jack Dempsey and Gene Tunney retired and Tex Rickard died.

The state of decline in boxing had far a reaching implications for much of the populace. Heavyweight champions have often reflected the mood, spirit, hopes, aspirations, and beliefs of their societies. As late as 1934, America still did not have a champion who met heroic standards, reigning heavyweight king, Max Baer appeared a strange mixture of crackpot and genius, whose role seemed more entertainer than athletic hero. Thus the fight game, like other sports needed uplift from a hero who could stir interest, restore integrity, and produce revenues. As in baseball, the answer came from an unlikely source— Joseph Louis Barrow, a poor, virtually uneducated black, who emerged as Joe Louis, the "Brown Bomber."

Sensing the potential of Louis not only as a boxer, but as a symbol, Louis's handlers groomed him for his multifarious roles. More than anything he had to overcome the image of Jack Johnson who gave whites easy rationalizations for excluding blacks from heavyweight championship fights. As a result of natural ability and proper training, Louis took on a Dempsey-like ferocity with a quiet unassuming clean-cut character in order that he would "be a credit to his people and undo what others had done before him in the ring."

Louis became much more than a great boxer and race hero. With the rise of Adolf Hitler, international unrest compounded domestic problems, thereby heightening a need for symbols to help combat threats to capitalism, democracy, and world order. With the aid of the press, public opinion, promoters, and boxing skill, Joe Louis loomed as a fighting symbol for 15 years, helping to knock out menaces from within and without the ring, while reviving a moribund sport.

Joe Louis captured the heavyweight championship in 1937 from James J. Braddock and was the first black in 22 years to fight for the title. As champion he expected to defend not only his own honor, but that of his people—the American people. By the time of his second match with Max Schmeling of Germany in 1938, black and white citizens put the fight in a racial and patriotic context. American democracy stood trial against Aryan fascism and Joe assured his public, he would "go to town." and "go to town" he did with a stunning first round victory. Coupled with Jesse Owens's incredible track performance in the 1936 Berlin Olympics, Louis's feat tarnished Hitler's notion of Aryan supremacy and greatly lifted American morale and confidence. Yet neither man's accomplishments significantly changed Hitler's course of action nor markedly altered the pattern of race relations in his own country. The walls of racial segregation stood as firmly as ever, even in the world of sports. No blacks played major league baseball or professional football and few played on integrated college teams. Louis and Owens were for the most part shining examples of what a black man could accomplish in sport, not active crusaders for black rights. Significant adjustments would wait until war's end.

When America entered World War II, Joe Louis and other leading athletes did their patriotic duty by enlisting, performing for troops, or by just playing and keeping America's games alive. Despite necessary sacrifices and drastic curtailments in many areas of American life, this nation's citizens strongly supported the continuance of professional and college sports during the war. Suggestions that professional sports be discontinued met with opposition from even the President, Franklin Delano Roosevelt. Aware of sports symbolic importance, Roosevelt did not want anyone to believe that the war was causing undue hardship on the home front. He reserved his greatest concern for baseball, enough to warrant a letter to Judge Landis concluding, "I honestly feel that it would be best for the country to keep baseball going." After all, war movies promoted World War II as, in part, a struggle to protect the right of children to play the national pastime. Even the Japanese recognized the importance of baseball in their battlecry, "To Hell with Babe Ruth."

Unavoidably, the war did have some negative effects on intercollegiate and professional sports, brought on by the depletion of manpower, the lack of athletic supplies, and rationing. Despite the hardships, sports sprang up from the war with increased vigor and public support because of their supposed connection with victory, nationalism, and democratic ideals. In fact sport loomed so large after the war it not only became a persistent theme in everyday life, but an imitator and initiator of changing racial values, a treasured weapon of the Cold War, a stamping ground for corruption, and a massive commercial institution. Many observers considered the changes revolutionary. Perhaps none drew more attention than the integration of athletics.

America had gone through two world wars and a depression with its black-white athletic separation intact. At war's end, however, many white colleges began to reassess their policies of excluding black students in general and black athletes in particular. It is important to note that the National Association for the Advancement of Colored People (NAACP) focused its attack on the "separate but equal" doctrine through forcing selected institutions of higher education to admit blacks. Thus the combination of legal pressure, changing mores, and the prospects for athletic and commercial success led to the recruitment of black student-athletes. By the mid 1950s black football and basketball players were recruited into big-time athletics in significant numbers. Despite the publicity, significance, and symbolism attached to the integration of baseball in 1947 by Jackie Robinson of the Brooklyn Dodgers, America's college campuses were numerically far more important in the quest to integrate sports. Even ten years after Robinson's historic feat, there were only 18 blacks in major league baseball.

While sport had long played a role in international affairs, its spectacular growth combined with post-war conditions to intensify governmental concern for and use of it. As nuclear proliferation brought on military stalemate, confrontation in other areas, particularly the sports arena, assumed correspondingly greater political meaning. As Hitler had proven earlier, sport could be a potent tool of national policy and a powerful medium through which evidence of superiority could be demonstrated. International sport by 1952 became an arena for ideological conflict, mirroring many of the same tensions evident in the political realm. Attesting this fact, a senator warned his countryman not to, "forget that Americans chalked up an amazing record of performance at the 1952 Olympic Games, because our free system of government and vast educational network paves the way to athletic excellence." The Soviet Union retaliated with accusations that bourgeois countries used sport as a means of "preparing cannon fodder for a new, aggressive war," whereas it used athletics in the "struggle for friendship and security of the people for peace in the whole world." From an incipient awareness of the significance of international sport in 1952, official United States interest in sport increased to the extent that many sports programs had become formal functions of government by 1963.

If athletics were not living up to the Olympic ideal as promoters of international harmony and good will, they fell short domestically as well. Sports related gambling, point shaving, and game-fixing scandals plagued intercollegiate athletics in the post-war years. Indeed it seemed as though intercollegiate athletics had a much closer affinity with business than education. In July, 1946, the National Collegiate Athletic Association (NCCA) met to establish the "Principles for the Conduct of Intercollegiate Athletics." Events of the early fifties vindicated the concern when collegiate sports were rocked by a series of scandals. In 1951, the most honor bound of all academic institutions, the United States Military Academy at West Point signaled the need for change when officials expelled 90 cadets for aiding football players on exams.

Of all the post-war developments, perhaps no single one had more of an influence on the growth and direction of spectator sports than did television. Before the war the extant technology relegated TV to the realm of novelty, but shortly technical improvements made the invention commercially viable. By the late 1940s this technological marvel enabled millions who had never witnessed a major sporting event, to see and hear the spectacles in their homes. After 1950 sports officials and the television industry shaped athletic events for potential television viewers rather than the fans who attended the games.

Before long, television had solidified, more than ever, the connection between sports and the entertainment and advertising industries. As a result the new industry gave millions of dollars for broadcast rights to major league baseball and major college athletics. The medium's influence on sports was not without side effects. Escalating video earnings contributed to numerous franchise shifts and a proliferation of baseball teams. Moreover attendance fell considerably in both major leagues and the minor league system withered to a mere skeleton of its old self. Boxing, because of its highly circumscribed action, was the most successful of early television sports. Yet over exposure forced repetitive fights and mismatches, while nearly destroying the local clubs, which produced the talent.

From the 1890s America moved steadily forward in the realm of play. Old, negative attitudes held less sway, as the forces of government, big business, and the public advanced the cause of sports. From a once taboo status, play became identifiable with the American people. By 1952 the technical and structural foundation for recreation and sports, as they presently appear, had been firmly established. The most commercially successful nation, also led the world in recreation and athletics. Once viewed as inimical to industry, play became an industry in its own right.

Sources and Suggested Readings

Altschuler, Glenn C. and Martin W. La Forse, "From Brawn to Brains: Football and Evolutionary Thought," *Journal of Popular Culture,* Vol. 16, No. 4, (Spring 1983) pp. 75–89.
Baker, William J. and John M. Carroll, eds., *Sports in Modern America* (1981).
Brown, Gene, ed., *Sports and Society: The Great Contemporary Issues* (1980).
Coakley, Jay J., *Sport In Society: Issues and Controversies* (1978).
Filene, Peter, *Him/Her/Self* (1974–75).
Lipsyte, Robert, *Sports World: An American Dreamland* (1975).
Rader, Benjamin G., *American Sports: From the Age of Folk Games to the Age of Spectators* (1982).
Riess, Steven, *Touching Base: Professional Baseball and American Culture in the Progressive Era* (1980).
Sammons, Jeffrey T., "Boxing as a Reflection of Society: The Southern Reaction to Joe Louis," *Journal of Popular Culture,* Vol. 14, No. 4 (Spring 1983) pp. 23–33.
Somers, Dale A., *The Rise of Sports in New Orleans 1850–1900* (1972).
Twin, Stephanie, ed., *Out of the Bleachers: Writings on Women and Sport* (1979).